FAR
2/14

How Karl Rove and the Establishment Lost...Again

C. EDMUND WRIGHT

To Sheldon Adelson, Charles and David Koch, and others who have invested their treasure to save America for future generations: Since you "built it," and have earned more than enough to shield yourselves and your families against the theft of the country, your motives are manifestly pure – and anyone who thinks otherwise is blinded by class envy.

So thank you for your generosity. But please, I respectfully suggest a change in whose advice and wisdom you invest in going forward. There are a lot of brilliant and talented people in America who understand what is at stake, but very few of them are in establishment Republican circles. They are where you are, in the real world, chasing their American dreams.

TABLE OF CONTENTS

INTRODUCTION

In analyzing Barack Obama's Second Inaugural Address, conservatives and liberals agree on at least one thing:

> *"Obama said he wanted to model himself more after a Reagan than Clinton. He thought Reagan made conservatism mainstream, and so this was an attempt to make progressive liberalism mainstream."* — **Chuck Todd, NBC News**

> *"I was listening to a Democratic Ronald Reagan. Where Reagan was unapologetically conservative, this was unapologetically progressive."* — **Jonathon Karl, ABC News**

> *"Obama basically is declaring the end of Reaganism in this speech. He said ...that Reagan had changed the ideological course of the country."* — **Charles Krauthammer, Fox News**

> *"Obama hates Reaganomics...and what he seeks to do is erase every trace of Reagan from America."* — **Rush Limbaugh**

From all of this, we conclude that Barack Obama understands something the GOP Establishment has denied for two decades: that Republican electoral and governing successes are defined by the principles of Ronald Reagan. Although Obama received a big boost from Bill Clinton at the Convention, and effectively ran against George W. Bush twice, he made it clear that a man named Reagan, and not *anyone* named Bush or Clinton, is his main historical concern. The paradox that both Obama and the Republican establishment want to roll back Reagan's influence conveniently verifies a major theme of this book. Karl Rove confirmed as much in early February, and by openly declaring war on the Tea Party and other conservatives, added perspective to words I wrote before the Inauguration — Obama's *first* Inaugural that is. From American Thinker, January 19, 2009:

> George Bush's legacy will be the end of Ronald Reagan's impact and the beginning of Barack Obama's.
>
> From the start, Bush and Rove's "new tone" strategy was a circular firing squad — doomed by a basic design flaw. But as it failed, Bush and Karl Rove's answer was not to re-examine the strategy, it was to make the firing squad circle even rounder. The more "new tone" they got, the more their enemies hated them and the less their supporters liked them. Down down down went the "Republican brand."
>
> Thus, it can be said the defeat of the party of Reagan had been self-engineered by this administration for at least eight years. Since Presidential terms are not isolated in a political-historical vacuum, the following election result is by definition part of the previous President's legacy. An administration's *perceived* successes or failures have more to do with the next election than perhaps any other factor.
>
> All the new tone did was to guarantee that Bush — and by extension his party and his supporters — never got credit for anything good yet got blamed for every problem.
>
> Connect the dots. This, not reality, led to the historically tiny approval ratings — which led to the nomination of a candidate like McCain who wanted to run against Bush —

which led to the 2008 election defeats — which will lead to God knows how much trouble in the near future under extremely liberal governance.

Pardon me for saying so, but this "decent man" (and I'll cede that point) whom I voted for twice appeared somewhat naïve and perhaps arrogant in "misoverestimating" his Texas charm's ability to bring about a "new tone" in Washington.

Moreover, *he was not elected to do that* by his supporters — nor was there ever a shred of evidence that his detractors wanted a new tone. As Bush came to find out, leftist rattlesnakes are not vulnerable to his charm. They bite back, period. Was this really such a surprise?

Say great words about Clinton in the White House? Let Ted Kennedy and John Edwards write legislation? Give the UN months to act? Throw Rummy and Scooter under the bus? Sign CFR? Play nice with Putin? No matter. The left still called Bush a cowboy and a terrorist and a Nazi and to this day hate him more than they hate anyone on the planet.

More to the point, by extension, they also hate us, and what we stand for. That is, they hate much of what America has stood for.

Memo to President Bush: this was NOT your fight alone. This was not YOUR office. It is our office and our fight. You shouldn't have capitulated on our principles to establish a new tone that only you wanted.

This misguided strategy (including compassionate conservatism) is merely an extension of Bush 41's "kinder and gentler" America. It is a rollback of official support for Reagan's successes by embarrassed Republicans who seem not to understand it. Since Reaganism was good for America, the weakening of it necessarily hurts America.

And this will be his defining legacy. Bush's refusal to fight back has allowed the left to define conservatism, capitalism, business, profit, terrorism and Reagan. The born again Christian Bush has some admirable ideals, but he appears to have missed how he should have applied the Biblical principle of stewardship of the ideals his supporters elected him to uphold.

The failure to use the bully pulpit to explain and define key principles has contributed to an ignorant American electorate now poised to drive us further and further left. No one in the White House had the faintest notion of how to use that pulpit to fight this.

In the early days after 9-11, Bush "the cowboy" had approval ratings in the '90's and was making cocksure statements of moral clarity about the "axis of evil" and being "with us or against us." But somehow he tired of the cowboy image. Or he ran scared of it. Never mind that he *is* a cowboy and that people (except for American liberals) LOVE cowboys.

So he became a nice decent meek man who preferred not to dirty his hands with political realities, and he thought it was noble to fall on the sword at every calamity. We need nice decent meek men in this country. We just don't need them as President. Sometimes we need the confident cowboy. Frankly, the institutions that made this country great have lost too much blood from Bush's misguided thinking that he could fall on his sword alone. The Presidency does not work that way. The nation will suffer from this blood letting, which is largely Bush's responsibility, and his legacy will ultimately reflect that.

The eight years of Bush 43 are a pivotal part of the twenty-year history that led to Mitt Romney's defeat in 2012. Bush and Rove codified the erosion of truth from the previous eight years - while setting the stage for the four years that followed. Perhaps you were thinking the same as these events unfolded.

1

SO WHO IS THIS ESTABLISHMENT, AND WTF HAPPENED?

A lot of very self-important people will insist there is no such thing as a Republican establishment – and, of course, most of them are part of it. There is indeed such a thing, nebulous though it may be, and defining it is a bit like describing pornography or the odor of a rotten egg: you'll know it when you run across it.

To be sure, the term Republican establishment (shortened to GOPe) refers to a certain mental infirmity as much as it does to a specific group of people. This is a way of thinking that is weak-willed, prissy, out of touch, and decidedly Washington-centered. This focus leads to an emphasis on keeping certain people in power instead of keeping certain limits on that power, and includes an unseemly reverence for Ivy League failure and antipathy towards real world accomplishment. This affliction is often accompanied by liberal views, especially on social issues, but that's not always the case. The more definitive trait is being unsure of, and sometimes ashamed of, conservatism, even on positions one ostensibly agrees with. As a result, establishment figures rarely articulate truth effectively, demonstrating their Reality Deficit Disorder (RDD). They often flaunt a faux bipartisanship to gain Washington credibility by trashing other Republicans, especially more conservative ones.

It is certainly possible to be in the establishment while not in Washington geographically, like, say, Mitt Romney. Conversely, one can be in town and fight the establishment, like Jim DeMint. And then you have Newt Gingrich, who can at times be the most potent thorn in the side of the establishment, and at other times be their quintessential groupthink poster boy. In fact, the tension between the "good Newt" and the "bad Newt" will be referenced often as the raging struggle inside this one person mirrors our battle with the GOPe. I'll define "our" and "we" in a minute, although if you are reading this, you are probably one of "us," and you already know who the establishment is.

Establishment psychosis is often caused by living in Washington too long, where over 90% of the residents you rub shoulders with loathe everything you once stood for. This cancer has invaded once good people like Jack Kemp and John Boehner, turning both into political eunuchs barely resembling the men first elected to Congress. This disease is a complication of RDD and is particularly malignant in those beset by an infantile yearning to be loved by the social elites and media mavens of Washington.

Many GOP operatives are infected by spending their entire adult lives in Washington, which can happen several ways, such as getting a Congressional staff job right out of law school thanks to daddy's connections. These staffers exist primarily to buffer members of Congress from those bothersome constituents, who live in a very strange place known as the real world. Over time, these perpetual children gain entrenched power and influence over citizens they know absolutely nothing about, even as elected officials come and go. On the DC career ladder, these kids never get term limited, and they often carry the disease further afield by becoming lobbyists who moonlight as so called "consultants" and "strategists" every two years.

The great unreported story is how this group is mostly invisible, devoid of any real world experience, not very intelligent, and yet so damned influential. These are "the cool kids" orbiting the Beltway universe, and they reinforce DC focused groupthink to insecure new members of Congress.

The establishment includes the "kept cons" that depend on government funding for their think tank or non-profit group salaries, as well as sell-outs for liberal media enclaves such as Matthew Dowd, Joe Scarborough, David Brooks and Peggy Noonan. Some people of higher intellect and character, like George Will and Charles Krauthammer, haven't sold out in order to sustain media jobs, yet they have clearly drifted away from a nation they are no longer familiar with.

Together, these groups make up a powerful, if amorphous and loosely defined, cabal. With a never ending desire to appear reasonable, they are often at cross-purposes with us, and don't appear to understand the concept of serious political enemies. They are typically much more concerned with a few soccer moms in southern Ohio than mysterious 145% turnouts in northern Ohio.

So, who do I mean by "us?"

"Us" is best defined as people who share a common set of core convictions as opposed to sharing specific group memberships. Primary among these convictions is opposition to big government liberalism and bureaucratic control. We believe America is under serious attack and is in grave and immediate danger as a result of the last two Presidential elections in particular, and we understand that liberals are indeed mortal enemies of our country as founded. This is a major point of contention, as the establishment foolishly looks at all of this as merely business as usual. To specify, many of us are part of one or more of the following: Reagan or base Republicans, Tea Party members, conservative talk radio listeners, message board visitors, Libertarians and libertine leaning conservatives, some social-issue-only conservatives, third party advocates, and others who just know something has gone very wrong.

And much is wrong indeed. We observe that our best

and most productive citizens are now under assault from a government that is growing in size, reach, power, scope, cost and intrusiveness by the minute. Our nation is being ripped away from the producers and systematically given to the very bureaucrats who are doing the ripping, all of which is, ironically, financed by us. What is not being redistributed to government bureaucrats is being given to powerful union interests.

It's the perfect crime and the grandest of all larcenies. America is being stolen in broad daylight.

Not understanding this larger reality is the fundamental blind spot of the establishment, as they are obsessed with the party per se and miss the big picture. Frankly, much more than a party is at stake here. We don't even particularly like the party per se, except that it's all that stands between us and the guaranteed end of the country as we know it.

With the breathtaking speed that Obama's government and union buddies are stealing the country, there may not enough time to erect another party to stand in the way. Oh, it would be damned satisfying to destroy the GOP, but perhaps counter productive to our own interests. And to be accurate, where this takeover is being rolled back on the state and local levels, Republican officials and their supporters are the ones doing it. If this were not the case, there would be no reason to bring the term "Republican" into this conversation. Confident conservative Republicans have won and governed properly, but for several decades these successes have had little to do with the DC Republican party. We can't replace the entire party, but we must replace this Beltway establishment.

The subtitle of the book is "How Karl Rove and the Establishment Lost...Again." They lost for the same reasons they've lost for the past twenty years. Moreover, it's why they'll continue to lose if the current players maintain control of the party message. We must defeat the GOPe to transform the party, and then we must defeat the liberal statists to save the country.

To win either, we must understand what's been going on for at least twenty years, and how it ties into the 2012 campaign. As such, this is not a second-guessing or Monday morning quarterback analysis. These two decades have been agonizing as I've sensed the party and the country slipping away, including the eight years of Bush. I have written extensively about this, and a lot of this book comes from those writings. Allow me a moment of bluntness: these articles have been way ahead of the curve, especially related to how the establishment has contributed to this slippage. If this were not the case, I'd have no business criticizing Rove and the establishment for being behind that curve.

This slippage has really been a twenty-year betrayal of the foundations of America and a betrayal of truth itself, and the book should be read in this context, as these betrayals and the 2012 loss cannot be separated.

This has long been my passion. I hope you enjoy it, not in the sense that it's good news, but in the sense that you will know that you have not been alone, and in knowing that there are solutions to the problem.

Now, a few revelations from the 2012 campaign....

WTF just happened?

One certainty — beyond any doubt — is that absurd narratives trumped truth in this election, and truth itself is the ultimate casualty of 2012. The fundamental breakdown of the GOPe and their consultant class over years is the failure to defend the truth in the face of liberal narratives. Instead of trying to persuade voters with information, consultants take a poll or focus group to figure out how badly the public is misinformed, and then position their candidates to appear to agree with that particular piece of misinformation.

Thus, liberals are constantly riding their false storylines and templates to victory as the truth is buried; and these falsehoods only harden over time. Instead of complaining about low information voters, perhaps our consultant class should realize that the low and mis-information problem is partially the result of their own tenuous and failed communications strategies.

And speaking of lies that have only hardened over time, one that currently threatens the very future of our county is that over half the voters still blame George Bush for the economy. Many Americans have wondered how long the Democrats can get away with blaming Bush and free enterprise for the economy. That's easy: forever. That is, until someone bothers to counter this foolishness. John McCain never did during his campaign, nor did John Boehner in the recent PR battle over the Fiscal Cliff. Mitt Romney and Paul Ryan failed to challenge this notion, literally agreeing with it time and again during 2012. No doubt their consultants told them to.

We also know that many voters are under the impression that Obama parachuted into Osama bin Laden's compound with Rambo's knife clenched between his teeth and took out the terrorist leader while Seal Team Six merely watched in awe. We also know our brilliant boy President had all the intel he needed without relying on Guantanamo Bay or waterboarding because we're assured that only dumb, old, rich, white Republican Presidents need such crutches. Apparently, our establishment candidates and consultants agree with that, too. Perhaps they should have checked with Leon Panetta first.

We also know that millions of Americans actually believe Obama's business wizardry alone rescued GM, among them Mitt Romney. Yes, he actually agreed (more than once) that a major corporation, which is still technically insolvent by the way, was saved through the business acumen of a community organizer who's never signed the front of a paycheck in his life. Not only that, but Obama's bailout model is what autoworkers cling to as the solution to their problems as opposed to say, cheaper domestic energy. (Does anyone remember Keystone, ANWR, or the Gulf oil moratorium?) We know that 73% of Americans actually do want more domestic oil and gas production, and yet *at least a third of those* still voted for the man standing in the way of just that.

We've also recently discovered that women have never had access to birth control while any Republican was in the White House, and unattractive old white women, who look nothing like Hiawatha, can climb the affirmative action ladder as a Cherokee. We have confirmed that it is a law school's responsibility to provide wealthy middle aged grad students' free birth control, and Mitt Romney's responsibility to cure cancer in a woman he never met and who never worked for him.

We can add with certitude that a portly B-list journalist from CNN vaporized three weeks of reality about a deadly attack on Americans in Libya, and that a portly governor from New Jersey reminded voters that Republicans were at fault for mishandling hurricane response seven years ago. Never mind the fact that both New Orleans and the state of Louisiana had been paralyzed by the iron hand of Democrat controlled corruption for generations.

We also have learned that some inner city precincts reported voter turnout of nearly 150%, a phenomenon about which our establishment remains remarkably uncurious.

Ah yes, all of this after a primary season where the sorcerers in charge of the establishment messaging machine, including Mitt Romney's campaign and his Super PACS, found it necessary to call the only candidate running hard against Obama the devil incarnate, but found it vital to insist that Obama himself is "a nice guy."

Imagine.

Since Newt Gingrich is supposedly "the Gingrich who stole Christmas," the GOP establishment felt safe, even justified, in savaging him. Since Obama is "still so personally popular, so likeable, such a great dad, the most amazing figure to visit our lowly planet, so elegant, so brilliant, so Ivy, so pragmatic, has such a sharp pant crease" and so on, they ran a frightened campaign that stopped just short of endorsing him.

Now, they actually thought this was the way to win, and the jaw dropping thinking behind that is explained later. At any rate, this personality obsession is the main reason conservatives and Republicans generally perform better in mid term elections, where campaigns have a chance to be about ideas instead of particular people. It's been said that small minds are focused on personalities while large minds are concerned with ideas. Small minds ran a Romney Campaign that was incessantly concerned with both candidates' reputations, and small minds ended up turning out in larger numbers in 2012. This is no coincidence.

* * *

Political pollster and commentator Pat Caddell knows a lot about failed Presidents, as well as good and bad campaigns. He worked for Jimmy Carter, and campaigned against Ted Kennedy, Gerald Ford and Ronald Reagan. Caddell detests both parties and is very critical of a media complex that has become nothing more than an arm of the most radical elements of Obama's Democrat Party. He is not a Reagan/Tea Party guy by any means, but he is not an anti-American radical liberal either.

After the election, he reiterated, "The Romney campaign was the single worst campaign in modern history." In context, he was referring to both the official campaign and the Rove-driven Super PACs. His contention is that it was a campaign of, by and for the GOPe consultant class.

"This consultant class is very, very dangerous," added radio host and author Mark Levin, a former member of the Reagan Administration, and a prominent historian. "They're not only pulling the Republican Party in the wrong direction, they are losing campaigns."

Indeed. What happened in 2012 is simply inexcusable. The establishment consultant coterie, led by Karl Rove, had their dream candidate and control of all the meaningful messaging money. The big money was strategically and purposefully combined, and donors who thought about going in other directions were given offers they couldn't refuse. This gave Rove and the establishment every messaging card that they needed to be successful.

And yet, this GOP establishment lost to the worst and most vulnerable President in modern history, with historically poor approval ratings, running the smallest and most absurd of all possible campaigns. Against this backdrop, there are many theories as to what went wrong, and most analyses are concentrating only on the 2012 campaign season. This is not a wide enough focus, as this campaign was merely an extension of the establishment's sacrificing of the truth in favor of shallow formulaic messaging for at least two decades.

"More than anything, they think they can overcome a narrative that builds over time with just a single message," says Caddell of this very problem, adding they "must move away from a bureaucratic, top down approach to messaging… and be more imaginative." He is right, and the problem is hardly new.

Thus, the following pages will focus not merely on an election analysis of what went wrong in 2012. The loss of 2012 has been in the works since at least 1992, and, in some ways, longer than that. The year 1992 is chosen for a number of reasons that will become evident, but primarily because this is the general career range for the current media/establishment/consultant class. It's also when the establishment abandoned Reagan, which was disastrous for them to attempt.

This current group of leaders in the GOPe now controls the main messaging outlets for Republican candidates and their top Super PACs. Never has a group of scared party apparatchiks been so out of touch with the base of their party, not to mention the truth about the history and greatness of America, as these people are today.

Rove certainly epitomizes this current group, and he controls more levers of power, influence, and money than any other single person. His fingerprints are all over the Party establishment mess, as well as on their estrangement from the rest of the country (and reality).

More damning, Rove is largely responsible for the fact that voters still blame Bush for the economy and still give no credit to Bush and Cheney for the eventual death of bin Laden. Rove's previous strategies can also be linked to the belief that the Hurricane Katrina response, dominated by Democrats and bureaucrats, was somehow a systemic Republican management problem. As 2012 played out and voters believed all of these fictions, they naturally concluded that Obama was the man to save the economy, restore America's place in the world, and to save New Jersey and New York from Sandy's damage.

Say what you want about the media's influence on low information voters, the fact remains that neither Romney, nor Ryan, nor their campaign, nor Rove's Super PACS ever bothered to counter any of the cockamamie notions above. While it's obvious that our side must fight institutions beyond our control, including the media, the education industry, and the entertainment industry, the problem is that we have the wrong people making the decisions over what we *can* control. In fact, the establishment often impugns talk radio hosts, conservative columnists, non-establishment PACS, and certain feisty candidates who are trying to counter these liberal institutions.

The thinking is that, if a few of their hand-picked wizards can control every message, spend enough money late in the game, and cherry pick some single issue zealots here and there in enough key areas, they will win a campaign. And they think they can do all of this without ever offending a single moderate soccer mom in Ohio, which apparently happens whenever you tell the truth. Above all, they insist we only campaign like we mean it when we are campaigning against other mean spirited Republicans.

They say we must muzzle those who are not willing to toe this line. MSNBC's Joe Scarborough recently said as much, calling talk radio hosts "cowards" and "bullies," and insisting that Republicans run against them. Someone should remind Joe that criticizing conservatives on MSNBC is actually the most cowardly profession on the planet and that McCain bombed by running against talk radio in 2008.

Scarborough is totally ignored inside Republican circles, as he should be, but Rove is still the single major influence there, and he agrees with Scarborough that certain conservatives should be stymied. One problem with Rove, the so-called "strategist," is he that has the mind of a tactician. Any business owner or military historian can confirm that these are profoundly different skill sets.

This really clicked for me when I discovered that Rove's background includes nineteen years running his own direct mail firm, Karl Rove and Company. Direct mail is the ultimate left brained, type B, small picture, tactical industry. In fact, to be good at it, your mind must, by definition, ignore over-arching themes. Yes, Rove can discern what corner of Ohio is filled with voters who care deeply about a specific issue and effectively target that area shortly before an election to generate freakishly high turn out. This is a valuable tactical talent.

It can also be a very expensive talent, as tactical thinking led Rove and Bush to target certain voters by pushing the monstrosity known as No Child Left Behind (NCLB). As you and I continue paying for this massive federal ambush written by Ted Kennedy, Rove considers it fabulous, since Bush got more "education voters" in 2004 than in 2000.

This tactical mono-vision prompts Rove to emphasize shallow temporal metrics like focus groups while not putting enough focus on deeper permanent metrics, like, say, reality and truth. A strategic campaign with a compelling big picture appeals to voters as individuals, not as "education voters" or "NASCAR voters" or "soccer moms." Such a campaign would have buried Al Gore and John Kerry, the two worst candidates in modern history. Reagan, with Lee Atwater, might have won similar elections by ten and twenty points respectively.

Oh wait, they did!

This strategic blind spot is related to the reality that Rove and most of the establishment class are not believers in the conservative vision in the first place. True to our nature and to the Constitution, our goal is to be left alone by bureaucrats and politicians in order to control our own destinies. This is not possible with a large intrusive government, and yet the establishment remains unfamiliar with this fundamental problem that impacts us every day. How? Think control.

Liberals naturally crave the power to control others while taking cover behind the TV screen, the bureaucratic cubicle, the academic podium, or the immunity of elected power. The allure of control is precisely why all of these people were initially attracted to the business of politics and government. Rove and our establishment enjoys this control almost as much as the left does, and yet they are in charge of messaging for the party that ostensibly opposes centralized control. This contradiction is not working.

Washington is a company town, and "the company" is government. So it naturally follows that any creature of Washington would struggle to craft an effective message about de-emphasizing government, a grand message that would mitigate the need for galactic turnouts in certain precincts in Ohio, Florida or anywhere else. Crafting such a message requires a strategic mind as well as core beliefs, plus the ability to articulate those beliefs without a teleprompter. A little real world experience outside the Beltway wouldn't hurt, either.

This message incoherence is what Caddell was referring to when he said it's impossible to combat narratives that build over time with a series of single, temporary messages. It should be obvious from human nature, not to mention GOPe electoral history that he's right.

The book will systematically demonstrate that the consultant class has destroyed our party's message and brand for years, and continues to misdiagnose the very problems they created. As you read sections that may not seem relevant to 2012, consider them in that light. On numerous occasions there will be an emphasis on Bush's refusal to fight ideologically on any issue. This was a colossal mistake by Bush and Rove, and is primarily why Team Bush left the White House with a 26% approval rating.

Yet forget about Bush's personal legacy for a minute. The salient point is that, as conservatives, we are still paying for Bush's unpopularity to this day. Consider the fact that 53% of the country still blames Bush for the economy and most of them just voted for Obama. You and I will suffer the consequences of that for a long time.

Rove, in his 2010 memoir, finally admitted that the new tone was a failed strategy, at least with respect to not countering the "Bush lied, people died" platitude. In truth, it was a failure on all issues. Just think, it only took him ten years to figure out what many of us knew instantly.

In the last election, Romney needed some sixty-five to seventy million votes to beat Obama, a figure impossible to obtain precinct-by-precinct or issue-by-issue with "a series of single messages." That kind of sum requires a compelling big picture strategy and a galvanizing message that is bold enough to motivate the core voters and coherent enough to change the minds and hearts of some percentage of the others. Only well articulated conservatism, repeated over and over, could deliver this.

This strategy necessarily includes aggressively engaging the other side and their phony maxims in the arena of ideas. Uncontested story lines will always become more powerful with time, a fact not difficult to deduce from human nature. And yet, on this score, Republican consultants have less understanding than the great philosopher Barney Fife. "Nip it, nip it in the bud!"

Somehow, the left-brain, type B, consultant mind is immune to this big-picture reality. Their turnout formulas assume that voters are all trifling, simple entities, to be mined and pampered to on their pet issues right before Election Day. This is something you must do while not appearing too confident in yourself. While this foppish approach might work on some people, these sterile formulas completely miss the defining moods of the nation.

The defining mood the GOPe missed in 2012 was the tectonic groundswell of anti-Obama, anti-government sentiment and the reasons for it. The establishment was so determined to be enlightened enough to understand the brilliance of the first black President that they were blind to this, even though it started emerging immediately after Obama's election in late 2008 and early 2009. This mood is why every single election of consequence went against Obama from late 2008 through mid 2012. None of these victories had anything to do with the establishment. It took Romney's GOPe campaign to allow Obama to win again.

* * *

The mood was in response to the greatest crime of all time. Government is in the process of stealing the country, as our economy, our freedoms, our energy, our health care, the very American experiment as founded, are all being consumed by a parasitic government and the bureaucratic class. This is the big picture, and it should be the fundamental message for every Republican campaign. This message defines Obama and the modern Democrats and explains every issue with a clear perspective. In 2010, with no single genius pulling the strings, this indeed was the big over-arching narrative. It sprung up organically and it was powerful, as well as historically successful.

In 2012, however, the combined Romney and Rove directed Super PAC message was an empty, non-confrontational and non-philosophical campaign. It was a centrally controlled and elitist campaign, and it worked just as well as centrally controlled, elitist government works. Which is to say, it didn't work at all.

The following chapters will tell this predictable story as it unfolds for some two decades, beginning in 1992 and ending with the Romney Campaign. There will be a considerable emphasis on how the establishment's messaging problem is directly related to their reality problem, and how they are somehow completely ignorant of the fundamental "government versus citizen" cross current roiling across the nation. These dots are connected and related, and thus our messaging problems cannot be solved until we resolve our reality problem.

2

TEAM CLINTON CHANGES THE NATURE OF THE GAME

Elections do not occur in chronological vacuums, and 2012 is the sum of many years and not merely many months. Frankly, this analysis could start with the Vietnam era, or Reagan's election, or perhaps the Robert Bork hearings, as each seemed to usher in a new tenor of political discourse.

For purposes of this discussion, 1992 works, since the Clinton campaign team certainly ushered in a new era of political narratives. He and his team are still pertinent, and many of the current Republican gurus have careers spanning this time. The 1992 race is also the campaign when many in the Republican establishment turned away from Reagan after shamelessly riding his coattails in 1988. Barack Obama's preoccupation with Reagan reinforces this as a good starting point, as well.

Bush Quayle '92

Through the oddities of fast moving and hectic campaigns, I landed as Communications Director for the N.C. Bush Quayle campaign two weeks after walking into the headquarters as an unknown volunteer. This is only significant in that it afforded me insider access to the party and campaign, and the first lesson I learned is that the GOP of 1992 was no longer Reagan's GOP.

This may seem obvious now, but in 1992, the Reagan Presidency was just four years removed, and his Vice President was in the White House. George H.W. Bush, known now as Bush 41, was in a tough re-election fight against Bill Clinton and Reform Party candidate Ross Perot. Perot was taking a lot of votes from Bush, which was painfully ironic since about 80% of what Perot was scoring points with was conservatism, while 20% was a folksy "look under the hood and fix it" set of banalities. Clearly, Perot disliked Bush and Republicans more than he disliked Clinton and Democrats, which philosophically made absolutely no sense.

Whatever Perot's motives were, Bush had no one to blame but himself for the fact that Perot was even a relevant candidate. The obvious strategy would have been to articulate a conservative vision to draw sharp distinctions between Bush and Clinton, which would have had the added bonus of exposing Perot's popular ideas as conservatism. But this was the Bush wing of the GOP, and they couldn't do that. Thus, the 1992 race had no philosophical definition at all, which is what Clinton needed.

To set the stage, Bush 41 was enjoying approval ratings near 90% in 1991 when campaigns were being contemplated. The real heavy hitters in the Democrat Party declined to run since 41 looked unbeatable. Strangely, that's the only reason Clinton, James Carville and George Stephanopoulos ever emerged, as Clinton was just a backbencher at the time.

Bush had high approval ratings because Stormin' Norman Schwarzkopf had Saddam Hussein's troops on the run in Desert Storm, live and in color on CNN. People actually watched CNN back then. The best spokesperson for Bush was the General himself, who was spirited, direct, and pulled no punches with the press in his widely watched briefings. He was very popular, and his blunt demeanor was probably worth twenty points for Bush, showing how a conservative should handle the media. At the same time, cowed by the inane charge that we were "trading blood for oil," Bush refused to admit what every adult knows, which is that the war was indeed about oil, as all wars in modern history have been. Protecting natural resources from the bad guys is nothing to be ashamed of, because those resources are crucial for the life and liberty of the good guys.

(As a related aside, it amazes me how our country has not yet matured to the point that we can talk about oil like grown ups. This includes the oil companies, who run ads ashamed of their own industry. This squeamishness is related to our over all truth-is-dying theme, but I digress.)

At the time, Bush could have easily removed Saddam Hussein from power, but stopped Norman from stormin', and politically, it was downhill from there. And as we all know, we had to deal with Saddam later on, too. Of more immediate impact, aborting the mission cut short the positive impact of the general's fabulous press conferences.

So with the magic of Schwarzkopf minimized and Desert Storm out of the news, the economy became central to the 1992 Campaign. Actually, the economy was not nearly as bad as the Clinton-Carville team insisted it was by using the phrase "the worst economy in 50 years" over and over and insisting that 1992 was "about the economy, stupid."

Bush had walked right into this trap by signing a 1990 budget deal that included Democrat tax increases as a bargaining chip. This was especially problematic because he had issued the famous "read my lips...no new taxes" pledge during the 1988 campaign. The resulting narrative was this: Bush the Republican was at fault for a bad economy because he had agreed to Democrat tax increases. Therefore, we must elect Democrats to straighten all of this out.

That's the storyline our establishment couldn't figure out how to fight, and while Perot muddied things, he was only able to do so because of the weak Bush message.

Speaking of muddying things, during the campaign a

certain Senator from Arizona was starting to establish himself as the media darling of the GOP. I remember thinking at the time that, if we don't shut this guy up, we're going to regret it. Senator John McCain's chief mantra, even then, was how the GOP was becoming too extreme. I couldn't help thinking, "Bush extreme? Extremely what? Extremely non-extreme?" McCain has always been opportunistic bad news, even if it took most people until the 2000, or perhaps the 2008 campaign to figure this out. McCain's confusing message only added to the unhelpful murkiness of a campaign that Clinton's team had already successfully clouded. It was not the last time McCain would help destroy his own party, either.

Election Disaster

Bush received only 38% of the popular vote, feeble for an incumbent. Clinton won, but with only 43%, and Perot got most of the rest (19%). Clinton had solid Democrat majorities to work with: 57 Senators and 258 House members.

As he took office, a couple of major changes were about to take place that have context today. First, a Congressman from Georgia named Newton Leroy Gingrich started to come to prominence, replacing Minority Leader Bob Michel as the top Republican. Michel had been the perfect establishment Republican, serving thirty-eight years in Congress with fourteen as House Minority Leader, He was, in fact, happy to be in the minority. The Democrats were happy with Michel, too, and controlled Congress during his entire tenure, thanks to people just like him.

Gingrich, however, was not at all happy with Michel, or with being in the minority. He had been saying for years that the Republicans could win the House if they would stand up for limited government and run a daring national campaign.

Another related game changer in 1993 was the emergence of Hillary Care. Controlling the individual by access to medical services has long been a dream of the liberal statists, and Reagan predicted this as the ultimate statist ploy in 1961. Hillary Care, just like ObamaCare, was all about control. Reagan, by the way, was fifty some years ahead of naive Republicans who think ObamaCare has anything to do with health care.

The nation largely recoiled at the thought of government-run health care, so Newt and the Republicans jumped on this opportunity. Focusing on Hillary Care, along with an assault weapons ban and a number of corruption issues, they ran a national Congressional campaign in 1994. Front and center was a document called the "Contract with America" (CWA), co-written by Newt and others, including Dick Armey, Tom DeLay, and a newcomer named John Boehner, none of whom could be considered establishment figures in 1994. A Reagan speech from 1985 was the outline for the CWA, which was more or less a Tea Party platform of limited government, albeit twenty years early.

Boehner's history is so illustrative of the current problem with the GOPe. Elected in 1992 as a small business owner, Boehner was quite Tea Party some seventeen years before there was such a thing. He could never author the CWA today, and in 2001 he helped Ted Kennedy write NCLB (No Child Left Behind). This is a Speaker who still doesn't understand the election that gave him the gavel, which is ironic since 2010 was similar to 1994 in so many ways.

The CWA was scoffed at in the media and was given little chance of success. Undeterred, Newt, Boehner, Armey, and others like Jim Nussle kept making their case. And here is the lesson: while the CWA faced competing liberal narratives, these particular Republicans fought back with persuasion and repetition and refused to cede the discussion to the liberals.

There was no reaching across the aisle or backing down. There was no new tone or talk of "compassionate conservatism." The CWA was unapologetically conservative and quite partisan. The only outreach to moderates and independents was to persuade them to vote conservative and vote Republican.

History was made as the GOP flipped fifty-four House seats and assumed control in January 1995, promptly electing Newt as Speaker. The outgoing Speaker, Tom Foley of Washington, lost his seat altogether. Showing the arrogance that was also an issue in this election, Foley had literally sued the people of his state for their audacity to vote in favor of term limits. Foley won the suit, and then the people term limited him anyway. He was the first speaker in one hundred and thirty-two years to lose an election.

The Senate was flipped as well, with the GOP winning a whopping net of nine seats, giving them a 52-48 majority in that body. But make no mistake, Newt, the House Republicans, and the CWA drove this ideological and partisan election.

* * *

Clinton had won the White House in 1992 by effectively clouding the differences between the parties with help from Perot, and Newt had taken Congress away from Clinton's party by effectively re-clarifying those differences in 1994. This doctrinal differential is foundational, as for over 30 years Republicans have fared best when the doctrinal differences were clear, and conversely Democrats have generally won when differences were fuzzy.

I know some people will say, "Yeah, but that was 1994, and this won't work today." If that is true, and I contend it is not, there are self inflicted reasons for it, and the establishment's self inflicted damage is my premise in the first place.

Starting in early 1995, the Democrats and their pals in the Jurassic media threw a collective and coordinated tantrum over the GOP's takeover of Congress. As Newt and his new majority tried to enact the policies they had run on, the media and the Democrats went into overdrive, accusing the mean spirited Republicans of draconian cuts, and starving old folks and kids. All of these narratives were forerunners to the GOP pushing granny off the cliff in 2012, not to mention the union outrage in Wisconsin. This reaction was nothing new, but it was taken to a whole new level of degree. The GOPe shudders to this day thinking about the 1995 media ambush. Consider the Fiscal Cliff debates of 2012 and 2013 as evidence of this fact.

It is important to remember that there was no political internet to speak of in the mid '90's, no Fox News, and Rush was just coming into national prominence. The many spin-offs he inspired were not yet spun off. The media was more or less CNN, the three networks, the three big papers, and C-Span. C-Span exploded onto the scene and quickly became a conservative refuge, with callers that were on the order of 90% conservative. That is until founder Brian Lamb panicked and instituted a mandatory 50-50 formula. C-Span quickly became irrelevant, and still is today. There are lessons in that for our establishment, and maybe for Fox, too.

At any rate, Newt and his newly powerful Republican caucus were clearly caught off guard by the intensity of the onslaught. It was an unforeseeable black swan response, since the modern media and GOP control had never met before. Newt was visibly shaken at times, and the CWA momentum was mitigated. Certainly, part of his unreliability today results from the media beatings he took in the '90's, and he is one of the few people in the country who can relate to Sarah Palin in this regard. He was personally attacked above and beyond the general attack on the GOP, including the infamous "Gingrich Who Stole Christmas" meme.

Nonetheless, his Congress did get welfare reform and some other conservative legislation passed and onto Clinton's desk for signing. Hillary Care went nowhere with Newt's Congress, and momentum for it was weakened when a young restaurateur named Herman Cain gave Clinton a lecture on economics and reality on national TV. Imagine, well articulated conservatism was dominating Clinton's agenda at every turn.

Clinton remained popular because he was credited with the success of legislation he was clearly against, sent to him by a conservative Congress he clearly despised. This is one of the great media/political ironies of all time, and he took advantage of it with the "triangulation" strategy designed by Dick Morris. Morris and Clinton knew it was the Democrats who were advantaged when the differences between the parties were blurred, and no one could blur them and take credit for conservative successes like Clinton. Why do you think Obama picked Clinton to Keynote his convention in 2012? The Democrats still need that blur!

1996 Election Cycle

Unfortunately, the Republican Presidential nominee in 1996 didn't help clarify much of the blurriness. There was an excellent fiscal conservative, Steve Forbes, in the field, but he faced very long odds for a number of reasons. Pat Buchanan ran again and continued his counter-intuitive mix of fearless social conservatism plus a dose of a blurry populism/protectionism that frankly borders on liberalism. He had two small niches of support, but neither he nor Forbes were much competition for another perfect establishment candidate, Bob Dole. Dole had given Bush 41 a reasonable run in 1988 and had the "my turn" credibility so deeply valued by the establishment. In June, Dole resigned from the Senate after a few hundred years, allegedly to run as "Citizen Dole from Kansas." Puh-leeze. Who showed him Kansas on a map?

The problem with Citizen Dole and his wife Elizabeth was that they had been on the citizens' dole their entire adult lives. Dole had no understanding of the core voters he needed to motivate to win, let alone any ability to persuade undecided voters about anything. The Doles are also a lot like the Clintons, both families having won high office from two states they rarely ever visit. This necessarily leads to an increase in one's Reality Deficit Disorder (RDD.)

Dole listed his greatest accomplishment as the passage of the Americans with Disabilities Act (ADA), a government fiat that forced businesses who may have one or two wheel chair customers a decade to spend tens of thousands of dollars putting in ramps. Dole is completely unfamiliar with the private sector, something else that made him the perfect establishment candidate. Business people and reality can be so extreme, you know. (Consider that Mitt Romney ran away from his own private sector success in 2012.)

Citizen Dole eventually picked Jack Kemp as his running mate. Kemp was once a great supply-side advocate, and, as a Congressman, was key in the successful Reagan economic agenda. He had run for President himself in 1988. As the campaign wore on it became obvious that Jack, too, had been domesticated, and he is best remembered for a cringe-worthy moment in the Vice Presidential debate with Al Gore. Kemp's awful, "Thank you, Al," reply came in response to Gore congratulating him on being unusually kind for a conservative, and by inference, totally different than the typical mean spirited, racist Republican. Or, as Obama would clarify in 2008, a *typical white person.*

Kemp walked right into that one, and for some reason, I was reminded of this during the 2012 VP debate as Paul Ryan meekly ceded the point to Joe Biden that poor Obama had "inherited a big mess" from Bush and the Republicans. Thank you, Paul. Very helpful.

Kemp was, at one time, fearlessly clear when explaining how and why conservative economic policies worked. Now he was a sniveling poodle next to Gore. This is what living in Washington will do for you. He demonstrated the psychosis of the "new tone," which really is the same thing as "compassionate conservatism" and "reaching across the aisle." Predictably, Dole-Kemp was never competitive. Perot ran again for no particular reason, and polled about half of what he received in 1992. Clinton won re-election while getting less than half the vote for the second straight campaign.

If you're scoring at home, the establishment had run their candidate in 1988, 1992 and 1996, with their only win coming in 1988. That's misleading though, since Bush 41 ran as the *assumed* extension of the Reagan Revolution. By 1992, his establishment thinking had come out of the closet, and he was embarrassed, as was Dole. Conversely, Newt ran the non-establishment CWA campaign in 1994 and rolled Republicans to their historic victory. Are we spotting a trend regarding conservative campaigns versus establishment campaigns?

1998 Mid Terms

The results of the 1998 mid term elections were a strange mix, and not much of it was good for Republicans. Still, it is a great tutorial. Though Clinton was weakened by the Monica Lewinsky affair, his party picked up five seats in the House. This was unusual for a second term, mid term incumbent, although the GOP did out poll the Democrats by about 1% in the national popular vote. In the Senate, the split stayed 55-45 in favor of the GOP, but the party should have picked up seats due to Democrat retirements and weak incumbents. Of note, two rising Democrats defeated GOP incumbents, as Chuck Schumer beat Alphonse D'Amato and John Edwards beat the ideologically squishy Lauch Faircloth.

Perhaps the most exegetical lesson was Jesse Ventura's stunning third party victory in Minnesota's Governor race. Ventura, a former professional wrestler, ran an aggressive common sense campaign, with an emphasis on personal responsibility. He never seemed to realize it, but his campaign was to the right of Republican Norm Coleman, and way right of Democrat Skip Humphrey. How he governed is something else altogether. Lessons just keep popping up in the strangest places.

Elsewhere, the unreported story is that conservative referendums won handily everywhere in 1998, even in liberal states. So while it was not a great night for the GOP, conservatism won everywhere it was tried. It just wasn't tried everywhere. As for Clinton, he had lost some shine, but his party had survived the dreaded lame duck mid term.

His second term was dominated by the Lewinsky scandal, and his major accomplishment was surviving it. He was aided by a Republican Party that kinda sorta wanted to pursue it, but maybe only a little bit. Nonetheless, the liberal version was the Republicans failed because they were all foaming at the mouth over the issue. Much has been written on this subject, but my quick take is that the GOP should have either gone full speed ahead or not pursued it at all. The thread-the-needle approach they took failed on all counts, as it always does. It's also par for the course that pliable Republicans believed the liberal spin, including a young Congressman from South Carolina named Graham, who was never the same after this affair. Clinton emerged as the underdog victor, but did little else of note in the second four years.

2000 Election and the Bush Cheney Years

The eight George W. Bush (Bush 43) years that followed are a case study in how not to use the bully pulpit. The damage done to conservatism was enormous, including creating a stage perfectly set for Obama. In that context, this history is still part of our reality today. It all started with the memorable 2000 campaign.

A Lewinsky'd Clinton, even though personally popular, could not generate a lot of momentum for Al Gore going forward. Bush 43 had a lot of momentum, having crushed a fairly popular sitting Texas governor, "Ma" Richards, by nine points in 1994, then rolling to re-election in 1998 by more than thirty-seven points. That margin is astounding in any state, let alone one the size of Texas.

Along with momentum, he had money, a big organization, and almost had the GOP nomination wrapped up before it started. He was the choice of fifty out of fifty-four Republican Senators, which is interesting because Senator McCain was also running. Normally Senators stick together regardless, so it's obvious that the more you know about McCain, the less you like him. This validated my thoughts about McCain, and as the public has gotten to know him better over the past 12 years, they seem to like him less, also.

McCain was running his "Straight Talk Express" in 2000, which, of course, was anything but. It was just his thinly veiled Democrat disguise. He had also carefully cultivated his reputation as the "Maverick," a brave reformer not afraid to take bold, courageous stands against his party.

Boldness schmoldness. In Washington's culture, the easiest thing for a Republican to do is to oppose his party. The straight talk maverick shtick was all just a bunch of flapdoodle from the start. The reforms he favored always thrilled the media and the Democrats.

Since they like that kind of weak Republican collaborator in New Hampshire and other states with cross-over primary voters, McCain had some primary opportunities. He beat Bush in New Hampshire.

Then it was on to South Carolina, a state where both men had somewhat of a natural constituency. Bush was popular in general and with evangelicals, and McCain was strong with the state's very large military vote. The S.C. contest was nasty, with claims of dirty pool, phony push polls, and the like, and McCain even threw a tantrum at Bush during a commercial break in one of the debates. Rush Limbaugh, who now clearly had McCain in his sites, aided Bush by pointing out that McCain was trying to win the GOP nomination with liberal Democrat voters. Voters recoiled at this, and it was the biggest factor in Bush's 54% to 42% win in the state.

The next week, with momentum from South Carolina, Bush routed McCain in Florida 74% to 19%, and the race was all but over. McCain later won his home state of Arizona and a few others with heavy Democrat cross-over voting, but those were immaterial.

As an aside, the Maverick was not through, and he was not 'over it,' either. His multi-year vendetta against Bush and voters who supported him still haunts our cause today, as

McCain remained an intentional thorn in Bush's side for all eight years of his Presidency. He would pop up right at the rare moment when Bush was actually trying to apply some conservatism and sabotage those efforts. Thus, McCain bears much of the blame for the Republican brand being in so much trouble in the first place. This irony led to all kinds of unhappy dynamics for the party in the 2008 cycle and beyond.

(In fact, the McCain-Bush tension is a large reason why Bush was considered the 'Republican right' in the first place, even though that was never the case. To me, this is another good reason to dislike McCain, as this confusion still tortures us today, and it certainly did in 2012.)

As the 2000 General election campaign neared the finish line, Bush seemed to have a slight edge in momentum and polling over Gore. This could have been due to Clinton fatigue as much as anything else, as the Bush Cheney campaign was not overtly philosophical by any means. Everyone figured Florida and Ohio would be key states, and in some ways the 2000 election cemented the importance of those two states in everybody's mindset.

Schwarzkopf, still a popular figure, campaigned some for Bush in Florida, and would also wade into the upcoming recount scuffle regarding overseas military ballots, thousands of which were not accepted in Florida. This controversy would be very important, since Bush was winning those voters almost two to one, and we were all about to learn the lesson of counting every single vote.

Now, if you're wondering what the relevancies are to 2012, they will unfold before long. Think of the 2000 election as a fish story, where the stinky fish has grown in size over the years.

Five days before Election Day, one of the classic late surprises of all time exploded onto the scene. The story about a DUI incurred by Bush in Maine in 1976 dominated the news for the final few days. A local cop tipped off a WPXT reporter named Erin Fehlbau, who broke the story on November 2. As luck would have it, the exact dates and docket number for this 24-year-old case just happened to be available to Fehlbau from a guy named Tom Connolly. Connolly, coincidentally, is a lifetime Democrat operative and former candidate for Governor. The Gore Campaign was 'strangely prepared' to maximize this opportunity, with blast faxes already written raising the possibility of systemic substance abuse. Another phony narrative was born.

Alan Simpson, the former Wyoming Senator, told Chris Matthews "if anybody doesn't believe that this came right out of Gore headquarters, you ought to sprinkle some Peter Pan twinkle dust on them." It's not clear whether Simpson was indicating that Matthews carried twinkle dust or not, but the broader implication was clear.

At any rate, the story obviously caught Bush off guard, and like Hurricane Sandy in 2012, it was a story that caused an discernable last minute shift in what had been palpable momentum. Gore strategist Chris Lehane later said he was convinced it changed the dynamic of the popular vote altogether.

And that popular vote was extraordinarily close.

Even so, NBC decided to call Florida for Al Gore before the polls even closed in the Panhandle of that state, and the lemmings in the other networks followed shortly. This was critical, since Florida's most Republican-leaning districts are in the central time zone, and everyone knew Bush had no chance without winning Florida. The phony early call for Gore sent thousands of dispirited Bush voters home from the polls, not only in the Florida panhandle, but all across the nation in the two western time zones. Who knows how many hundreds of thousands of Republican voters left voting lines at that time? Keep this question in mind, because all of what was about to transpire led to the narrative that Bush was an illegitimate President. This illegitimacy is an underlying theme that has been considered a fact for the entire adult lives of many voters in the 2012 electorate. As such, it tends to poison their perception of all Republicans in general, and it is sophistry to pretend that this is not an underlying factor in our current political climate. This is exactly why the Democrats have continually pushed this meme as part of their revisionist history on the Bush years.

As we know now, Bush rallied and the Gore projections for Florida were removed around 10:00 by most networks. In fact, Bush had moved slightly ahead and was even declared the winner in Florida, and thus of the entire election, shortly after 2:00 the next morning. But wait....

That prediction lasted about two hours and then was rescinded by the networks at around 4:00. Wednesday morning came, people were exhausted, the media complex was thoroughly embarrassed, and the nation still had no President-elect. And as you know, we would not have a winner for another thirty-seven days. The initial raw vote difference in the entire state of Florida was just over five hundred votes in favor of Bush. Again, keep in mind that the errant call for Gore impacted the actual behavior of many thousands in voting lines, while the premature call for Bush was after all the polls were closed.

NBC, according to Tom Brokaw, did not merely have egg on its face; it had "the whole omelet." (NBC's boss at the time was Jeff Zucker, who was recently hired to salvage CNN. That should work out just great.)

What transpired over the next thirty-seven days in Florida, with the hanging chads, the voter confusion, and the Florida and U.S. Supreme Courts, was nothing short of bizarre. It's been well chronicled elsewhere, but the upshot is that Bush limped into office under a cloud of perceived illegitimacy. That cloud still drops some rain on us from time to time today.

This perception was due primarily to two factors, one being that the conservative majority on the U.S. Supreme Court ultimately decided the case by only 5-4 (even though one key vote was 7-2), and the other was the popular vote interpretation. No doubt you remember that Gore won the popular vote, and officially, he did. But remember that the margin was just over half a million votes, and many thousands of voters left polling places across two entire time zones after the phony Gore call in Florida. To clarify, I'm not claiming that Bush would have won the popular vote without the network mistakes, but I do contend that an uncontested liberal interpretation of these events now perverts everyone's memory. The narrative morphed into one where Gore routed Bush in the popular vote and probably won Florida, but Bush cheated his way into office with one Republican Supreme Court Justice's vote.

This doggone fish was not nearly that big in 2000, but we never told the other side of the story so it has grown over the years. It still haunts us.

At the time, it was more widely understood that the vote was for, all practical purposes, a statistical tie. The Senate raw vote was just about dead even, and Republicans won the House popular vote by a hair. God only knows the actual Bush-Gore count, and I mean that literally.

Moreover, it was known in 2000 that the voters in the Panhandle who abandoned polling places would have certainly given Bush a clean win in Florida. The same holds true for the military ballots from overseas that Schwarzkopf was concerned about. Without any doubt, a cleaner win in Florida would have greatly softened the idea of illegitimacy, as would a closer popular vote interpretation. All of this could have reduced the impact of the "re-defeat Bush" mantra from 2004, which may the closest thing Democrats have ever come to campaign humor. But Bush and Rove decided not to pursue any of these available avenues, and frankly did nothing to try and mitigate the "Bush really lost" meme.

I was sick to my stomach, thinking that if we don't at least blunt this template somewhat, we're going to wish we had. It was an early moment when the new tone stuff tweaked my radar. In fact, I think the Florida recount might have inspired that regrettable strategy.

The Democrats, who never stop campaigning under any

circumstances, immediately hammered the popular vote parable, the biased Supreme Court theory, and the supposedly dirty Florida count, and those are still clouds over the GOP today. Why not? The Democrats constantly campaign on all of their pet narratives all the time. Our side never counters, which is why no one seems to remember our narratives. We never narrate!

Apparently the Bush Rove team thought that, if they tiptoed into the White House politely, both the Democrats and the voters would reward them. This misguided, naive notion was the implementation of the new tone that Bush thought he could bring to Washington, and the official beginning of Rove's vice grip on the Republican messaging and communications strategy. For the most part, he has had that control up through 2012.

History Intervenes, At Least For a While

Of course, the recount, the hanging chads, popular vote totals, the Supreme Court, and just about everything else was to be temporarily blown out of the national discussion by what transpired on the morning of September 11th, 2001. It's certainly untoward to mention this awful world-changing event and immediately segue into the political ramifications, and yet this book is about political ramifications.

And the main political impact of 9-11 is that, for a while, any whiff of Bush's illegitimacy was wiped away. In fact, there was sort of a "seller's remorse" dynamic going around, with some Gore voters conceding that Bush was the right man for the times after all. Some of this was the natural "rallying around the flag" that always occurs when a nation is attacked from outside. But a lot of it was the cowboy responding in a way most Americans thought a President should respond. Even Chris Matthews, before his apparent sex change operation, said, "We're sort of a cowboy, kick ass, kind of a country," and meant it as a good thing!

The image from the World Trade Center rubble with Bush, that bullhorn, and his arm around the old fire fighter, became a national symbol. Suddenly all of that conservative patriotism stuff that liberals normally hate was apt. Bush 41 had General Schwarzkopf, but Bush 43 had his bullhorn and the fire fighter.

His approval ratings touched the 90% range. (Are we spotting a trend here?) Certainly, a good part of this was simply unsustainable, regardless of how Bush had handled the rest of his administration, and yet there are teachable ideas here.

Like his father, Bush 43 had his best moments when he was self assured, strong, and unapologetic. When Bush 41 allowed Norman to storm, Americans responded to his audacious leadership. When Bush 43 flat out said the people who "knocked these buildings down...are gonna hear from all of us soon," people responded then, too.

Which brings me to a vital truth that consultants are apparently unable to process. Regardless of what kind of bipartisan, can't we all get along garbage people tell a pollster or a focus group, when the stuff hits the fan, human nature longs for leadership. You can't duplicate stuff hitting the fan in a focus group. Leadership involves the unapologetic articulation of what you believe and why you believe it, as well as follow through. Leaders change the hearts and minds of voters through their words and actions, while followers and their consultants obsess over poll results.

Both Bushs showed everybody this kind of leadership at various times, and yet neither man, nor our consultant class, ever understood the dynamic. As we all witnessed, the Romney Campaign never did, either.

3

TONE DEAF: BUSH ROVE PREPARE THE SOIL FOR THE MESSIAH

Obviously, the attacks of 9-11 and related stories continued to dominate the news and politics for the rest of 2001 and most of 2002, leading up to mid term elections in 2002.

Now keep in mind that Democrats and liberals in the media talk about the "eight years of Bush Cheney" as if those years were some kind of monolithic, extra terrestrial occupation, forced upon an unwilling and helpless American people, and that nothing good ever happened during this time. This is absurd, as there were ups and downs, not to mention several elections, where the voters reconfirmed their support for the Republicans. The mid terms of 2002 are one of those occasions, and they're a fascinating object lesson in messaging. It was a strange turn of events, having nothing to do with the GOPe, which made this mid term cycle a moment of true clarity. Not only that, the still crucial "Bush tax cuts" came out of that 2003 Congress. History matters!

In 2002, Bush was in the 55% approval range and his approval was heading downward into the mid terms. That's not good news for the party of the White House in mid terms, since unhappy voters turn out in larger numbers to begin with. Bush was "not trending," as we say today, and any chart of his approval over eight years shows a stunning ski slope downward.

On the other hand, the Democrats had not fully re-engaged their Bush derangement syndrome since the smoldering rubble of the WTC, and the attacks of 9-11 were barely a year in the past. In fact, Congress had just voted to authorize the use of force in Iraq in early October of 2002. At the time, a very strong majority of both houses agreed that Saddam Hussein did indeed have a dangerous stockpile of Weapons of Mass Destruction (WMDs). Democrats have conveniently forgotten this agreement on WMDs, of course. What do you expect from folks who were for the war before they were against it? Or was it the other way around?

In other words, there was no real ideological shape to the 2002 mid term elections, even into late October. That is, until Minnesota Senator Paul Wellstone, two family members and five others died in a tragic plane crash on the 25th. Wellstone, who had spent time as a community organizer and a college professor before becoming a politician, was always on the far left edge of the Democrat Party. (Does this sound like anyone else we know?) His nickname was "the conscience of the Senate," meaning that he was the most liberal. He was favored against Norm Coleman, the same guy who managed to make Ventura look like a raging right-winger in 1998.

Wellstone's death might not have had a major impact on the elections, at least outside of Minnesota, were it not for an event known as "The Wellstone Memorial." Just to set the mood properly, the Wellstone family had gone out of their way to make it known Dick Cheney was not welcome at the service. You mean three Wellstone family members had barely assumed room temperature, and yet the family was already thinking politics? Uh yeah, those compassionate bipartisan Democrats, you know.

So six days before the election, in a large sports arena, the Wellstone Memorial service morphed into a far left loon pep rally. Moreover, the media thought they were helping Democrats by showing this on national television. Tom

Harkin, the ultra liberal Senator from Iowa who is perpetually stuck in an Upton Sinclair time warp was perhaps the most shamelessly political of all the speakers, and Wellstone's own son didn't help matters, either. The event was so tasteless and so partisan that Governor Ventura stormed out. I can't remember the last time an event was so tasteless that a pro wrestler's sensibilities were insulted.

Even the left leaning Slate was horrified at the scene:

> But the solemnity of death (is) overshadowed tonight by the angry piety of populism...Sharply political speeches urging Wellstone's supporters to channel their grief into electoral victory. The crowd repeatedly stands, stomps, and whoops...each time Walter Mondale...who will replace Wellstone on the ballot, appears. "Fritz! Fritz!" the assembly chants. (And) as the evening's speakers proceed, it becomes clear that to them, honoring Wellstone's legacy is all about winning the election.

> Repeating the words of Wellstone's son, the assembly shouts, "We will win! We will win!" Rick Kahn, a friend of Wellstone's...challenges several Republican Senators in attendance to "honor your friend" by helping to "win this election for Paul Wellstone." What can he be thinking?

Mr. Kahn was thinking the way all liberals think: that politics and government are all important — even more important than life and death. This display clarified for everyone that the Democrats were a nasty coterie obsessed with big government and politics, and thankfully our consultants couldn't swoop in and mitigate the damage they were self-inflicting. Without a doubt, this spectacle impacted the 2002 elections, at least around the margins, and the margins were critical in this election. Defying the polling data of September and October, the Republicans picked up eight House seats and won the raw vote by 5%, neither of which would have happened without the Wellstone Memorial. More importantly, Mondale lost

Wellstone's seat, and the GOP took 51-49 control of the Senate with a gain of two seats. Yes, around the margins, indeed.

Once again, the GOP won an election when there was clarity between the parties. Oh sure, it took the liberal moonbats to demonstrate it, but the clarity was there nonetheless. As we know, this kind of lucidity was avoided at all costs by the Romney and Rove messaging machine in 2012. The newly elected Wellstone GOP Congress soon passed the "Bush tax cuts," and those cuts, plus the visibility of the war finally starting with its quick success in Iraq, spurred an economy decimated by the attacks of 9-11 and the dot com bubble bursting. GDP growth in 2003 was the best in twenty years. The aggressive use of superior military force plus those tax cuts were perhaps the closest Bush ever came to actually applying some real conservatism, and it all worked.

* * *

The year 2004 was not so good, at least at first. Early on, the national discussion focused on Bush's immigration reform plan, widely criticized by conservatives as being an amnesty plan. It wasn't enough amnesty to make the Democrats like it though, making it a lose-lose proposition. Immigration is a difficult and complex issue, worthy of a separate book or ten, but suffice it to say that the establishment is totally wrong if they think it will help the GOP to join the amnesty train. Calls for doing just this have emerged from the establishment after Romney's loss. History informs us that Hispanic voters are more motivated by government services than amnesty, and they'll be a reliable Democrat voting block regardless of what the Republicans do. Increasing the size of that block will only destroy the GOP's chances of ever winning again, not to mention the damage to our culture, our laws, and our economy. Exhibit A on all of the above: California.

Complicating the conservative case is the reality that many small business owners have suffered legitimate staffing problems as a result of a native work force disfigured by union demands, workers comp fraud, and a government that pays laborers handsomely to sit at home. Thus, the GOP was split about three ways on the emotional immigration issue, and this split continued to weaken the party.

Then, in the spring, the 9-11 report came out, which whitewashed everything, including the Clinton-era shortcomings. Contrary to just about every available narrative, 9-11 was largely dreamed up, planned, financed and set in motion on Clinton's watch. It occurred on Bush's watch, facilitated by a wall of separation between our intelligence agencies that was developed on Clinton's watch. The author of that deadly wall was Jamie Gorelick, a Clinton appointee at the Justice Department with no relevant qualifications.

(As an aside, Gorelick has gotten wealthy by failing upward, as many insiders do. She is the perfect foil for the two very different ideas about what real intelligence is, and as such, she'll make a number of appearances in the book.)

Meanwhile, since Bush was reticent to act like a legitimate President due to the turbid ending of the 2000 campaign, he never got around to replacing many of the bureaucrats from the previous administration. The entire intelligence complex and most of The State Department was still populated by Clinton appointees on the morning September 11. And yet, 9-11 was George Bush's fault, a supposition we live with to this moment.

No one on Team Bush or in the GOPe, has ever bothered to mention this simple, direct and correct perspective. As a result, Bush and all non-liberals will be considered at fault for 9-11 forever. Clinton will eternally get a pass. And in a related story, Obama will always get credit for killing bin Laden. Can you say festering narratives?

Another issue that came to light in the spring of 2004 was the Abu Ghraib controversy, which was blamed on Donald Rumsfeld as well as Bush and Cheney. To hear the liberal version, you'd think Rummy personally raided Laura Bush's underwear drawer, hopped a Halliburton jet, ordered our soldiers to put Iraqis into homo-erotic poses, S&M leather and women's underwear, then posted photos on Facebook, all to insult Allah. Oh, while smoking a cigarette, no doubt.

The only reason this affair became so dominant is that it was a convenient avenue of attack for the Democrats. Not only was it ridiculous to blame Rummy and Bush for this, I'm not sure why the liberals were in a snit in the first place. Aren't they the ones who tell us the gay, transgender, BDSM and cross-dressing lifestyle are perfectly fine? By liberal standards, our soldiers were doing the prisoners a favor, showing them an enlightened way of expressing themselves through gender bending activities, something that homophobic Sharia Law probably rewards with an amputation of some sort. Frankly, the Abu Ghraib photos were not even sketchy enough to qualify for federal funding from the National Endowment of Arts. And oh, by the way, there WAS a war on. There are about three thousand Americans who would gladly exchange their fate on 9-11 for an Abu Ghraib photo session, even with the cigarette burns.

Let's not forget the ever-helpful John McCain's role in this narrative either. He was prosecuting a one man media war against Rumsfeld, tying Abu Ghraib to waterboarding, no doubt as an excuse to mention — ahead of 2008 — that he was a tortured war hero himself. (I wonder if McCain was surprised in early 2013 when Leon Panetta admitted the obvious: that water boarding was successfully utilized in the hunt for bin Laden.) Rove made himself feel better by publicly opining that it "would take a generation" to heal the damage. McCain and Rove were damaging the GOP brand simply to appear enlightened and appropriately outraged.

Moreover, this drip of negativity sullied all conservatives by association. Millions of people who voted in 2012 lived through these days as an adult, and it is fanciful to think that surrendering on these issues in the arena of ideas for a decade had no impact on how they voted. History connects, and when our own establishment throws people like Rumsfeld under the bus for immediate convenience, they are contributing to the erosion of truth in our national discourse.

Another issue that was hurting Bush was the WMD issue. That is to say, no massive stockpiles of WMDs had been found. There would be two reports issued on WMDs, the Duelfer Report for the CIA in October of 2004, and the Silberman-Robb Report in March of 2005. Both concluded that Saddam did not have stockpiles at the time of the U.S. invasion, but both reports acknowledged that they had existed at one time, and admitted to not knowing what had become of them. They further confirmed that Saddam had gone to great lengths in order to deceive the world, and that he intended to re-tool when he could do so. Think Syria.

Silberman-Robb also specifically exonerated the Bush Administration of the "Bush lied People died" charge, but wasn't released in time for the 2004 election. All those Democrats who agreed with Bush in 2002 suddenly had lapses into mass deception and tried to establish the fiction "Bush lied us into war." Thank goodness they didn't have much time to run with this, since less than a third of the public believed Bush lied about WMDs at the time.

As his Presidency wore on, the "Bush lied" attacks would continue, and, in the end, more than half of the country would come to believe it. This, again, demonstrates the power of sticking with a false narrative, especially when the other side refuses to counter it. Rove's admission in 2010 that he regrets not contesting this charge was a case of too little, too late. That most of us knew at the time it was a mistake is more evidence of the RDD within the establishment.

* * *

As the 2004 election approached, the very animated liberal anti-war Democrat base was driving that party's primary process way to the left. This was good news, since Republicans win when there is plenty of philosophical room between the parties. The loon who led in the early going was Howard Dean, and he was setting the Democrat agenda.

Bush was simultaneously backing off his cowboy persona, which was central to his inspirational appeal after 9-11. Since people like cowboys, they naturally started to like Bush less as he purposefully abandoned this image. This was another awful, consultant-driven decision, designed to appease those who would never like him under any circumstances. All this did was weaken the resolve of his supporters, not to mention the war effort, as well as his mantle of command. He was also getting hit pretty hard by the mantra "re-defeat Bush," alluding to the popular vote from the 2000 campaign.

Inevitably, Dean's campaign imploded. Out of the pack emerged John Kerry. Kerry more or less made his public debut as a liberal anti-war hero in the '70's, and 'made' his fortune by marrying not one, but two rich widows. The second, and richest, inherited a lot of Republican cash that was earned by her first husband's family when the private sector really was doing fine. Kerry preserves this inherited wealth by living off the public dole, and he works against the private sector every chance he gets. After all, he's "got his, you get yours," an attitude perceptible among rich liberals.

How certain people view Kerry's wealth is interesting. Apparently, when a thin white guy from Massachusetts donates his entire inheritance to charity, then gets rich from the private sector like Romney did, he is bad. When another thin white guy gets rich by marrying into money meant for others' inheritances, and living off government checks and perks, he is good. Go figure.

Kerry was simply a typical Massachusetts liberal, yet with his campaign dead in the water, what saved him was his paradoxical emergence as a swash-buckling, right wing, John Wayne military figure. A former Swift Boat mate, James Rassman, surfaced and started recounting how Kerry saved his life in Vietnam. The upshot is that Kerry had some conservative war hero street cred to help disguise his ultra liberal candidacy. It's always interesting how liberals will conveniently find the nearest flag in certain circumstances, isn't it?

Fearing that this was not quite enough to blunt Bush's advantage on foreign policy and the military, CBS News' Dan Rather contributed to an evolving strategy of 'Kerry as the hero versus Bush as a draft dodger' with his fraudulent Bush National Guard story in September. This fabrication aired on 60 Minutes. The impact was to blur the issues of torture, Homeland Security, manliness, and all national defense in general, as well as making Bush look privileged, hypocritical and weak compared to the serial inheriting, wind surfing, aristocratic Kerry.

It damned near worked. Not only had the liberal cabal managed to erase Bush's advantage in military related issues, they had successfully reversed it. So what did the Bush campaign and the GOPe do? Not a thing. In fact, they got in the way of their own rescue at times, trying to play the Bush-Rove "above it all" drivel.

Other Swift Boat veterans were not so worried about staying above it all. In order to clear up the exaggeration of Kerry the hero, some vets formed a 527 group, Swift Boat Veterans For Truth. They raised money and ran an aggressive media campaign, giving their side of the Kerry as hero story. Let's just say their version didn't validate the Kerry/Rassman version. The Swifties' campaign was very successful, yet Bush, Rove, and their campaign publicly criticized the efforts. This was yet another flaccid iteration of the "new tone," not to mention particularly unappreciative.

Simultaneously, Rather came under attack for the preposterous National Guard story, but not from Bush's campaign or Rove. Who blew the whistle? Bloggers! Yes, the supposedly 'lowly' bloggers did the heavy lifting. Ratherbiased.com, Wizbangblog.com, and Powerline.com were the first to demonstrate the lies in Rather's story, then the Drudge Report and talk radio took those blog reports and made them worldwide news. Rather's 60 Minutes' report was mitigated just enough, and Bush was saved, and not by his campaign or by Rove, but by the Swift Boat Vets, bloggers, Drudge and talk radio. As a nice bonus, Rather's career was effectively ended, too.

Yes, I know, Rove gets credit for churning out niche voters in certain areas of Ohio, and that was helpful. But without the Swift Boat Vets and the blogs, Bush would have been buried. Thirty precincts turning out in Ohio wouldn't have mattered. The Swift Vets and bloggers accomplished this because they fought back hard on two phony liberal narratives and refused to accept a single liberal premise. They did not back down, nor did they run for cover when they took flak and faced push back. It's the narrative, stupid!

Rove was christened "the architect" after 2004 due to Ohio, though a case can be made that his last minute genius ultimately had little to do with Bush's 2004 win. For the record, Bush won the popular vote by roughly 62-59 million, a 2.4% advantage. He won Ohio by over a hundred thousand votes, or about 2%, meaning that Ohio roughly tracked the rest of America in terms of the raw vote.

The solid margin was a pleasant surprise in light of some fatuous exit polling, and there was a palpable collective sigh of relief. That sigh was as good as it would get for the entire Bush Presidency going forward. The second term was to be one dominated by bad news and a constant erosion of Bush's standing with the public. All of this impacted 2008 and 2012 significantly.

* * *

While it's hard to keep up with all of the spikes in energy prices over the past eight years, the first spike was in Bush's second term in 2005, when oil crested at over $55 a barrel. (Oh, for those days). This was putting a drag on the economy, and Bush and Cheney, the so-called "oil men in the White House," were blamed precisely because they were "oil men."

Now, to conservatives, having people in the White House

who understand the realities of energy is a good thing. Liberals don't think that way, but then again, neither do establishment consultants, demonstrating that they are almost as out of touch with America as our political enemies are. Bush and Rove ran scared of this idea, too. If anything, official Republicans tried to outdo Democrat outrage regarding supposedly obscene oil company profits. (I remain amazed at how certain Republicans don't understand the reality-driven need for profits.)

To make matters worse, Bush was buying into too much of the man made global warming hooey — the very hooey that would be exposed by the East Anglia emails for all to see in 2010. Thus, as an oilman and a semi-warmist, he was hated by liberals and not trusted by conservatives. This kind of flawed bipartisan attempt to thread the needle is how you earn a sub 30% approval rating, not to mention being the way to insure that bad policies and high prices continue.

During this time, the Iraq war still seemed to be dragging on with no end or specific mission in sight. War fatigue worsened as the Valerie Plame "yellow cake" affair reached critical mass in 2005, with Scooter Libby resigning as a result. Bush and Rove were certainly willing to dump on Libby, and by extension Cheney, for the purpose of protecting Bush's personal approvals. Rove had been against Cheney being on the ticket from the beginning, and, in his small way of thinking, he figured Bush should try and curry favor with liberals who hated Cheney by distancing himself. This kind of tactic never works, and only served to strengthen unflattering liberal narratives about the administration.

Shazam!! Who could have possibly seen that coming?

In another poll driven story, the Supreme Court dominated the news for about ninety days in the summer. In July, on the recommendation of the poll driven Rove, Bush picked poll driven John Roberts to replace Sandra Day O'Connor. When Chief Justice William Rehnquist died a few weeks later, Robert's nomination was "upgraded" to that of Chief Justice. Roberts was a politically safe pick, as he had clerked for Rehnquist in the '80's and had almost no written record. He was the perfect pick for an administration that wanted to be loved more than they wanted to be right. Roberts was confirmed quickly in 2005. In June of 2012, we found out that Roberts suffers from a need to be loved, too.

With O'Connor's seat not yet filled in September, Bush chose Harriet Miers, who had worked with Rove on the search that landed Roberts. (Don't you love the fail upward world of the properly connected?). The unqualified Miers was an unqualified disaster for Bush, and her nomination was removed. Eventually Bush named Samuel Alito, who was confirmed. To date Alito has proven more reliable than Bush, Rove, Miers or Roberts.

Republicans Lose '06, '08 and 2012 AT ONCE

At 6:10 a.m., August 29, 2005, the Republicans lost the 2006, 2008 and 2012 elections. Well, that was not the exact spin at the time, but it might as well have been. Hurricane Katrina made landfall as a Category 3 storm at Buras-Triumph, Louisiana. Yes, I know, the story is that Katrina was a Cat 5 storm, developed by evil scientists at Halliburton, and directed specifically into New Orleans 9th Ward by George W. Bush in order to kill negroes.

Or something like that.

More to the point, we know that Bush, Dick Cheney, Donald Rumsfeld, all Republicans, conservatives, free enterprise, pro-lifers, supply-siders, Rush listeners, NRA members, church goers, SUV owners, homeschoolers, Wal-Mart shoppers, Tea Partiers, and any other racists who might not like Barack Obama were all at fault for the misery that ensued. Thus, we need wonderful Democrats like Obama and Chris Christie (give him time) to come save the day when this happens again in 2012! Hold on, you say. The Tea Party wasn't around when Katrina struck. So what? Guantanamo Bay wasn't around when 9-11 happened, either, but details like chronology can never be allowed to get in the way of a good liberal narrative.

While we will never be able to determine the exact impact on Katrina on the 2012 election by way of Sandy, what we can establish is that Bush, and by extension all Republicans including Romney, are still haunted by the ghosts of this storm. (CNN even tried to bring Katrina and Bush into their coverage of the Carnival Cruise Ship disaster, asking passengers if they felt like Katrina victims as they disembarked.)

As we all watched on live television, New Orleans seemed to have weathered Katrina better than expected until late morning on the 29th. That's when 65-75% of the levee failures occurred, and the Crescent City was filled with water "like a soup bowl." Levees, pumping stations, and the like continued to fail for another day or so.

One would think that the logical place to assign blame for the aftermath would fall on the levee system. That's what failed catastrophically, and without that failure, most of the other dire situations would never have happened. There was, however, a political obstacle to blaming the levee system.

In 1998 and 1999, when Clinton was in his sixth and seventh years as President, the new levee upgrade was started. By the beginning of the hurricane season in 2005, the system was supposed to be in good shape. From where I sit, these failures are on the people who contracted for and built the levees, and I don't see Clinton or Bush as responsible.

Frankly, I would be more interested in why Congressman William Jefferson of New Orleans had $99,000 in cold cash in his freezer. Maybe it would be a good idea to look into Jefferson's ties to contractors working on the levees, since we hear the occasional rumor of some minor corruption coming out of Louisiana.

Having said that, since Americans tend to blame the party of a sitting President for everything — not counting the Obama economy of course -- it's fair to say that the failed levees were indeed redesigned and planned "on Clinton's watch." They were built on the watch of a Democrat governor in Louisiana and a Democrat mayor in New Orleans.

In other words, this was just another bungled, crony, government program. Many studies show this was the case, disputing any evidence that the levees were over topped. They failed due to workmanship and material deficiencies.

And speaking of bungled government programs, most of the decisions that directly led to the loss of life in New Orleans can be laid squarely on the shoulders of that city's wonderful mayor, Ray "school bus" Nagin. In case you have forgotten why he is called "school bus Nagin," he earned that moniker by refusing to mobilize hundreds of school buses and drivers under his control ahead of the storm. In an interview with WWL afterwards, he confessed "they were talking about getting, you know, public school bus drivers to come down here and bus people out of here. I'm like, you're kidding me. This is a natural disaster. Get every doggone Greyhound bus line in the country and get their asses moving to New Orleans."

I'm not sure why a private company should "get their asses moving" and abandon their entire national operation to evacuate New Orleans, nor am I certain if it's even possible. I am certain that buses and drivers already IN New Orleans, and already paid for, were not used. Ironically, the New Orleans buses were flooded where they sat. To the shock of no one, Nagin was recently hit with massive corruption charges stemming from his dirty contractor relationships while mayor. Come to think of it, checking *his* relationships with levee contractors might not be a bad idea either. Oh, did I mention Nagin is a life long Democrat?

Yet as bad as Nagin's performance was, he was not the politician most responsible for the disaster that Katrina became. No, it's not Bush, either. This honor belongs to another Democrat, Governor Kathleen Blanco. Her devastating incompetence started well before Katrina made landfall and continued for days. Now, keep in mind, Governors have a lot of say about if and when a President can intervene in their state. When Feds intervene by sending in the National Guard without an invitation, it is legally termed an "invasion." Bush, having a "fetish" for the Constitution, did not invade Louisiana. Perhaps he should have.

To recount, Governor Blanco delayed the suggested mandatory evacuation of the area until twenty hours before the storm hit, a known minimum of twenty-eight hours too late. She hesitated again after the storm, not asking for Federal troops until Wednesday the 31st. By this time, Shep Smith of Fox News along with the entire media had blamed Bush, Cheney, Halliburton, and all Republicans. In a whispered conversation recorded by CNN between Blanco and one of her aides, she conceded that perhaps she had sort of screwed the pooch on that one (paraphrase). Shep Smith was not watching, apparently.

Demonstrating even more incompetence, Blanco failed to mobilize the Louisiana National Guard in a timely manner, and these troops are under her direct command. Her hesitations made the situation at the Super Dome and everywhere else much worse than they should have been.

Certainly FEMA's response was flawed, but FEMA was not designed or staffed by Bush. It's a massive bureaucracy that's been wrapping itself in red tape for years. It was preordained that FEMA's response would be flawed in Katrina, as it will be in every single catastrophe. Government bureaucracies are always flawed. (This is why we're so excited about ObamaCare!)

Besides, the levee failure was an event for which no preparation can be adequately made under any circumstances, and certainly not by government bureaucrats. It's highly likely that bureaucratic screw-ups and the attendant corruption were the reasons the levees failed in the first place. In fact, every Katrina problem was the result of bureaucratic bungling. So I ask again, why is this bureaucratic bungle the fault of the very party that wants to reduce bureaucracies?

Bush had nothing to do with the fact that the levees broke and flooded New Orleans, thus making it impossible for FEMA or anyone else to get around town. Nagin's school buses were not under Bush's control, and neither was the Louisiana National Guard. Very little, if any, of this was the fault of Bush — or any other Republican, for that matter. And yet the Bush White House decided to absorb all of the blame that should have gone to the Corps of Engineers, Mayor Nagin, Governor Blanco, and government bureaucrats in general. What a wonderful stroke of genius that was.

So, just days before the election in 2012, when Governor Christie assured the nation that Obama was "doing a terrific job" just a day after Sandy hit, the obese one had to know he was tapping into the ghosts of Bush and Katrina. Obama had heroically donned a bomber jacket and flown into town to embrace Christie, after all.

This Katrina narrative was self-inflicted, and obviously still has impact years later. It's one of many storylines that exist simply because our consultant-establishment class decided not to fight it in its infancy, even though it's fundamentally false. This also re-establishes that all of this blame that Bush was graciously accepting because he wanted to remain above the fray was not his to accept in the first damned place. *We* are caught up in the fray and *we* bleed as a result of his capitulations. It's a kind of soft arrogance that Bush demonstrated by treating the bully pulpit as his own private public relations tool. A President's bully pulpit ultimately reflects on the supporters of the man who occupies the office more than the man himself. As was so often the case, Rove and Bush allowed all of the liberal bull and took all of the bully out of the pulpit.

* * *

Under the withering attacks from the media related to Katrina, 2005 ended poorly for Bush and 2006 followed suit. On top of more Katrina coverage, Iraq continued to putrefy as an issue throughout the year. Adding to this negative momentum, the Jack Abramoff lobbying scandal broke, and although it was a bipartisan scandal involving mostly liberal interests, the narrative was that of a purely Republican scandal. For a party already struggling, this was not helpful.

In case you forgot (or never knew), the issue underlying all of this Abramoff lobbying was gambling rights for Native Americans. In other words, it was a liberal scandal of establishment lobbyists, working with establishment politicians, and doing so with classic smoke-filled-room, crony-capitalist ventures. Frankly, everything about Abramoff reeked of typical liberalism, but the perception was that of a Republican, i.e. conservative, scandal.

And as if Katrina, Iraq, and Abramoff weren't enough, things were about to get even worse. On October 4th, 2006, reports surfaced that Congressman Mark Foley, a six-term Florida incumbent in a leadership position, was involved in a gay sex scandal. Except there was no actual sex. Nonetheless, Foley was indeed guilty of sexting young male pages and former pages.

This was embarrassing, and it naturally played into the typical liberal cliché about Republicans, family values and hypocrisy. Of course, there was no hypocrisy, as Republicans demanded and immediately got Foley's resignation, as they always do in these kinds of situations. Hypocrisy would apply only if Republicans acted like Democrats, which is to circle the wagons, make excuses, and attack those who deign to bring up the subject in the first place.

For the record, Foley is classic establishment, serving six terms in Congress and holding the position of Deputy Whip. Yes, I know, that whip title is kind of unfortunate in light of the nature of the scandal, isn't it?

The 2006 election was awful as a result of all of these factors, not to mention a conservative base that was livid with Bush over federal spending, immigration, and his conciliatory tone in general. Pelosi got her over-sized Speaker's gavel as the Democrats gained thirty-one seats in the House, six in the Senate, and rolled to a raw vote margin of almost 10%. This failure can be traced to a number of factors, and all of them involve Bush, Rove, the GOPe consultants, establishment lobbyists and establishment politicians.

The upshot was that Louisiana Democrats and bureaucrats, a phony gay sex affair, too much spending, too many crony back room deals, and gambling led directly to more power for the party that openly supports gay sex, crony back room deals, more spending, endless bureaucrats and gambling. Indeed, the Republican brand was in an awful state, as was the country.

* * *

So damaged was it throughout 2007 and 2008 that Republicans took all of the blame for the bad economy, which was a case of perception and reality being out of sync. To be brief, liberals made borrowing too easy and drilling too hard, and our economy tanked as a result. Yes, the root of everything bad can be traced to those two problems, and yet Republicans and free enterprise took the hit.

Part of the problem is that low information pundits and low information journalists like to talk about the housing crises, energy prices, unemployment, regulations, taxes, the deficit and so on as if these are separate, and even unrelated, issues. This is economic nonsense, spouted drone-like from a media class with absolutely no talent for discerning cause and effect. They never connect these issues economically, so they certainly never link them politically to certain policies. Low information Republican strategists, who probably don't know the difference anyway, never bother with connecting any of these dots, either. Certainly no one on the McCain Campaign ever did.

Come to think of it, a pretty decent campaign for McCain could've been based on the slogan that "Democrats have made borrowing too easy and drilling too hard."

Allow me to establish some linkage for the consultants. Since the 1970's, liberals have passed and enforced regulations that have indeed made borrowing money, especially for home mortgages, too easy, and drilling for oil or building an oil refinery too hard. They have done this through legislation, such as The Community Reinvestment Act of 1977, and through bureaucrats and various regulatory agencies like the EPA and OSHA. With laws and regulations on the books involving both lending and drilling, the floodgates were swung open for liberal protestors, activists and trial lawyers to bring suit against lenders and energy producers. It became damned near impossible to say no to a minority borrower or yes to a refinery. In fact, the last refinery was built on our shores before the first Starbucks was.

Fast forward to the mid 2000's across America, where we had millions of people living in houses they could barely afford and energy prices, specifically gasoline, rising rapidly. Businesses were starting to cut back on employees a bit due to energy, as well. On Wall Street, we had all kinds of convoluted esoteric investment derivatives like credit default swaps flying around, since the banks had repackaged and sold the bogus mortgages the government had forced them to make. Fannie Mae and Freddie Mac bought many of these mortgages, and in Washington, Democrats like Barney Frank, Chris Dodd and Maxine Waters were blocking any Republican investigations of Fannie and Freddie. These institutions, like many Wall Street banks, were depending on home prices staying strong, since the houses were the ultimate collateral for everything. To this point, the home prices had held up.

In other words, our economy was one big shaky domino table, and the only thing needed to knock everything down was to have the wrong domino tip. In 2005, that first domino was the price of gas, which shot up 40% during the year. This lightly bumped into the subprime domino, since those borrowers were the shakiest to begin with, and a few more defaults than usual started to pop up. It wasn't too bad for a couple years; while the seeds of destruction had been planted, there was still the appearance of a healthy economy. In fact, borrowing was becoming even easier.

Energy prices then came down some in 2006, but started

back up in 2007 and rose steadily all year. As this played out, more subprime borrowers started to default under the strain of the price shock. The price of oil was around $100 a barrel at year's end. There were many factors at play, including the weak dollar policy of Ben Bernanke, a growing international demand including China, but the over-riding factor was that American supply had not kept up with American demand in either crude oil or refined gas. If it had, all of the other issues would have been mitigated, as the law of supply and demand is not flexible. Liberals continue to be vexed by this law, and insisted that the problem was the few pennies per gallon profit made by the oil companies.

In 2008 the price continued to shoot up and finally peaked at nearly $150 a barrel. Gas was over four dollar in most places. While this was happening, all the dominos on the table started tipping. Sub prime defaults started impacting the price of houses, which then started motivating prime mortgage borrowers to default. This lowered home prices even more, motivating even more people to default and walk away from their homes.

Businesses, slammed by energy prices and the related inflation, started laying off employees and buying fewer supplies. This tipped even more dominos, as unemployed workers tend to default on their mortgages, too. The economy was caught in a vice between skyrocketing energy and food prices, and declining real estate values, employment, and consumer demand. Every problem made every other problem even worse, and in the swirl the dominos were flying off the board.

Meanwhile, back on Wall Street, it was becoming evident that the entire investment house was built on sand, and in September of 2008, the financial world was rocked by the failure of Lehman Brothers. The collapse was inevitable, since so much "value" was undergirded by residential real estate. Naturally, there was a sharp decline in the value of most stocks, completing the carnage across the economy. Families depending on 401K's and their home equity had their futures ripped out from under them, and many had lost their income sources, as well.

Not all was lost, though. Democrat cronies running Fannie Mae and Freddie Mac got wealthy giving themselves big bonuses, including Jamie Gorelick and Franklin Raines. Fannie and Freddie's biggest defenders on Capitol Hill, including Chris Dodd, got sweetheart mortgages from Countrywide Financial, the lender closest with Fannie under the sheets.

John McCain didn't help anything by suspending his campaign in a self-righteous panic and complaining about "unfettered capitalism." The problem was actually unfettered government, which had made borrowing too easy and drilling too hard. None of this would have happened without those factors.

And yet, all of these problems were laid at the feet of Bush, which to the low and mis-information voter and others automatically meant all Republicans, including all conservatives. All the while, the Bush White House never said anything to counter this, and neither did anyone in the establishment. They were more comfortable rushing to blame big banks, big oil and Wall Street — no doubt because their polling and focus groups told them this was the path of least resistance. And they wonder where all these low information voters come from.

Then on October 3, 2008, eighteen days after the Lehman crash, Bush signed the Troubled Asset Relief Program (TARP) into law. TARP remains one of the most misunderstood pieces of legislation ever, as more than half of all voters think Obama signed it into law, and few know that most of the TARP loans have been repaid. Inspired by shameless commercials for certain candidates, gold, and refinance programs, people continue to think it was a give-away. In most cases, this is incorrect. Many voters also confuse TARP with Obama's Stimulus, which *was* a purposeful give-away in every sense.

All of this continued to cloud the public's perception

of free enterprise, Wall Street, cronyism, Republicans and Democrats. On balance, the public came down on the side of blaming Republicans and capitalism for everything, with McCain's campaign helpfully leading the way, I might add.

Bush didn't help all of this confusion when he made perhaps his single dumbest comment ever in referring to TARP: "I've abandoned free-market principles to save the free-market system." That was totally incorrect and played into Obama's hands by indicting capitalism in the tiny minds of mis- information voters, not to mention confusing the minds of many others. If Bush really had any idea what the hell was going on, he would have said something like, "Government interventions have finally destroyed our free market economy, so now we will make some loans to ease the pain everyone is feeling as a result of too much government meddling."

Wherever you come down on TARP, and chances are you were against it, at least the second statement accurately portrays what TARP was supposed to do. More importantly, such an interpretation correctly assigns blame to big government regulations. If you really want to get sick, do some research on how the brunt of the crisis might have been avoided simply by suspending the "mark to market" regulation imbedded in the Sarbanes-Oxley bill. This law, a bureaucratic accounting illusion to begin with, turned a future balance sheet challenge for some banks into an immediate cash crisis for the entire world.

You could say that, in addition to making borrowing too easy and drilling too hard, liberals in power have made accounting impossible. The end result is yet another historical media and political irony, as the blame fell on Republicans and free enterprise, simply because there was a Bush in the White House when liberalism came home to roost. And neither Bush nor Rove nor any of our brilliant pundits or consultants, could put three words together explaining these rather obvious and pedestrian observations.

The economic issues were not the only problems the GOP

were facing, either. The Republican base continued to be angry with Bush and Congress over spending and immigration reform, among other issues, meaning Bush was just about out of constituencies. In the interim, the fact that ultra liberal Harry Reid and Nancy Pelosi were now in charge of Congress didn't seem to matter to a media totally inept at applying cause and effect. Everything that went wrong was still Bush' fault, and ours, too, for deigning to support him.

Consider: a bridge collapses in Minnesota. This is Bush's fault because certainly that the bridge would be fine if we were not spending money in Iraq. The IPCC issues a report confirming man is at fault for global warming and that is Bush's fault because he's an "oilman," after all. Never mind that he bought into all of this phony data that was to be discredited three years later.

It's our fault too because we don't feel guilty enough about driving our SUV's while the rich liberals jetting about in their Gulfstreams do.

All of this trouble is what led to the nomination of a man who clearly dislikes Republicans to run as the *Republican* nominee. In a perfect stroke of dark comedy, John McCain clinched the 2008 nomination in Florida thanks to the strong endorsement of the sitting governor... a man named Charlie Crist.

Oh yeah, this McCain thing was destined to work out just great.

4

MCCAIN CAMPAIGN: NOTHING TO FEAR FROM OBAMA

The McCain nomination signaled a subtle shift in Republican leadership. While Bush refused, or was unable, to defend conservative principles, McCain had a history of openly attacking them. This was categorically a shift in the wrong direction.

Before McCain could make things worse by suspending his campaign and muttering incoherently about "unfettered capitalism," he had to secure the nomination. This fight was one that could have only unfolded the way it did in light of the GOP brand issues. Romney's presence in this contest clearly colored how we would fight the next one, as well, and validates the theory that elections are sequential and not isolated events.

For the record, former Arkansas Governor Mike Huckabee technically finished in second by staying in the longest. Huck had his niche but was never truly a threat after Iowa. The technical term for the extension of a campaign like Huck's is known as the "Fox News Channel audition period."

Romney, Fred Thompson and Rudy Giuliani were considered the early favorites, and many conservatives favored Thompson. His campaign started slowly, as he seemed not to want the nomination as much as others wanted him to have it.

Giuliani, for some reason, decided to more or less skip Iowa, New Hampshire, and South Carolina and rely on a super firewall in Florida. His candidacy was a study in contradictions, given that he is fearless towards the press, and yet socially liberal. On terror, he was far and away the feistiest and most conservative of all the candidates. He was also very conservative on taxes and regulation, giving him great marks on two of the three legs of the stool of conservatism. So what about the third, the social issue leg?

With his oft repeated pledge to appoint justices in the model of Antonin Scalia, a case could be made that Rudy might have actually governed more conservatively on a net basis than the others, with the courts doing the heavy lifting on social issues. This is counter-intuitive, given his lifetime policy preferences and personal beliefs on social issues, and we'll never know. Still, a low tax, low regulation guy who was not afraid to use the phrase "Islamists war against us" and not afraid to support water boarding and who never backs down on anything, would have been a more interesting candidate than McCain or Romney. Doctrinal moderation or liberalism is one problem with the GOPe, but their scaredy-cat prissiness in the face of liberal narratives is an even bigger problem. Rudy may suffer from the former but not the latter, and it's important that we nominate candidates that don't.

His Florida strategy failed miserably as firewall strategies almost always do, and the Scalia pledge would have been a tough sell to social conservatives to begin with.

Which brings us to the Romney campaign of 2007-2008. Romney was not the hand-picked establishment moderate in 2008. Mitt was considered too conservative on taxes, regulations, and other economic issues back then. This seems strange now, but think back to those odd days of 2007-2008. This was a meme that was almost universally agreed upon by the pundit class, including Krauthammer, Luntz, Morris and many others.

This is not to say that Mitt didn't have the same challenges with some conservatives that he carried into 2012, but his business background and views on taxes and regulations put him closer to Reagan and the base than McCain was.

While few remember this today, somewhere deep inside of Romney was the realization of what the fundamental problems were. In 2007 and 2008, he very correctly stated that America's problems were all "the result of too many Republicans acting too much like Democrats," which was, and still is, profoundly correct. He added that we were in trouble because "bureaucrats had more opportunities than entrepreneurs," in response to statistics showing that public employees had passed private sector employees in compensation. Again, Mitt had stumbled upon a critical profundity, and those are the two crusades we are fighting now. This begs the question: what happened to *that* Mitt? Romney's words were even more accurate four years later, yet as the establishment candidate, he was too domesticated to say so.

At any rate, the net result of this anti-Republican sentiment on our own side was the nomination of a man who acts a whole lot like a Democrat most of the time, and who (in a related story) is a lifetime government employee. As a Senator, McCain is more or less a grandiose bureaucrat himself, and thus Republicans were once again going to war with a nominee with no familiarity with the private sector. Like his good friend John Kerry, McCain is in favor of marrying into the private sector; he just doesn't understand it. Thus, there was no chance that McCain could understand, let alone articulate, what the contest of 2008 was really about. He still can't.

Against this backdrop and against Bush's approval marks, McCain ran against Bush and capitalism instead of running against Obama and socialism. This is what the establishment wanted, which is another perplexing non sequitur since establishment messaging is what led to Bush and capitalism being so unpopular in the first place.

* * *

For all of McCain's phony "Maverick" babbling, he is classic establishment. Some might say "but McCain went counter to the establishment with his pick of Sarah Palin as his running mate." Fair enough, but let's examine this. McCain stumbled into the Palin pick out of misconception, as he fancied Palin as Alaska's young McCain, not a young Reagan. People may say there's no way he was that ignorant of what Palin was about, and yet McCain proved ignorant of almost everything about Alaska, including ANWR.

Keep in mind that Palin had established some anti-Republican bona fides in Alaska, which is what interested McCain. Her appeal to the conservative base stunned him and his consultants. His campaign never understood the only smart move they ever made. They still don't.

Setting your particular views of Palin aside, consider the long-term dynamics this pick set in motion. She has been a major player from the moment McCain named her, was crucial to the 2010 election cycle, and I doubt her days on the big stage are over. She is considered an unsophisticated, poorly educated hick by Washington standards, yet her decisions and successes provide an astonishing contrast with the bungling disasters brought about by many who are thought of as highly educated and sophisticated by the elites. Like, say, Obama. Palin's mere existence illustrates the establishment's reality problem, which is foundational to their messaging problem, and for this reason she appears often in this book.

I wrote a lot about the relationship between the establishment and the rest of the country between 2008 and 2012, and many of those columns will make up much of the next few chapters. Each was chosen for a specific purpose, and it lends authenticity to read the words as they were written at the time. And frankly, if I have the audacity to claim that Rove and consultants have been wrong for years, the onus is on me to demonstrate that I, along with others, have been right for years. As for Palin and her warfare with the elites: I saw this coming when she first exploded onto the scene.

WHY SARAH PALIN MAKES SUCH A BIG DIFFERENCE FOR THE GOP TICKET

American Thinker, September 10, 2008

It is pretty obvious that the liberal media's reaction to Sarah Palin is driven by their two camps: those who don't understand her, and a small but growing number who do and are scared to death. Either way, their superficial analysis that Sarah Palin was picked as a calculated decision to "appeal to the base," and to "disaffected Hillary supporters," is to miss the point of the relationship between thermometers and thermostats.

Palin clearly does appeal to the base, and an opportunistic appeal to Hillary voters is wise since a flip of merely 10% of her primary voters means a net gain to McCain of the margins of the 2000 and 2004 elections combined.

Sarah Palin, however, is more than a pawn in a one dimensional chess game to figure out where the electorate tailwinds are and help the McCain ticket get in front of it. The choice of Palin is a potential reboot of the political thermostat. She has turned the heat up on conventional political wisdom across the country as she has done at every level of her new but accomplished political career.

The Alaska Governor is far more than someone who appeals to the base; she is someone who can make the base appeal to the rest of America.

She is more than a token to take advantage of disaffected Hillary voters, she can replace Hillary as the authentic female role model - and is more in line with how the base lives. That's why the base is beyond happy. They are electrified. And fear of this game-changing dynamic is panicking some on the left (and in the center, too.)

Palin believes and lives what she says, and that is why her

story and her opinions are so authentic and compelling. It seems like she was trying to live a life free from government interference when corruption, regulation, schools and bad energy policy made that impossible. So she joined the political game to change it, not to play at it. To get government out of the way for Track and Piper and the gang, she took the season off as team mom. (Snip)

When she says that the opinions of the pundits and reporters and insiders are not of concern to her, it is more than a good line. It is reflective of her history. The public gets the impression of someone who would rather be back at the snow machine races than live the compromised life of a DC politician.(Snip)

As such, Sarah Palin *is* the base, as in those who believe in the basic principles of smaller government, lower taxes and a strong national defense. She is more of the base than George Bush 41 or 43. She lives a Reagan life. She lives a Contract with America life. She lives the life the Founding Fathers envisioned when they crafted a Constitution to guarantee everyone a shot at such a life.

The base instantly recognized her as one of them and fell in love. No one has done this since Reagan. Bush was never this loved or considered "one of us," but next to Al Gore and John Kerry he was positively adorable. He was a diluted representative from the start and continued to go out of his new tone way to "de-base" himself, causing a substantial fraction of the country not to like him and more importantly, distorting what Republican base means in the first place.

Palin's appeal to Americans who for various reasons would not consider themselves conservatives is obvious. Be they Reagan Democrats or independents or undecideds or disaffected Hillary voters, many will like what she says, does and is and want to be a part of it.(Snip)

She doesn't appear to care what middling moderate temperature the pundits think the political temperature is. She is not interested in adjusting. She knows what the temperature should be and has lit the fire in this campaign to reach it. We can only hope she'll level her moose rifle at any pundits or consultants foolish enough to attempt to adjust her thermostat.

Reagan won nearly 60% of the vote in 1984, and no one has come close since. Reagan's principles are still valid, although the understanding of conservatism has been disfigured by the Bush 41's "kinder gentler" America and Bush 43's "compassionate conservatism." Those concepts just reinforced the liberal supposition that conservatism is not compassionate to begin with, which

is the kind of screwy idea you get in the Ivy League or in Washington focus groups, not in Wasilla, Alaska.

The base is not deceived. McCain is not one of us. He won't run like Reagan, and he won't get 60% of the vote. If he gets a tad over 50%, he won't govern like Reagan. But what we do know is with Palin on the team, reaching 50% is suddenly possible in 2008. With her youth and authenticity, the days of 60% are at least worth dreaming about again.

Palin's relevance to 2012 and today is that liberals fear her for the same reason Clarence Thomas spooked them. She threatened every liberal template about women the way Thomas threatened them about African Americans, so the left reacted with unprecedented campaigns of phony and hateful narratives against both. These contemptible batteries against Palin were successful in that they marginalized her in the minds of too many on "our" side, not to mention independents. These onslaughts also collaterally defaced the entire idea of what a non-government conservative life is about, and that concept cannot be separated from Republican victory.

Spearheaded by the pusillanimous Steve Schmidt, perhaps the worst campaign manager in history, Team McCain spent the rest of the campaign trying to pretend they didn't have a VP pick. This was awkward since the only half of the GOP ticket that *either* side cared about was Palin. McCain was almost irrelevant, which is hysterical considering he has spent every waking moment for forty years desperate to remain relevant. Part of the Schmidt/McCain strategy was to help facilitate the trivialization of Palin, especially on key issues. (Too bad she didn't level her moose gun at Schmidt, who would qualify as fair game for such a weapon by weight.) Palin's understanding of ANWR and energy, for example, clashed with McCain's and Schmidt's blithering ignorance on these subjects. Her non-bubble, non-government existence from the wilds of Alaska was also a refreshing contrast with McCain's staid Senate chamber, Fox News Sunday lifestyle.

We've mentioned McCain's lack of familiarity with the private sector and life outside of government, but by choosing Palin he had actually stumbled into some credibility in these areas, as well as someone from the other side of the divide between Washington and the rest of the country. Succinctly, McCain had stumbled onto the very themes the 2008 campaign should have been about, and yet he kept stumbling around, never understanding the tremendous opportunities he had.

In 2008, the moment was right to explain how excessive government meddling and spending brought about our problems. Sure, Bush and the GOP Congress were guilty of that to a degree, but a turn to Obama, Reid and Pelosi would only accelerate the problems. This was not that hard to understand or explain in 2008, and should have been McCain's campaign theme.

It's infinitely harder to make that case now. Given that some 53% of the country still blames Bush, not to mention all Republicans and conservative policies for the economy, there is no way to overstate the importance of this absurdity. And yet, neither the Bush Administration nor McCain's Campaign ever countered this fairy tale. Again, we have more proof that it is always devastating to allow faulty suppositions to take root over a period of years.

We can only wonder what might have happened in 2008, or even 2012, if McCain and the GOPe would have taken the advice below, which was featured on Rush's show:

TIME FOR MCCAIN TO NAME NAMES
American Thinker, October 1, 2008

There is but one issue in the 2008 election. The economy. Or more to the point, the economic meltdown. Whoever wins this debate will win the election. Or perhaps more accurately, whoever loses this debate will lose the election. Period.

It is important to understand this for anyone trying *not* to lose this upcoming election. This would ostensibly include Arizona Senator John McCain. The housing-mortgage virus is eating up billions of dollars of wealth daily, and this tends to irritate those who are losing the wealth. That includes everyone in the country who owns any stock, mutual fund shares or real estate. In other words, a large share of voters.

When folks are this angry, there is hell to pay, and "hell to pay" includes figuring out who to blame. For all of McCain's wanting to stay "above the fray" and his too-clever-by-half comment that now is not the time to assign blame, he is simply not hearing the public. It is indeed time to assign blame. With this kind of financial destruction on the part of most American families, someone is going to get blamed. You can count on it.

Let me repeat. Someone *will* get blamed. You will either enter that debate or you will *lose* that debate. Period.

And short of properly assigning blame to the liberal

policies and politicians who are responsible for this mess, the blame will automatically fall to the current Presidential administration and by extension, his party. Right or wrong, that's how our politics play out. McCain simply has no choice now. He will start doing what he claims he loves to do related to government corruption — naming names — or he will be thrown on the ash heap of electoral shame alongside Bob Dole, George H. W. Bush and so on.

The good news for McCain, should he decide to grasp it, is that the party against which he is (supposed to be) running can easily be pegged with the lion's share of the blame regarding our economic meltdown. There is no doubt that liberal policies on energy and housing have combined to put the country in this situation, and only unwinding these policies will lead the nation out of this problem. Naming names properly will name a whole lot of folks with "D" beside their names.

The very people who put us into this mess to begin with now lead Congress. If McCain thinks he can thread the needle in a bi-partisan fashion here, he is sadly mistaken. If he does not point out the facts, then his party will take the blame for and he will not win the election. It cannot happen. As far as he has run from President Bush, he will never get as far away from Bush as Obama can.

Bush has actually been on the right side of the energy production debate and the Fannie Mae-Freddie Mac regulation debate all along. The President has been an inadequate advocate of the correct positions on these issues to be sure, but at least one can legitimately claim that the administration was intellectually correct on Fannie, Freddie and oil.

McCain himself pointed out problems with Fannie and Freddie back in 2005 and 2006, only to have the reforms he wanted defeated by Democrats in Congress. President

Bush was with McCain on these issues. Obama benefitted from more Fannie Mae contributions in two years than all other Senators not named Chris Dodd, and was on the wrong side of these issues. This is a slam-dunk waiting for McCain simply to take advantage of it.

Recently he has been out rambling on about government spending, CEO pay and earmarks. All of this is a big yawn in light of our economic disaster. None of this is pertinent unless you point out that Fannie Mae and Freddie Mac were Democrat earmarks and that the worst CEO pay abuse in recent memory is Franklin Raines' incentive compensation from Fannie. McCain didn't bother to point any of that, because "we must not assign blame."

The simple fact is this: if the Democrats do not get their deserved blame for this economic situation, Republicans will experience a bloodbath on Election Day. The way our elections work, it is up to McCain to make that happen. The fact that he seems not to understand it is why many conservatives loathed the idea of a McCain nomination to begin with.

It can be argued that if McCain will not assign blame, he will not win the White House. He says he wants to lead. That sometimes mean calling out friends and colleagues in the opposition. We soon will see whether McCain has it in him to put his country ahead of his instinct to reach across the aisle. If he does not show this ability, he will never occupy the Oval Office.

As we know now, McCain never did assign blame or in any way articulate what happened to the economy. He never got over his proclivity for "reaching across the aisle," which seemed like McCain's answer for every situation. Frankly, I doubt McCain, Schmidt, or even Rove could put two sentences together today explaining what went wrong with the economy. Again, since Republican consultants are so worried about low information voters, perhaps they should consider the role played by low information candidates and handlers in causing that problem.

The closest thing to economic coherence from the 2008 campaign came unwittingly from Obama himself, when he bumped into an unemployed plumber named Samuel Joseph Wurzelbacher on October 12. Chatting off-teleprompter with 'Joe the Plumber' about owning a successful company, Obama murmured something about the advantages of "spreading the wealth around" once that happens. The confrontation was instantly famous, and many conservatives immediately understood that Obama was admitting to being a textbook socialist. The key was that Obama was finally caught on tape, since anyone paying attention had known this for a long time.

McCain toyed with the "spread the wealth around" theme a bit, but he refused to press the larger issue of Obama's economic doctrine, insuring everyone that we had "nothing to fear from an Obama Presidency." Funny, many of us do fear socialism.

When you step back a minute and look at the long view, this "spread the wealth" conversation should have been part of an ongoing narrative about the wonders that free markets have unleashed for all of mankind, not to mention the major role our free economy has played in America's history. It should be Exhibit A in every Republican campaign. In a slightly shorter view, it should have been, at the very least, the perfect bookend to the "you didn't build that" speech in Roanoke in July of 2012. All of this is an extension of the Obama interview with Chicago Public Radio in 2001, focusing on the flaws in our Constitution related to redistributive policies. Statements like these would have naturally formed a powerful ongoing narrative, if the establishment wasn't so scared of defining Obama.

Contrast this with how liberals keep hammering away at a narrative, even if they have to fake it. The phony "war on women" was obviously a sham, but the Democrats kept at it. Thus, when Todd Akin and Richard Mourdock came out with insanely inarticulate statements on abortion, the impact was magnified because they were instantly part of a very established theme. By comparison, Obama's "spread the wealth around" and "you didn't build that" comments were merely single events with impact for just a few days each.

And as predicted, since McCain refused to name names, we were in for a bloodbath.

Obama Wins Big

In round figures, the popular vote count was sixty-nine million plus to something over fifty-nine million in the Presidential race, giving Obama a margin of almost 8%. In the House, the Democrats picked up twenty-one seats for a strong 257-178 margin, within one seat of the exact ratio after Clinton's 1992 win. In the Senate, the Democrats picked up eight seats on Election Day, and managed to sneak one more seat through weeks later in the Al Franken race for a 60-40 margin. These devastating ratios in Congress were now the result of the 2006 and 2008 elections combined, brought to us by the cumulative establishment messaging during the eight years of Bush. That 60-40 Senate margin was to become even more important than normal for a number of reasons.

There was all sorts of universal euphoria throughout the country, with the hope and change bug now infecting even some McCain voters, according to most approval polls. People bought into the "first black President" thing, not to mention the perception of Obama as some kind of brilliant, pleasant centrist, who simply wanted to govern better than his predecessor. His approval numbers were in the 70% range, though there was an anti-liberal, buyer's remorse panic brewing beneath the surface.

As expected, there were many campaign autopsies.

GOP DEFEAT AND THE 'NEW TONE'
American Thinker, November 6, 2008

Tuesday's debacle was some 8 years in the making. Or more.

Consider: Eight years ago, George Bush rode into town from Texas with one thing on his mind: bringing a "new tone to Washington." He was going to use his Texas charm and drawl to end all of the partisan bickering. This was a tad dispiriting to some of us who had supported him frankly. We were thinking more along the lines of some partisan victories in Congress to roll back some liberalism. Actually, only Bush wanted a new tone. *Neither his supporters nor his opponents had even the vaguest interest in it*, dooming it from the start.

(What does this have to do with McCain v. Obama? Everything. Stick with me.)

Nonetheless, with the new tone, its architect Karl Rove was going to fashion a "permanent Republican majority" governing coalition. We're not sure what this new permanent coalition was going to accomplish exactly, since the operational foundation of the new tone turned out to be giving in on your principles so as to be universally loved. Nonetheless, Bush and Rove were confident it would work. To ensure it, they were quick to "reach across the aisle" to let ultra-liberals like Ted Kennedy and John Edwards dictate policy time to time.

Well damned if Bush didn't pull it off after all, albeit not exactly as he envisioned. There is indeed a new tone, and a new governing coalition in Washington as of Wednesday, and they are determined to make it permanent. They have the numbers to give it a good shot, too. And that other new tone? That is the clanking of widespread hatred of a President who, above all else, was determined to be loved. This is sad and unjust, since his tax cuts, the Surge, and the war on terror are all vitally important successes.

Even last night, this new tone, "compassionate conservative" President who was almost nowhere to be found during the entire campaign, could peer out his window from the White House and see how well his eight year capitulation had 'worked.' He had not thrown a single elbow in this entire election cycle, yet the hatred of him was running thick. This was a classic "in your face" demonstration against Bush. Forget the vapor at Grant Park in Chicago, there was red meat in D.C. These anti-Bush protestors have no idea that his terror policies perhaps saved some of their lives, probably because he never bothered to tell them.

The man from Texas is indeed profoundly hated by the left. But that is not the point. The man from Texas is not hated alone. The left has projected their hatred of him onto us. His refusal to fight back was not the individual "falling on the sword" he thought it was. When he refused to fight, he let us all down.

The result has been a directionless party with no effective titular head. Too much liberalism crept into policy and caused problems. Those problems, with a new tone leader not willing to point fingers, got laid right at the undeserving doorstep of the Bush Administration. That is our doorstep too, however, and *Bush never seemed to understand this.*

(We *are* getting to McCain v Obama, I promise)

Remember that the attacks of 9-11 were dreamed up, planned, staffed, financed, practiced and set into motion during the Clinton Administration, but it was deemed to have "happened on Bush's watch." Hurricane Katrina exposed decades of corrupt and inefficient Democrat control of New Orleans, but Bush (and by extension, all Republicans) took the blame. Thirty years of liberal energy policy came crashing down on us this year with four-dollar gas, yet Bush, Big Oil and free enterprise took the hit. Two decades of liberal political correctness, fraud and crony capitalism in the form of Fannie Mae and Freddie Mac collapsed and took an over-leveraged economy with it. Again, Bush and free enterprise took the fall even though Bush actively fought the bad energy and lending policies. Interestingly McCain was at times quick to help this negative inertia with his public "straight talk."

Conversely, the Bush tax cuts have done a great job of undergirding the economy for nearly eight years and bringing us out of the tech bubble and 9-11. Bush and conservatism, however, received no credit for this. There had not been another terror attack on this nation since 9-11 — an amazing feat no one thought possible — yet Bush and his hawkish efforts were not recognized as the reasons for this success.

You see, all the new tone did was ensure that Bush received no credit when he deserved it, and he deserved it often. Yet, he often took all the blame when he did not deserve it. This led to a candidate like John McCain for the 2008 race.

Bush lavished his "a new tone" on the Republican left, supporting moderates in their primaries against upstart conservatives. But they would never return the favor when they got to Washington. Led by maverick John McCain, this wing of the party worked against Bush on almost every major legislative initiative. Some even say McCain took great satisfaction bashing Bush in the press, in retaliation for the 2000 primary season.

The result has been almost a total lack of conservative leadership anywhere. On the few occasions when Bush actually tried to practice conservatism, McCain and various permutations of the "gang of 14" were always there to torpedo the efforts. Making things worse, the inarticulate Bush would often trot out some lightweight like Scott McClellan to occupy the bully pulpit. There was no message, no leadership, and no cohesion. There was, however, a 25% approval rating. Thus, when McCain emerged from the primary pack as the pundits' candidate of choice for the GOP, a run against Bush himself was the natural inclination.

This amounts to one of the great political ironies of all time, since in practice there is not that much difference between Bush's "new tone" and McCain's incessant need to "reach across the aisle." You can make the case that Bush›s low approval numbers were to a degree the natural result of McCain›s Bush-bashing, plus Bush›s new tone refusal to state his own case.

As we know, McCain made his willingness to work with Democrats a centerpiece of his campaign. He made a big issue of numerous pieces of legislation where he did so, and some of them are unmitigated disasters, chief among them is Campaign Finance Reform, which was going to take the money out of politics. *Perhaps that did not go exactly as planned Mr. McCain. Just sayin...*

And neither did the flawed notion that McCain would swoop into the White House on this great wave of bi-partisan fever on the part of "independents." This is one of the great tealeaf misreads of all time. In my view, there *is* no great clamor for bipartisanship; there is only the flawed conventional wisdom that there is such a clamor. Surely, if such a public hunger really existed, McCain would have won by double digits. He did not. He did not even win the moderates themselves. He lost them by ten points, and he also lost notable moderates like Colin Powell, Chuck Hagel and Lincoln Chaffee.

Ronald Reagan, on the other hand, carried the independents by convincing them he was right, not that he was one of them. Newt Gingrich and the Contract with America Congress won them by exposing the liberal Democrats as the corrupt political animals they were. There was no reaching across any aisle or any new tone with those successes. No one prattled on about so-called "compassionate conservatism." There was simply unabashed constitutional conservatism, which is compassionate by nature, and it was proclaimed boldly and repeatedly (and at times with humor), and it resonated. You might even call it partisan.

Conversely, McCain would rarely mention conservatism or Reagan without quickly reminding us of times when he fought against them. Well no wonder it didn't sell. The seller doesn't even like it!

Conservatism did not lose last night as it was not on the ballot. The big winner was ignorance, and the biggest loser was the Bush-Rove-McCain brand of watered down Republicanism. Yes, the Bush-Rove-McCain brand. They gave us each other. Much as the two men cannot stand each other, they are ironically similar. And the result is indeed a new tone in Washington, and it is a scary dreary leftist tone.

We will never beat it back until the watered down bi-partisans are flushed from the system. Thomas Jefferson loved partisanship. Hugo Chavez does not. That should tell us all we need to know about this flawed path our party has been on for many years. Tuesday, our aisle-crossing, new tone chickens came home to roost.

Rush's take was the same, as he opened his Wednesday post election show by saying, "Well friends, the new tone has come home to roost." The implication was clear.

One specific shock was North Carolina, a great case study for the GOP today. After Clinton had come within a single point of beating Bush 41 in 1992, the Tar Heel state had returned home as solid Republican Presidential territory in 1996, 2000 and 2004. Then in 2008, seemingly out of nowhere, Obama edged McCain by fourteen thousand votes, a tiny margin in a state that size.

To be sure, North Carolina has some trends working against Republicans in the macro. The state's economy is part of the demographic problem, attracting a lot of liberal high tech workers from the northeast and the west coast, along with a growing Hispanic population for the growing labor sector. To top it off, Senator Elizabeth Dole was up for re-election in 2008. Dole, like her husband, and McCain for that matter, were quintessential establishment figures. Liddy Dole was not a very good Senator to begin with, and ran an awful campaign, thus contributing to the perfect storm for Obama. More to the point, the pertinence to 2012 and today's combat inside the GOP is astonishing.

SAFE SEATS AND CAROLINA BLUES
American Thinker, November 13, 2008

The voting shift in this nation is largely about two dynamics: safe seats and the Carolina blues. To get a really good close-up glimpse of what demographic problems the GOP is facing in the national electorate, one has to look no further than the Senate race lost by Elizabeth Dole.

The loss by Dole was not simply a result of the self-inflicted headwinds that all GOP candidates faced in 2008, though they were a factor. The Dole loss was more than that. Dole lost a Senate seat held by Republicans since 1972, the "Jesse Helms" seat. Truth be told, she never filled it adequately, but at least she did hold it in 2002 against Clinton Chief of Staff Erskine Bowles.

Consider: Counting the 36 years total that Helms and Dole occupied that seat, and the multiple terms served by conservative Democrat B. Everett Jordan before Helms, this particular seat is soon to be occupied by a liberal for the first time in modern American political history. The other N.C. seat has gone back and forth between the parties for the past four decades, including the John Edwards era, but this is a *loss of the Helms seat.* This is seismic.

For decades, the Senate has balanced on a Helms-Kennedy continuum. It wasn't an official delineation, but the conservative Helms and the liberal Ted Kennedy counter balanced each other. Until Barack Obama came along, all U.S. Senators were somewhere left of Jesse and right of Teddy. Oh I know that technically Socialist Bernie Sanders of Vermont and Joe Biden of Delaware vote a bit more liberally than Kennedy, but of the big time figures, Helms and Kennedy set the philosophical boundaries. There was *a semblance of* equilibrium — or so it seemed. Helms tugged from the right and Kennedy from the left, and most legislation ended *up somewhere in between.* (Snip)

Since liberals leverage their safe seats to great advantage, Helms mere presence in Washington was vital. Consider elected officials like Kennedy, Barney Frank, Henry Waxman, Maxine Waters, Chris Dodd, Robert Wexler, and others who fit the liberal safe seat category: It doesn't matter how wrong they are on policies, or how unhinged they are in hearings, or how corrupt they are with money in their freezers, sweetheart mortgages from Fannie Mae lenders, not to mention gay prostitution rings in their apartments - these folks are lifers. Not pro-lifers mind you, they are Congressional lifers, and there seems to be no way to abort their lifetime selections. Their collective voice tugs the two houses of Congress to the left, and without Helms, there seems to be no counter balance anymore.

Unlike the safe liberal seats, the Helms seat was always

tenuous. Every time Jesse was up for election, millions upon millions of dollars of out of state cash flowed into the coffers of his opponent, and it mattered not whom the opponent was. And this is true of many of the most conservative members in the House and Senate. Their seats are vulnerable, and the left mobilizes huge throngs of donors and 527's and ACORN voters each cycle to target a handful of them. And they are picking them off, one by one, and this cycle they picked off the Helms seat.

This strategy works for Democrats, mainly because they face no such countering vulnerability with their liberal leaders. Their locked up safe seats allow them to funnel the most money and emphasis to incumbent Republican seats. So why are the liberal seats safe, and the conservative seats vulnerable?

To illustrate, understand we are not a nation of red and blue states as much as we are a nation of red and blue counties, or red and blue precincts. In the big cities, the electorate is blue. Very blue. In many of these cities, run down by decades of liberal rule, the vote turn out is massive, and it is often 95% Democrat.

Conversely, many more counties and many more precincts in this nation are red. This is true even in the 2008 debacle. But they are only about 60-40% red. The vast majority of this country is fairly conservative, yet we are being governed by enclaves of slums and limousine liberals that are extremely liberal. Look at the map, and this becomes clear.

If we could vote by acreage, the GOP would have routed the Democrats. (And a good case could be made for that, but that's another book). But the Democrats can run up enough of a vote tally in one urban ward full of housing projects to balance several rural counties. (This is especially true when they can have turnout of 145%).

And it gets worse. In a state like North Carolina, there is a disturbing and counter productive trend going on. Liberals are fleeing northern states due to high taxes and other business-killing liberal policies and coming to North Carolina for jobs. And damned if they aren't now voting for the same kind of politician they tried to flee by leaving New York, New Jersey, Michigan and so on in the first place. They are turning Carolina blue, but thanks to the inner cities in the states they left, no such reciprocal effect is taking place in the states they fled.

As has been said, you can't fight demographics. So what is the GOP to do? Some inside the Beltway will say the party must diversify and moderate to prevent destruction. These are the folks who ran the McCain campaign. McCain lost the big tent moderates by ten points, so clearly this is not the answer. The only answer is to start winning some arguments. We have to start changing some minds. We need to educate. You know — like who really caused 9-11 and the collapse of Fannie Mae — as we look back. As we look ahead, perhaps the argument of how liberal oil policy and confiscatory union thugs are the reason Detroit and Michigan are in the tank, not George Bush and capitalism and so on.

But to win some arguments, *you must HAVE some arguments*. This is something people named Dole, Bush and McCain don't seem to understand. If we don't start, Carolina blue is just the beginning.

Today, our establishment is telling us exactly what they told us before and after 2008. They insist we moderate our message, our views, and accept false diversity at all costs, especially with regard to immigration issues. And they still don't have the appetite to engage in philosophical arguments.

Yet consider what has happened since 2008. In many elections across the country, conservatives made these arguments in the public arena and won them. In fact, almost every single election of consequence after November 2008 was won with fearless conservative ideology being contrasted with liberalism. The arguments were not made by the party hacks, however. People like Palin and Herman Cain and Scott Walker, or any number of Tea Party speakers and organizations, made them. Yet still today, our GOP establishment is insisting that we take the opposite course of action going forward. More of their RDD.

As hard as it is to fathom now, at the time of Obama's election, we had been assured by many of the elites that Obama was a pragmatic centrist. Many so called conservative pundits, all in the establishment, rushed to join this analysis. In Georgia, however, the voters didn't buy into this. In very early December, less than a month after conservatism had ostensibly been wiped off the face of the planet, there was a purely ideological special election for a key Senate seat in the state. It was Saxby Chambliss versus Jim Martin in a run-off election.

This special election resulted in a panic vote against Obama getting his filibuster proof Senate. In other words, this was a vote up or down on an America totally controlled by Obama, Reid and Pelosi, just weeks after Obama's 2008 win. It was Obama's first loss, and yet few remember it since it took place before he was sworn in.

This result is incredibly important because it started a long losing streak for Obama, a streak that only the Romney Campaign and the Rove message machine could break. This result, which is stunning in retrospect, shows what can happen when the GOP runs a daring, philosophical campaign against the Democrats and their ideology.

Saxby's Win: 08's Most Intellectually Pure Contest
American Thinker, December 4, 2008

For all of the talk about "bi-partisanship," the Georgia

Senate run-off was nothing if not blatantly partisan. It was, simply, ALL about the party, and by extension, *was the most intellectually sound and pure election in all of the 2008 cycle.*

Six years ago, Republican Saxby Chambliss routed incumbent Max Cleland by running a partisan and aggressive campaign that "infuriated Democrats" at the time. Since then, Chambliss has often wandered off the conservative partisan plantation and infuriated mainly his own base. He even got chastised for a "reach across the aisle" energy vote in an appearance on the Rush Limbaugh show when oil was over 100 bucks a barrel. (If you heard the interview, you know the helpless Chambliss didn't even realize he was being mocked.)

This philosophical meandering had the conservative base less than thrilled with Saxby, to the point that a libertarian candidate polled strongly, and kept Chambliss from winning 50% plus one on Election Day in November.

This rightward bleeding, plus Obama mania and the attached voter drives, had Saxby in a run-off against a charismatically challenged and unknown state legislator named Jim Martin.

As we know, it has been trendy for years for voters to claim an aggressive lack of party affiliation, and to proclaim that one "votes for the man (or woman) and not the party." It sounds so darned enlightened and open-minded. When turnout is high, many who fit this category get out and vote.

But with respects to Congressional elections, this makes almost no sense. After all, a vote for any single Democrat in 2008 for House or Senate was effectively a vote for one of only two people: Harry Reid or Nancy Pelosi. These are the people who are mainly empowered when there are more D's than R's in the Senate and House. Chances are, for any law that might actually affect your life, the D or the R mean much more than the name of your rep.

With this in mind, what happened this week in Georgia is not so much that Saxby Chambliss beat Jim Martin — as it is that Harry Reid lost to the Republican Party - or perhaps Harry Reid lost to the fear of a Democrat super majority. Martin was irrelevant. (Okay, his photo op appearance with Ludacris was relevant, but not in a good way.) Chambliss was not the issue either. He was merely the necessary Republican speed bump in the path of the prospects of a Harry Reid legislative super highway.

Sadly, one of the fruits of a government school system run amok and a leftist media is that only a small percentage of the voters in the country realize the critical party dynamic in Congress. In a related story, only a small percentage of the voters turned out for Chambliss v. Martin. For all of Chambliss' flaws to the conservative base, and he has many, he was suddenly critical due to the Senate party affiliation math to these same voters.

(As an aside, this race was a testament to the power and wisdom of small turnouts.)

In this particular election, money and effort from all across the country poured into Georgia on behalf of Chambliss. Websites hyped the need for conservatives and Republicans everywhere to donate to the Georgia cause. And all of the pleas were about one thing: keeping Harry Reid and Barack Obama from getting a "filibuster proof" Senate. Period.

There was no mention in any of these ads about Martin. There was nothing mentioned about the need to keep the wonderful Chambliss in office. Chambliss is not particularly wonderful. As is the case with the still on-going Minnesota contest, the pleas for help were all about keeping the total of Democrats in the Senate to less than

60 at any cost. Period.

And frankly, this is brilliant and appropriate. This makes the Georgia run-off the most intelligently pure contest in the nation. This race was ultimately decided on what is really important. It was decided on what the national impact would be, which had everything to do *with keeping the liberal machine in check.* (snip)

The only "firewall" against an all out leftward legislative lurch is the Senate, where an organized minority of 41 or more can use cloture rules to stall the wishes of the other 59. And the small percentage of Georgians who turned out for this run-off seemed to understand that as the key issue here, be they liberal or conservative. There were precious few of the now famous «Obama voters» from the John Ziegler video, who were clueless about whom Harry Reid is, not to mention how many Senators there are. Folks who think Sarah Palin said she could "see Russia from my house" and has "campaigned in 57 states" did not bother to show up in large numbers. In short, the ignorant stayed home. And so did the "I vote for the man, not the party" crowd. This election was all about party, or more specifically, governing philosophy.

All of which led to a really good and refined election. For years, we have been bombarded with the ideas that being undecided or non-partisan is automatically a good thing, and that every living being (and then some) should vote. I have always disagreed. With so much at stake in elections, especially this one, I cringe when I realize many who remain clueless and undecided and misinformed and arrogantly non-partisan will cancel informed votes. Call me close- minded, but I happen to think knowing how many Senators exists, and how cloture works, is a low bar requisite for voting in a Senatorial election.

I also think partisanship is a good thing. So did our founders, by the way, as long as it was based on principle.

> The genius of the American people — if such a thing really exists — will only manifest itself when the few interested and enlightened from both sides of the philosophical spectrum participate. Much like Chambliss v. Martin 2008, where folks voted against a party they rightfully feared.

> Perhaps we should start encouraging people not really interested to stay home on Election Day. I suspect more races would turn out like the run-off in Georgia did. Now THAT would be "change I can believe in."

In hindsight, this analysis stands up exceptionally well. Chambliss' win did forestall Obama and Harry Reid getting their sixty seats in the Senate. Unfortunately, a few days later, the forces of Franken were able to wrestle the Minnesota seat from Coleman, giving Reid his sixty-seat majority anyway. The fine folks in Georgia, however, had done their part. This was an immediate backlash on ideological grounds against Obama by ordinary citizens, taking place while the brilliant establishment pundits were rushing to jump on Obama's bandwagon.

Voters in Georgia were not the only group to understand the dangers of an Obama government. Business owners started their anti-Obama reactions in early November. They didn't need to hear the Roanoke speech in 2012 to know who Obama was, as they were not only years ahead of Obama, they were years ahead of the GOP establishment on the reality of Obama, as well.

BLAME ME FOR JOB LOSSES
American Thinker, December 11, 2008

When the jobs report for November came out last week, many so-called "experts" were shocked at the massive loss of an estimated 533 thousand jobs. Even a Time /CNN organization called "The Curious Capitalists" were at a loss to explain it.

Let me attempt to help out these "curious capitalists" (though I am still skeptical that anyone working for CNN or Time is either curious or a capitalist). I caused part of this job loss and I know precisely why; the 2008 election. Those results guaranteed big trouble for small business.

The job destruction process has started. We are about twenty% of the way through our ramp down process and on schedule to complete the shut down by spring 2009. Watch the financial news and you will see continued job cuts each month, as we are not alone in our strategy. Far from it, as Atlas has shrugged all over the country.

Like many business owners, we are no longer willing to take all of the financial and legal risks and put up with all of the aggravation of owning and running a business. Not with the prospects of even higher taxes, more regulation, more litigation and more emboldened bureaucrats on the horizon. Like others we know, we are getting out while the getting is, well, tolerable. Many who aren't getting out are scaling back.

We learned just this week that getting *out* of business is harder than we thought. Take Republic Windows & Doors of Chicago, where being out of money and out of paying customers apparently does not give a business the right to shut down. Nor does it give their bankers the right to withhold credit. According to the unions, Jesse Jackson and the Governor of Illinois (yes, BLAGO), this company must continue to pay its employees salaries and benefits.

But pay them with WHAT? Liberals seem to be clueless as to where "the money" comes from. They love to tax, regulate and redistribute wealth — all the while decrying the very profit motive that created it — something they do not understand. If they did, they would not naively insist that a business that is out of money, out of customers and out of credit stay open so as to pay employees.

And that is but one example of why the lay-offs of November 2008 - *which will be part of George W. Bush's statistical record* - fall in reality on the Obama election. Business owners understand that the election of 2008 just gave a lot more power to people who think like these liberals in Illinois. For crying out loud, an Illinois liberal is now "President elect" and he chose another one for his Chief of Staff. He chose Michigan liberals for his economic team. Illinois and Michigan are broke!

It is no secret that owners circulated endless emails leading up to election day discussing lay off plans were Obama to win. *Entrepreneurs instinctively understand* the danger posed by larger liberal majorities in power. The risk-reward equation and fierce independence spirit of start up businesses are anathema to the class warfare, equality of outcome and spread the wealth mentality of the left.

We have very little appetite to have our lives run by elected or un-elected officials like Barney Frank and Jamie Gorelick. We have no appetite to be taxed even more by the likes of Charlie Rangel. These clowns destroyed Fannie Mae, Freddie Mac and our entire economy as a result. Congress, by their *own admission*, cannot even run their own damned dining room with a captive customer base! Some of them refuse to pay their own tax burden. Why in the world would we subject ourselves to their ilk armed with the unchecked powers of the Oval Office and both houses of Congress and a massive army of bureaucrats?

The answer to that question is that we will not subject ourselves to this. We got into business to be independent. We will get out for the same reason.

This particular article went viral and elicited even more of a response than some of the works on Sarah Palin had, proving that many average Americans were ahead of the Republican pros – who, to this day, don't understand the angst in the small business community.

Needless to say, this piece was frightfully prescient for correctly predicting the "Atlas Shrugged" mentality that Obama's election would unleash. Moreover, it predicted, years in advance, how Obama would benefit statistically during his campaign of 2012, as the two million jobs shed between Election Day and inauguration day in 2009 are indeed still blamed on Bush and Republicans. This voter ignorance can be blamed in part on the Romney Campaign and on Rove's Crossroads groups, as they never challenged this false stipulation at any point in 2012.

The Republican message machine never managed to mention this in late 2008 or early 2009 either, as the job cuts were happening and people's opinions were forming. This is inexcusable, given that almost every entrepreneur in the nation was fully aware of what was going on. The establishment mantra was that we must give Obama's policies "time to work." Entrepreneurs understand that the longer you give socialism to work, the worse it gets. Had the correct jobs narrative been established four years ago, Romney would be in the White House today, regardless of how poorly his particular campaign handled the issue in the final weeks.

At any rate, Georgia voters and business owners had started what would be four bad years for Obama.

Winter of 2009: No Honeymoon

Negative momentum continued to build even before Inauguration with Tim Geithner, Obama's pick for Treasury Secretary. While not a major issue in and of itself, this was a startling halo-slip for a man who was sold as some kind of a god, and it kicked off what was an awful period for Obama during the first few months of his regime. Meanwhile, back at headquarters, the GOPe remained obsessed with the "first black President" thing.

Naturally, lily white Timothy Geithner had exactly the kind of resume that liberals worship. He was well connected, educated at all the right places, and hadn't sullied his life experiences with any kind of real world exposure. He is a white Obama in other words. Geithner was part of the wonder team of Obama sorcerers who the liberals assured us would use the levers of power, combined with their collective geniuses, to rescue America from the financial collapse. The GOPe never bothered to mention that the collapse was the direct result of the meddling of just such financial shamans in the first place. Mr. Geithner, that liberal genius, is apparently as lost with Turbo Tax as another Ivy League mastermind, Elizabeth Warren, is with Ancestry.com.

The upshot is that the Obama Administration was now working with tax cheats occupying the two most important positions in our entire government regarding tax law. The travails of Geithner and Charlie Rangel were a big fat opportunity for the GOP, teed up with a wide-open fairway.

WHY GEITHNER AND RANGEL MATTER
American Thinker, January 16, 2009

The Chairman of the House Ways and Means Committee and the U.S. Treasury Secretary are literally the two highest-ranking political figures with regard to the Internal Revenue Service. If any two people on the planet should set an example in their tax behavior, it is the two people who hold those positions.

Yet Charles Rangel and Timothy Geithner are apparently somewhat more casual about tax compliance than we can afford to be, taking hypocrisy and irony to new levels in the process.

As the Chair of the House Ways and Means Committee, Rangel is literally *the most influential* member of Congress related to taxing and spending. As we found out in September, Rangel decided that he was above paying taxes on rental income on houses he owned in the Dominican Republic And as we found out days ago, the man appointed by Barack Obama to run the Treasury Department — of which the IRS is a major part — has also considered himself above the tax laws that haunt the rest of us.

Please understand these two people will have tremendous influence on how our tax laws are written and that they will expect every damned one of us to follow that 66 thousand page tax code to the letter. Or as Joe Biden would say, they expect us to "be patriotic" and to do so accurately. Which makes the excuses rendered by Rangel jaw dropping. These are excuses I would not recommend you try at home. Consider the following explanations from Rangel, and his attorney Lanny Davis, along with some commentary.   —

"Mr. Davis said the Congressman did not realize he had to declare the money as income, and was unaware of the semiannual payments from the resort because his wife, Alma, handled the family finances and conferred with their accountant, John Viardi, on tax matters." (NY Times).

Yeah, right. Let you or I try to claim the ignorant wife and accountant as a defense to the IRS.

"While I now know is [sic] although I had not personally received proceeds in cash, the fact that [sic] any reduction of the mortgage actually counted as income and should have been reported as such." (Rangel news conference, September 10).

Well yes, it should. It is called "taxable income," an understanding that should not escape the man who wants to dictate tax policy for the rest of us!!

"I personally feel that I have done nothing morally wrong."

I am sure that will go a long way with IRS agents. By the way, just how low is your bar for "morally wrong?"

While Rangel was out digging an even deeper hole, Geithner has purposefully avoided public comment on the issue, perhaps because any comment will simply make his problems worse. While working for the International Monetary Fund, Geithner failed to pay taxes even though the IMF "grossed up" his pay to give him the money with which to pay his taxes. They also attached a stub showing how much his pay had been grossed up. This should not have been complicated for someone working for the International *Monetary* Fund! You would hope someone like that would understand, um, *money*!

Not only that, but Geithner himself prepared his own tax returns for several of years where this underpayment was made. Bottom line: He either is not capable of handling a rather pedestrian income statement for tax purposes, or he flat out cheated. Frankly, I am not sure that either explanation gives me the utmost confidence in the "only man smart enough to understand the TARP" program. Based on his tax return, why would we assume he understands the business impact of "depreciation recapture," let alone "credit default swap?"

Then again, he was appointed by the man who lost an impromptu debate on basic tax policy to a plumber from Ohio, clearly demonstrating ignorance of what a capital gains tax is in the process.

We have been told that these are the people who are going to lead our economy out of the Bush imposed wilderness and to the Promised Land. These are the people who will end the Republican's "culture of corruption" and "era of special interests" in Washington and clean things up. These people represent hope and change.

I think we can look at these people and easily understand

why the stock market is tanking. It is obvious why, for the second month in a row, the jobless report "stunned the experts." Investors and business owners do not live in the make believe world of Washington and its political gamesmanship. These people have skin in the game. These people suffer when they make bad decisions, and they are en masse deciding that to "take their ball and go home" as the only prudent decision. That's why people are dumping stocks and laying off employees.

When the people who make the rules are either too ignorant to understand their own rules or feel entitled to break them, the allure of playing is simply gone for the rest of us. Apparently, more than half the voters have no understanding of this concept. And no amount of bailouts will change that.

It was fully predictable in 2009 that Obama's 2012 re-election campaign would focus on tax rates, and would most certainly play the class warfare card. Thus, it is beyond foolish that the GOPe was not hammering away at Geithner and Rangel from the start, not to mention during the 2012 campaign.

The breathtaking sense of entitlement on the part of Geithner and Rangel was a fabulous example of the immense tension building between government royalty and everybody else. Instead of focusing on this in 2012, the GOPe had all kinds of tortured internal debates about Romney's tax returns. To the establishment, having incompetent felons running government is not a problem, while having a rich and generous nominee with competent accountants apparently is.

Another big topic at the time of the 2009 Inauguration was the legacy of George W. Bush. As we've mentioned in the Introduction, my contention at the time was that Bush's legacy was *always* destined to be the end of Reagan's impact on the nation and the beginning of Obama's. Obama confirmed this in his 2013 Inaugural. In January 09, as excerpted in the Introduction, I bluntly concluded the following about Bush, his new tone, and, by implication, Rove:

> George Bush's legacy will be the end of Ronald Reagan's impact and the beginning of Barack Obama's... All the new tone did was to guarantee that Bush — and by extension his party and his supporters — never got credit for anything good yet got blamed for every problem. The left still calls Bush a cowboy and a terrorist and a Nazi and to this day hate him more than they hate anyone on the planet. More to the point, they also hate us and what we stand for. That is, they hate much of what America has stood for.

At the time, the Bush Administration's only concern was a narrow focus on what would protect the President's reputation, which is a major problem. Even so, how did it work out for Bush's sake personally? Well let's see: Bush left office with an historically abysmal rating, with only about one in four approving. It is obvious the new tone didn't win him any new friends, while costing him roughly half his old ones. The lost friends would be those conservatives who sensed Bush was destroying the reputation of all of us, and not just himself.

Moreover, no President has achieved irrelevance so soon after leaving office. Jimmy Carter is more relevant today than Bush 43, and certainly Bill Clinton is. For that matter, so is Reagan, as Obama's second Inaugural verified. Heck, even Gerald Ford remained more relevant in the first few years after his short term than Bush is now after serving the full eight years. I think it's obvious that Bush's VP, Dick Cheney, is more pertinent today than Bush himself is.

From where I sit, the verdict is in: the new tone of compassionate conservatism did not improve Washington, nor did it help Bush' legacy, nor did he even get credit for trying. It did, however, manage to damage the brand of conservatism and the GOP. Succinctly, it is hard to adequately describe what a total failure it was. Frankly, all of this was foreseeable. Many did predict it, yet Mr. Rove, the genius, was not among them.

5

2009 WOULD HAVE ENDED
MOST PRESIDENCIES

Shortly after being sworn in the first time, Obama's first bill signing foretold the eventual smallness of his first term and re-election campaign. On the 29th, he signed the Lily Ledbetter Act, which is the Big Bird contraception binder of all legislation. Wikipedia says that Ledbetter amends the Civil Rights Act of 1964. Maybe so, but it also enhances the "Full Employment for Trial Lawyers," as Ledbetter rolls back the statute of limitations for filing equal pay lawsuits. Obama thought the first thing to turn our economy around would be to help trial lawyers destroy present day companies for decisions made many years ago. Do they teach that at Harvard Law or Harvard Business?

And at about the same time, Obama's first foreign policy declaration was a promise to close Guantanamo Bay. Yes, signing Ledbetter and a promise about Gitmo were the top priorities from the man who is a god, the man who would roll back the oceans, and the man who is the most brilliant life force to ever trod the soil of politics. Is there any wonder Big Bird, free condoms and "voter revenge" were part of his 2012 campaign? (We lost to this clown?)

So to recap January, Obama had been elected for eighty-seven days and in office for only eleven. In that short period, Georgia voters had said "hell no" to unchecked Democrat rule in the Senate, two million jobs had been slashed by panicked business owners, his key appointees had embarrassed themselves in front of the world, and his first two official actions were laughable. He was off to a terrible start and had handed the Republican establishment any number of narratives to run with. And yet the GOPe was still desperate to be counted among those who were brilliant and bipartisan enough to recognize the brilliance and bipartisanship of Obama.

Again, I suggest that perhaps the establishment should quit worrying so much about the low information voter until they solve their low intelligence consultant problem. The two are closely related.

February 2009: Stimulating!

February 2009 is historically significant for a number of reasons. The first is the passage of the massive stimulus bill, which we know only stimulated unions and government along with debt and deficits. While Obama was insisting the stimulus was needed for "shovel ready jobs," organized liberalism, including groups close to Obama, were doing everything they could to destroy jobs.

This is what liberalism has always done, by definition. To connect these dots for the low info voter, however, the party and our candidates must keep explaining the problems in the economy in just such terms. Having isolated issue, short-term messages and nothing connecting the dots to a particular philosophical persuasion just won't cut it. The following is relevant to 2012 in the context of the Romney Campaign's concession that Obama merely inherited a mess from Bush, free enterprise, and Republicans.

THE LAW LIBERALS ALWAYS BREAK
American Thinker, February 14, 2009

There's a law that liberals always shatter. (And no, I'm not talking about tax law.) It's the law of unintended consequences. Actually it's not that liberals per se that break it so much as it seems *liberal thinking by definition always runs afoul of this law*. Leftist policy always hangs itself if given enough rope.

The liberals now have the entire stage with a very liberal President, extreme leftists in control of Congress, and the mainstream media. Liberal failure has nowhere to hide, and no one to hide behind. So as the Obama administration attempts to attack the country's economic woes, they find themselves stepping in one pile of liberal voodoo doo-doo after another. You might say that the left hand doesn't know what the other left hand is doing. The world will watch as liberal policy for problem A destroys Obama goals for problem B, and so on.

Consider: with Obama, Reid and Pelosi screaming for the country to accept a ridiculous stimulus package to create jobs, jobs, jobs — liberals in Chicago are standing in the way of a Wal-Mart Super Center that would bring in construction and retail jobs jobs jobs to the messiah's hometown. By the way, liberals will also keep the lowest cost provider of food and clothes and home goods from being accessed by hurting Chicagoans.

The reason? The liberal principle of protecting union jobs at all costs. Remember, behind every economic disaster is a powerful union. And sometimes a community organizer.

Which leads to another example. Union jobs at the big three automakers have been supported for years by the high profit SUVs and pick up trucks. During that time, liberal environmentalists have long made the SUV a target, while limiting domestic energy production. Greenies are doing everything they can to destroy the SUV, and with it many union jobs, and they almost succeeded during the last energy price spike.

Oh, and should we mention the fact that those oil rig jobs

that pay a ton of money to union members - cannot be had in America thanks to drilling restrictions? The Russians and Venezuelans send their thanks to American liberals.

But it gets better. This contradiction, which has been obvious for anyone with some linear thinking ability, has escaped the minds of millions of Michigan voters educated by the liberal-controlled public school system. They have for decades voted for politicians illogically holding pro-green yet pro-UAW positions simultaneously. Voters of that very liberal state have no one to blame but themselves. They voted themselves out of an economy over a period of years. This is the state where Obama went to pick up a good share of his economic advisors. No wonder the Detroit Lions went 0-16 not long ago.

Meanwhile, back in Washington and New York, liberals in Congress and in the media are having a field day chastising corporations for buying jets, hiring contractors to renovate posh office suites, and giving big bonuses to executives.

Well guess what? Buying jets, hiring contractors, and giving bonuses stimulates the economy. They are jobs jobs jobs friendly activities. And that's what we need now, right? Liberalism simply cannot get out of its own way. Especially hurt is left leaning New York, where the economy is reeling from a number of factors, all liberal in nature.

Yet the liberal tenet of wealth envy is paramount to common sense. And apparently, to jobs jobs jobs. Speaking of which, if you break down the Starbucks corporate jet issue, it's especially rife with unintended consequences. The coffee purveyor, you remember, was mercilessly raked across the media's coals for taking delivery on a 45 million dollar jet while it was closing stores and laying off baristas. So they cancelled the jet order.

Think about that for a second.

Starbuck's deposit on the jet was lost, which is foolish under any circumstances. Further, that jet is now back "on the showroom floor" so to speak, reducing by one unit the need to manufacture such planes. So to keep some "hamburger flipper" type jobs that liberals make fun of, many high paying jet manufacturing jobs jobs jobs were lost.

Take California's government cash meltdown. The main culprit is retiree benefits for unionized government workers in the state. And the unavoidable result is that current unionized government workers are being laid off, furloughed and not hired. More jobs jobs jobs lost as a result of liberal on liberal crime. And we could go on like this simply with stories from today's headlines. It's a fact of life. Liberal policies in action always cave in on themselves. They always have, as demonstrated by any number of issues from history above and beyond issues related to jobs jobs jobs.

Liberalism's failure is universal because liberalism embraces a false view of human nature as perfectible, if only the right political arrangements exist. And it would be funny, except that the consequences are so devastating to so many people. And so often the victims are the very liberals the policy was supposed to protect. As such, these foundational flaws with liberalism should be the main message of every single Republican campaign.

The only good news is this: with liberal Democrats front and center on all stages governmental now, they will be opposed by a much more formidable foe than a Republican President and a Congress dying to just get along. They will be opposed by the obvious truth of their bankrupt philosophy.

Now I will admit that, in early 2009, I figured four years of Obama and Reid-Pelosi control would be enough for America. And in many ways, elections and other events that happened in the interim indicated that was the case. The emergence of the Tea Party comes to mind.

The Tea Party movement was formed as a response to Obama's proposed mortgage plan, one forcing people who were paying their mortgages to subsidize those were not. This nutty Obama idea inspired a guy named Rick Santelli to go ballistic on the floor of the Chicago Mercantile Exchange. Giving a passionate rant, he explained why this scheme was such an un-American idea. In the middle of his speech, he casually dropped the idea of "a Chicago Tea Party on Lake Michigan," causing me to spit out my coffee. Something told me this was big, even though I was one of only about forty-three people who watched CNBC at the time.

Some two hours later, Rush Limbaugh's show opened with the phrase "the pulse of the Revolution has started," and virtually the entire February 19 show was devoted to Santelli. Simultaneously, the Drudge Report featured a rare "end of the world" red headline about Santelli. It is significant that in early 2009, very few people knew of Santelli, yet within days his name and the words "Tea Party" were famous. Press Secretary Robert Gibbs even threatened Santelli from the podium in the White House Press room.

American politics were never to be the same after the Tea Party movement erupted organically. To this day, it is still widely misunderstood by the elites in both parties and across the media. The term "movement" is misleading to begin with, as "Tea Party" is a mindset more than a movement. The mindset is primarily one of returning to an America as she was founded, where citizens do not live in fear of a gargantuan, intrusive and destructive federal government that serves only favored constituencies. With their reality problem, the GOPe does not understand this concept, and are usually among those favored constituencies.

Now certainly, this movement would have bubbled up at some time, under some name, with or without the Santelli broadcast. These sentiments and emotions were already out there and building. Be that as it may, the match that fell upon this particular kindling was Santelli's speech, which was then amplified by the incredible reach of Rush's show and Drudge's website.

* * *

Frankly, it shouldn't take a movement like the Tea Party to make cogent arguments about the size, scope and reach of the Federal Government. Theoretically, this is why the Republican Party exists in the first place. Making the case should be the very reason GOP office holders, candidates, consultants and spokespeople have jobs. There should always be one party whose main objective is to reduce the impact of government, because there doggoned sure is always a party pushing to maximize it.

One inherent problem is that to be effective in reducing government, you have to be a part of that government. And once you are part of government, human nature being what it is, it is very easy to morph into being part of the problem instead of the solution. We see evidence of this all the time, and John McCain could be Exhibit A.

Since the 2008 election, Palin had become a much more influential figure than McCain anyway, and she naturally fit Tea Party thinking. After all, she had demonstrated the ability to be *in* government while not being *of* government, which she exemplified by resigning as Governor of Alaska. Palin's non-government focus was totally misunderstood by the elites in both parties, because their entire focus is government, government, and more government.

To reiterate, Palin is important because she is a lightning rod for anyone trying to live a non-government-centered life. Her enemies are our enemies, and her struggles are our struggles by definition, not to mention how she is contrasted with Obama and other good Ivy League liberals (like Gorelick) in media groupthink. Obama is considered brilliant, elegant, and a force more wonderful than any other being that has graced the planet, while Palin is considered a hick, a boob, poorly educated, and certainly not sophisticated. These templates are ludicrous when you stop and look at the facts, including the recent admission by Paul Krugman that Palin was right and all of her arrogant detractors were wrong about the ObamaCare "death panels."

Logic dictates that Republicans cannot possibly win elections consistently as long as someone like Palin is considered inferior to elites like Obama (or Gorelick, for that matter). And yet, for a number of years, we have seen this thinking get imbedded into our conventional wisdom. I was wary of this potential problem the day Palin resigned, and predicted that history would vindicate her decision. This piece could be called Palin versus the Ivy League, and also touches on the government employee siege we are all under.

PALIN V. PUNDITS
American Thinker, July 5, 2009

The accomplished Alaskan governor can gaze into the face of tiny Trig and inherently know that she still has much to learn, even from her "little guy." Meanwhile, her less accomplished critics gaze mostly into TV cameras, or mirrors, and remain convinced they already know it all.

Well gosh darn. Who is right?

Palin v. the pundits demonstrates a profound disconnect that not only explains how and why the pundit class remains so incapable of understanding her (and much of America), it is a decent microcosm of the larger political debate going on in this country.

To the Beltway-Big Apple pundit elites, the idea that

anyone would (or could, or should) live a life not centered on the government-Ivy League-media capital corridor is simply an idea that is not on their radar. That Palin did not have such a life, and was not interested in such a life, was by definition a disqualification in their minds. That she was not willing to change her behavior to curry their favor was simply not forgivable. The only possible reason was that she must be too stupid to realize that all wisdom worth having is contained within this rather closed circle of geographies, people and philosophies.

After all, what good is being able to hunt and prepare your own food when any decent speed dial will get you the maitre'd at the Four Seasons? Why learn to run a business and turn a profit, when real wisdom is running a deficit and taxing those who turn a profit to make up the difference? I mean, there is wisdom and then there is wisdom. There is Washington — and then there is the real world.

Thus, just as they were last August, the D.C.-focused pundits remain totally incapable of properly analyzing what she is all about. They continue to filter her decision through purely Beltway parameters. It is clear that they were not listening to her words.

Beltway pundits view the world through the template that everything in life is a calculated PR stunt with an eye on the next election because politics and government are everything. They also have a template that no one from a state university in Idaho could possibly play in a world dominated by Ivy League insiders.

Well, just for the hell of it, let's examine both templates.

Take Ivy League-educated and connected Jamie Gorelick. Harvard B.A., magna cum laude, Harvard Law School, cum laude. Now this is the resume the pundits have immense respect for. Gorelick held the position of Assistant Attorney General under Bill Clinton (not literally). From that perch, another one for which she had no qualifications, she authored the infamous "wall" that kept the CIA and FBI from comparing notes on some young Middle Eastern men who ended up driving jet planes into buildings on 9-11.

After that deadly misadventure, she managed to make tens of millions of dollars while a Vice President at Fannie Mae. Never mind that she had no background in real estate or mortgages. She was an Ivy Leaguer with connections. Policies enacted by her and Franklin Raines (another Ivy Leaguer with connections and no experience) greatly contributed to the crash of not only Fannie Mae but also the entire housing segment. Not all was lost, as she and Raines got filthy stinking rich for their efforts.

Come to think of it, maybe the pundits are right. No one from the University of Idaho could possibly screw up that much in one lifetime. Score one for the outsiders.

And then there are the brilliant and respected Republicans like Christopher Buckley and Colin Powell. While these two wizards were among many swooning at the elegant and brilliant Obama and chafing at the plain spoken Palin, they failed to notice that the elegant one was a socialist who was mentored by American hating radicals.

Dumb ole hick Governor Palin was never fooled. Now Buckley and Powell have chimed in publicly with various degrees of buyer's remorse. Maybe living near Soviet territory does sharpen ones sensitivity.

And let's not forget that brilliant strategists were preaching that Republicans must embrace the moderate platform of the McCains of the party to have any chance of winning. You know, global warming and government nanny state programs for every phase of life and so on.

Uh oh. That backwoods Annie Oakley would talk about limited government and drilling for our own oil whenever she could break free from McCain's handlers. She even had the audacity — as someone who has actually seen ANWR — to differ with the Beltway elites on what ANWR looked like. What nerve.

Now we know now that global temperatures have not risen in nearly ten years, and Americans didn't want to pay a cent more for gas due to climate concerns even if they had. And there are surveys indicating that their number one concern is government spending, too. Oh, and *now* Dick Morris is writing a book a week about Obama the socialist. Thanks Dick, but we could have used this in 2008 when you were assuring us we must moderate.

What Palin has — along with those in the conservative base — is a lot of common sense. The kind of common sense that is so easy to get while studying at the University of Idaho, hunting moose in sub zero temperatures or managing a little league hockey team. It seems out of reach for folks who all went to the same pretentious schools K thru Ivy, and who spend their entire adult life in the D.C. to Manhattan corridor giving each other jobs for which they are not qualified, and worrying incessantly over what the press is saying about them.

That is not how Sarah Palin thinks or lives. It is not how the people who made this country great think or live. And folks who are trapped in that mentality are simply not able to figure out someone like Palin, or millions of voters who were energized by her addition to the McCain ticket. So while it would be folly for me to feign insight into her heart and mind now, not to mention any kind of prediction into the future, I think it is safe to say that her calculations were not those of the pundit class so busily analyzing this resignation.

Maybe it was just some practical common sense. With her

star power now, she can surely make more money in a month on the rubber chicken circuit than she makes in a year as governor. A book deal could easily be done also. And she needs the cash since the politically motivated grievances left her family a half mil in the red in legal bills.

Such a strategy would open up all kinds of possibilities outside of politics (gasp!) while stabilizing her finances. The increased exposure would always be a plus if she ever does think about office again. In other words, *I think it might be wise to consider this as a "business decision" and not a political one.* I would never say political future considerations never entered her mind. But I do not think it's her obsession every waking moment.

Some folks just don't get this kind of thinking. If you can get Tony Rezko to finance part of your house, you don't have to think this way. If you inherited the Kennedy liquor zillions, you don't have to think this way. If you married a widow sitting on top of a business fortune of a Republican Senator, you don't have to think this way. If you can simply call up some Ivy League connection and get a cushy government job with seven figure bonuses regardless of performance, you don't have to think this way.

The Palins have to think this way. My family has to think this way. Yours probably does too. That's why the Beltway pundits and other Washingtonians will never understand the Palins, or most of us. And the conflict is this. Our way of thinking made the country what it is. Their way of thinking will destroy it. The Palin V. Pundit contest is but one battle on a titanic stage in a vital war.

As predicted, Palin's decision to resign was validated just three months later, and was a blow to the credibility of the establishment of both parties. Not only that, but it was once again evidence that this woman, looked down upon as stupid and ditzy, somehow always made really good decisions.

PALIN'S REVENGE: WHO'S LAUGHING NOW?

American Thinker, July 5, 2009

Now correct me if I am wrong, but didn't I hear the Jurassic media bury the career of Sarah Palin just last July? And weren't they joined in this mockery by the so-called conservative elites like David Brooks and Karl Rove and Joe Scarborough and so on?

Wasn't Maureen Dowd just delirious that the wicked witch (of her world) was dead? You betcha.

Well, just who is looking out of touch and foolish now? Hint: It isn't the former Governor from Wasilla. The temptation here is to rub the seven million dollar book advance in the face of all her naysayers — then add that the book is coming out early, and is breaking all kinds of sales records though not even edited yet. But we won't do that for Mo Dowd's sake.

Another temptation is to chide the Jurassics and the elites who were snickering at the thought she could command the six figures fees the big boys get for speaking engagements — with reports that she is currently sifting through some eleven hundred offers. We won't make a big deal over that either. It might make Colin Powell blush.

What is the real story here is that given a set of singularly difficult circumstances, Governor Palin made a counter-intuitive and gutsy decision that has already proven right for all parties involved. We call that brilliance. We call that effective leadership.

Perhaps inside the Beltway, those measures of wisdom and intelligence and instinctive leadership are out of date. All too often in that world, decisions are made by what is the safe play and by what will play well with the pundits. Damn the consequences to others, just pull that focus group report and make sure we look good to the media. That was not how Palin measured her decision. She was willing to look outside the box for a possibility, and when she found an idea that worked for everyone she grabbed it. Quickly. And she never looked back. Dan Rather might call that "...courage..."

Palin didn't seem to worry a bit about how her decision would look to the pundit class as she strode to the microphones and confidently gave a shocking announcement that she knew would bring down a hell storm of derision. She did not flinch. She made a decision, announced it, and went about making it work for all involved.

And it has. It has worked for the state of Alaska, where their small government is no longer burdened by over the top media scrutiny and an endless string of nuisance legal actions. Alaska can get back to being Alaska, and the state is governed by a man who shares Palin's vision for the state without having one of the biggest media targets in the history of the country painted on his back.

What? You don't know his name? Good. Alaskans probably like it that way, and most of them probably don't know his name either.

And the resignation has certainly worked for Palin's family and the former governor herself, as they no longer have the targets painted on their backs. A mountain of legal debt no longer burdens them either. Win. Win. Win. For the Palins, and Alaskans.

Heck, it looks like the family will be able to travel the entire country at the expense of many other people who are happy to pay a nice honorarium. Along the way, she will be exposed to millions and millions of American voters who will see her in person or see local coverage of her appearances. She will curry favor with many Republicans and other conservative candidates across the country.

Her Rolodex will be engorged with valuable contacts. Her work in this area is likely to have a major impact on the mid-term elections of 2010. If it goes well for the GOP, she will get much of the credit in all likelihood.

There will be sound bytes from her on any number of weighty issues, and even

Charles Krauthammer might be impressed. By the time 2012 rolls around - just in case she has that year circled in her day planner - any notion of her lack of depth or experience will have been clearly dispelled.

Tina Fey shooting the moose will be a distant memory. Charlie Gibson will be the one thrown to the curb in his chosen profession. And I doubt Katie Couric will age as gracefully as Sarah Palin will. To summarize, every single ramification of Palin's resignation has come up aces. For her, her family, her state and even for any future political ambitions, it was the right call.

It is almost 100% certain that she will come in to the year 2012 with a lot more money, a lot more exposure, a lot more commentary on the big issues, a lot more potential campaign workers across the '57 states,' and a lot more favors owed, than she ever could have by hanging around Juneau for two more years. Yes, even in purely political terms, Palin's business and personal decision has proven to be superior to what the pundits thought she should have done. This, even though it wasn't a political decision per se.

Now this validation is sending the pundit class in the D.C.-Manhattan corridor into the vapors, not to mention shock. They've never made one correct assessment about Palin and her relationship with the American people, and the reaction to their own ineptness is to hate Palin herself. Millions of Americans are not surprised however. Why do you think so many are buying her book? You can call those «votes," and also «future campaign contributors.» They are not caught off guard by the brilliance of her decision. They knew it all along. It is obvious that Palin knew what she was doing all along.

Who knows what she will do in 2012? It doesn›t matter at the moment. What matters is that her decision to resign as Governor of Alaska will put her in a far superior position for whatever she does or does not pursue, and is better for Alaska as well. I think that's hilariously ironic. Betcha she does too. So who's laughing now?

You would think that just once, maybe, Charles Krauthammer or George Will or Dana Perino would notice the outcomes of her decisions versus those of Obama and maybe say, "You know, she didn't go to an Ivy League school, but Palin's decisions do seem to be working out better than Obama's." Instead, they continue to murmur about how elegant and well-liked Obama is, while Palin must get up to speed if she wants to be taken seriously. When you exist in the reality-immune bubble, results just don't matter, I guess.

This is about much more than Palin, however. The country has thrived because ordinary people have made decisions in liberty, and accomplished extraordinary things as a result. We stumble when these decisions are exchanged for controlling edicts from elitist Ivy League bureaucrats. There is something deeply out of kilter in anyone who refuses to see this contrast for what it is. This comparison is about so much more than just politics, as it speaks to free enterprise versus centralized control. It illustrates the very essence of who we are, and whether or not we will remain free or become subjects of the elites who would rule us for our own good.

* * *

This chuckle over the Palin-GOPe kerfuffle was about the last good thing to happen to Obama for a while. He was about to step into a deep pile on the one issue his very election was supposed to instantly heal, race relations. The idea that electing a liberal, race agitating, income redistributing, black liberation, community organizer would heal anything racial is laughable in the first place, but the elites assured us this was the case. The race card is perhaps the biggest bludgeon in the liberal arsenal of falsehoods about conservatives, and being called racist is the only thing that scares the GOPe more than Palin. As a result, they refuse to fight the charge, much less attempt to turn it around on the liberals.

But there was Obama, giving them every opportunity to do so. In the world of enlightened liberals like Obama, Attorney General Eric Holder, Jeremiah Wright and Professor Skip Gates, everything is about race. It is where their analysis of every situation starts and stops, comforted by the knowledge that the Republican establishment will never challenge them. This race obsession was demonstrated by Obama's reaction to the Gates run-in with local Cambridge cops, when he instantly knew that the Cambridge cops "acted stupidly."

Now I remind you, this is the cause and effect wunderkind who, to this day, has not figured out what happened at Fort Hood, let alone Benghazi. But somehow, he was immediately sure about what went wrong at Gate's house. How did he know? Only one answer fits his assumption, which is that white cops still routinely harass blacks. That even in 2009, in a liberal bastion like Cambridge, lynchings are routine and lunch counters are segregated.

Don't laugh. When you deconstruct his conclusion, he couldn't possibly have assumed white cops stupidity without such a default setting. The truth is, Obama's election was predestined to highlight racial differences and thereby tensions, a point made often by the more intrepid talk show hosts and columnists. To buttress this point, big time Obama fan Jamie Foxx flatly declared in December 2012 "every single thing in my life is about race." (In addition to calling Obama god and lord and savior).

Keep in mind, Foxx said this right after Obama won his second election! If Obama's election were really a racial healing, then Foxx's reaction would have been that he *used* to view everything in life through the prism of being black, but no longer. Foxx was falling in line with Obama's "revenge" plea and looking at the Presidency the way Obama does, as a chance to make things right and to return the country's wealth to its rightful owners. Yet the narrative that the media puts forth, and the one that our establishment reinforces, is that the real racists in America are in the Tea Party, at the NRA, and in the executive suites at private sector companies.

In truth, Obama has never been post-racial. Any man who idolizes and widely quotes Jeremiah Wright can be nothing but a racist by definition. Foxx even said "as a black person, it's always racial," and Obama and Wright are both black persons after all. The reason Obama befriended Wright in the first place was to burnish his black street cred, which he needed after living a cracker existence in Kansas, Hawaii and in the Ivy Leagues. Wright is doctrinally Marxist and anti-white, and Obama needed some of that to win elections in Marxist Chicago. The bottom line is that Foxx, Gates, Holder, Wright and Obama all look at everything through the prism of race. Obama's election didn't heal any of that, it merely put it into action. The support for Christopher Dorner and his killing spree is evidence of this, as is the spread of the so-called UN-FAIR Campaign. UN-FAIR is an effort to indoctrinate college students with the notion that it's unfair just to be white, and that whites are not even able to see racism, or as Reverend Wright put it; *"Hillary ain't nevah been called no niggah."* UN-FAIR was started in October of 2011, almost four years after Obama's election brought racial healing to America, or so we were told. Apparently, racial healing will not be complete until the white race ends. Until then, whites must scribble slogans of guilt on their face with sharpies, one of which is "if you see racism, speak up." I just saw it, and I just spoke up.

Speaking of Obama's racism, the dirty truth about ACORN

and community organizers was exposed in September 2009 by James O'Keefe and Hannah Giles. In a brash video caper, O'Keefe and Giles demonstrated to millions of Americans that ACORN is nothing more than a racist, anti-capitalist, income redistribution junta working for certain select population subsets. They exist to funnel government grant money to certain people, many of whom are committing criminal acts. ACORN also keeps rather casual attitudes towards legitimacy in their voter registration efforts. This is scary third world stuff.

Obviously, the race dots were there for the GOPe to connect, from Pastor Wright to ACORN to Gates. No matter. The GOPe is still scared to death of any subject in any way related to race, and they remained extremely uncurious about it all. This racial fear is why a lot of Republicans went wobbly on the Ground Zero Mosque, yet went overboard about the threat by Terry Jones to burn a few Korans.

While Obama's blatant racism was being exposed, even if widely ignored, the debate over ObamaCare was also heating up. Late in the summer, with members of Congress in their home districts, town hall meetings across the nation were concerned with the continuing growth and reach of the government in general, and were specifically and vocally anti-ObamaCare. This strong push-back clearly caught Obama, the Democrats in Congress, and their media enablers by surprise. They figured out early on that their long held fantasy of total control by way of health care would not be easy.

October 2009: A Horror Show

While the racial issues and the push-back at the town halls defined the summer of 2009, the fall was not going to be any easier for Obama. Reliving some of this is important because voters are not beamed down onto a level playing field with the scoreboard at 0-0 as a campaign enters the final weeks. They enter the voting booth with opinions shaped by events and narratives they've been exposed to over many years. To use a war analogy, the battlefield is full of craters and booby traps and land mines from previous engagements.

The Republican establishment has stepped back and allowed liberals to lay all the booby traps and all the land mines darn near unopposed for a long time, so every election is softened in favor of the Democrats.

When voters stepped into the booth in 2012, they did so with false impressions about Romney and all Republicans, not to mention airy delusions about Obama and what his government had been up to. These misconceptions were the total of many past events and interpretations in voters' minds, and reflected their misguided understanding of the two competing visions for the future.

2009 offered incredible opportunities to reverse many of these fantasies, and October alone was a horror show for Obama. In a period of days, the GOP was served up real events that should have established Obama as a laughable socialist disaster, supported by only the most moronic among us, with no idea how to function in the real world. These few days could have doomed Obama's re-election, even though it was three years off.

It all started in Copenhagen in front of the International Olympic Committee (IOC). Once Chicago had made the final four in a bid to host the Summer Olympic Games, Barack and Michelle had taken it upon themselves to personally represent the city to the IOC. In their arrogant minds, this no doubt guaranteed Chicago's success. Consider the real world implications of this failure, not to mention Obama's breathtaking arrogance and lack of self-awareness and the political opportunities it all provided.

THE OBAMAS VIOLATED FIRST THREE RULES OF SELLING
American Thinker, October 4, 2009

Of course Barack and Michelle Obama failed in Copenhagen. Their strategy could not possibly succeed. In their academic arrogance, they thought they could sell a product they clearly do not believe in (the United States) and moreover, they could do so by stressing the benefits to the seller (Chicago) and not the buyer (the IOC). And to top it off, they committed the faux pas of talking too much about the sales force (themselves) and not about the product or the buyer.

Gee, what could possibly go wrong?

Anyone who has had to succeed in the real business world — and that includes few if any on Team Obama — instinctively knows that to get business done, you have to believe in what you are selling and offer a product or service that is focused on the benefits to the customer. In the Obama World of Chicago pay-to-play power, business gets done by flexing muscle and clearing the field of your competitors. You don't have to sell anything. You don't have to believe in anything. It is fine to be self-focused. You simply have to apply the power of the applicable political machinery and you win.

Which could explain why the First Couple was so lost in an attempt to actually have to make a sale to an audience not cowed by Chicago-style clout, inoculated by our own fawning Jurassic media, nor remotely interested in their life stories. Perhaps that is how and why they botched it so badly. This is not to say that Chicago was a slam-dunk in the first place. I have no way of knowing what their ultimate chances were. But the embarrassing first round knockout was a definitive rejection of both the Obamas and their approach. Their hearts were in selling Brand Obama, not U-S-A.

The Obamas' sales pitch was awful, and predictably so. How could our President, who has made his political fortune at the expense of the reputation of the country, sell our country to the IOC with a straight face?

The answer is he could not. And although it would have

been an out of body experience, I still thought he would at least attempt to sell America and some notion of our logistical competence and love of sports and so on. I didn't think he would believe it, but certainly thought the teleprompter would sneak in something good about the country for him to read.

Nope.

He and the First Lady did *not even pretend* to be proud of us. They went on an unseemly, surreal begging campaign that mixed in uncomfortable bits and pieces of their personal histories, with platitudes about what the Olympic Games could do for the children of Chicago. Oh, BTW, the Obama family would personally find it kind of a cool thing for the neighborhood.

So ask not what our country can do for your Olympics — ask what your Olympics can do for our city. Heck, that was the First Lady's closing argument:

"Chicago's vision for the Olympic and Paralympic Movement is about so more than what we can offer the Games — **it's about what the Games can offer all of us.**"

That was how she ended her speech. That was her "please sign here" moment. It's all about us! For the record, her talk mentioned NOTHING about what we could offer the games. Not a word. No wonder they didn't sign on the dotted line. Before that closing, some 40% of her speech was about her Dad and his M.S. Apparently the IOC didn't see the relevance. When she wasn't talking about her Dad, she was fantasizing about what a Chicago Olympiad would mean to her and the children of the city:

"But today, I can dream, and I am dreaming of an Olympic and Paralympic Games in Chicago...that will expose all our neighborhoods to new sports and new role models; that will show every child that regardless of wealth, or gender, or race, or physical ability, there is a sport and a place for them, too."

To which the IOC's answer was something like "get them ESPN and ESPN 2 if they need to be exposed to new sports and role models. And by the way, we're not so sure about that regardless of 'ability' concept either."

She was followed by the President — who in all fairness did shelve some his blatantly anti-American sentiment for the time being — but only couching positive things about the nation in terms of diversity or Obama-ness.

"Nearly one year ago...people from every corner of the world...gathered to watch the results of the U.S. Presidential election. Their interest wasn't about me as an individual. Rather, it was rooted in the belief that America's experiment in democracy still speaks to a set of universal aspirations and ideals."

Let me translate: That our experiment in democracy was hanging on by the thread of whether he won the election or not was his point, not to mention his point that the world was interested only because he was involved. But his stance that modern history started with his inauguration continued:

"Now, that work is far from over, but it has begun in earnest...(and) there is nothing I would like more than to step just a few blocks from my family's home, with Michelle and our two girls, and welcome the world back into our neighborhood."

Well where do I sign? How can I possibly turn down an opportunity to make the twenty16 Olympics so convenient for family Obama? After all, they are the family that has finally started — in earnest — the work of, well, whatever it is they are transforming in America.

Amazing.

When you consider these words in light of what Obama said about the United States last week at the U.N and the Gtwenty, it is clear to see that this is a man who really does think history started when he was born - and America's greatness started when he was elected. These thoughts dominate any sober analysis of the written words of his speeches. While our own Jurassic media is totally under his spell, the IOC and the much of the rest of the world media is not. They saw the Copenhagen sales pitch and rejected it out of hand. It came in fourth place out of four.

There is analysis out of the D.C.-Manhattan corridor already that the racists in the United States, and the Republicans and talk radio and Fox News and the right leaning blogosphere are to blame for the Denmark disaster. They are not. Neither is George Bush or Dick Cheney or even Donald Rumsfeld.

Elsewhere, there is talk that it was not-that-big-a-deal and that Chicago was done a favor by not getting the games. That may be true, but the Obama's and their Chicago buddies wanted it badly — and thought they had it in the bag. The bottom line is this: this was an Obama epic fail period. They were the sales force, they were the focus of the sales presentation and they were the product. The Obamas were there to sell the Obamas with the Obamas. All Obama all the time.

And the world said "no thanks."

This was a stunning personal rebuke of Obama as well as of his notion that America's history is all about him, proving how out of touch he is with a world not under the spell of Chicago thug power or his exotic race mix. He had no idea that someone might some day tell him no, and was unfamiliar with the need for a seller to emphasize advantages to a potential buyer. He thought he could prance in and get what he wanted on the premise that it would be a cool thing for him personally. As the Drudge headline said, "The Ego Has Landed."

Then again, none of these lessons got through to the buzz-kill establishment either, and they were quick to condemn those of us enjoying Obama's failure. This spectacular embarrassment had just set in when another imbroglio befell the messiah, when, for no particular reason, the Nobel Committee awarded Obama the Nobel Peace Prize on October 9th.

Now when you do the math, it is obvious that Obama's nomination had to have taken place just 12 days into his term as President at the latest, when all he had done was sign Ledbetter and threaten to close Gitmo. This risible award would still be an embarrassment today if liberals had any ability to feel shame. Frankly, I didn't know which was more embarrassing… losing the Olympics or winning the Nobel Prize.

And yet, October was about to get even worse for Obama. On the very same day, a Detroit reporter named Ken Rogulski filed the story featuring the famous "Obama stash" woman accompanied by chants of "O-bah-ma-Oh-bah-ma" from her peeps. Americans were once again hit with the reality that much of Obama's support was based on anticipated handouts. This sound byte is where the phrase "Obama stash" was born.

This "Obama stash" woman should have been the perfect bookend for an event that came along in October of 2012: the "Obama phone" woman from Cleveland. Taken individually, these events were slightly damaging to Obama. If our party elites knew anything about crafting a narrative, these events would have automatically built on each other and become more powerful. No doubt, the abject fear of racism motivated the GOPe's retreat from these very revealing events.

Had the GOP, its candidates, and the related Super PAC's taken advantage of these videos, there would have been no problem with Mitt's 47% comment. The obvious reality of the 47% would have been sequential to "Obama stash" and "Obama phones" in everybody's minds. Instead, Mitt ran from the 47% comment, and Paul Ryan and Marco Rubio continued to run from it after the election. Does it not matter to anyone in the establishment that the 47% comment is, in the larger context, TRUE? Does it matter that electronic food stamp cards are now being used to withdraw cold hard cash from ATM's in strip clubs by this 47%? Is this really something we should be scared to say? Will any of these potentially offended voters ever consider voting Republican under any circumstances anyway?

This is just more evidence that the GOPe will not do for the truth what the liberals routinely will do for a lie, which is to repeat it, even if it's initially met with some push-back. If we don't learn this lesson, and by learn I mean adopt as a strategy, we are doomed. And by doomed, I mean the country, not just the party. In fact, I'm going to add another GOPe ailment to the list, along with Reality Deficit Disorder (RDD). I think we have to add an advanced state, Reality Derangement Syndrome (RDS).

At any rate, these were nine devastating days to the mythology of Barack specifically and to the idea of a government-centered life in general. This was the perfect lead-in to campaigns in the fall of 2009, as reality was on display, Obama was in deep trouble, and there was nothing the GOPe could do to stop it.

6

TOXIC, NOT EXOTIC, AND
THE WINTER OF DEFEAT

One key race in 2009 was Virginia's race for Governor, notable since the state had gone solidly Obama in 2008. In this year of the halo freefall, all sober analyses pointed to a big win for Bob McDonnell over the largely irrelevant Creigh Deeds, as Virginians were having second thoughts about Obama. The state always would be among the reddest in the first place, were it not for the federal government attracting so many liberals into northern Virginia territory.

Meanwhile Democrats were embarrassed that Obama and Deeds couldn't decide if they wanted to associate with each other or not. Admitting that Obama was hurting Deeds would be devastating. Yes, Obama was incredibly weak, even toxic, just a few months into his term, another example of why losing in 2012 is just not forgivable.

Pumped up with all of this anti-Obama energy, Republicans were starting to believe that they might pull off the unthinkable: the New Jersey Governorship. Obama pal Jon Corzine, whose career is a testament to the power of arrogance combined with connections, had won easily in 2005. But along came plainspoken Chris Christie, who was not bashful about exposing Corzine's corruption or Jersey's spending problems, which were mostly due to government unions. (Set aside the quirky Hurricane Sandy related events late in the 2012 campaign, and Christie's likely jump to the Democrat Party in 2013. This was 2009.)

These two gubernatorial races were referendums on Obama and the general direction that Democrats were taking the country, even though the leftist media insisted otherwise. People couldn't formally vote against Obama, Reid or Pelosi in 2009, but they relished voting against them vicariously.

These races were capturing a lot of attention, along with an odd special election in New York's 23rd Congressional District. Palin became part of the NY 23 story when she endorsed third party candidate Doug Hoffman over the official GOP candidate, Dede Scozzafava. Newt Gingrich intervened on behalf of Dede and the party hacks, a mistake that dogged Newt throughout 2011-2012. Without a doubt, Palin won this little PR skirmish against the former Speaker. (Ironically, Sarah and Todd Palin later endorsed Gingrich for President in another act of defiance against the GOP establishment.) In the meantime, these three elections of 2009 were heralds to the elections of 2010.

NEXT TUESDAY'S LESSONS FOR 2010
American Thinker, October 29, 2009

OMG. From the "backwater" town of Wasilla, the naïve hockey-mom moose-huntress simply "Facebooked" a few thoughts into her device of choice, and damned if those words didn't bounce off a satellite and land squarely in the middle of New York state politics. Key among those words was the phrase "endorse Doug Hoffman."

Perhaps they landed in the middle of the run up to the 2010 mid term elections as well.

And from the glass towers of Manhattan to the stately low-rise buildings of Washington, self-important media pundits and Republican apparatchiks are once again slow to realize that they have been outmaneuvered, out-finessed, and outsmarted by their favorite target of derision, dumb ole Sarah Palin. Has David Brooks has quit staring at the crease in Obama's pants long enough to notice?

By her endorsement of Conservative Party candidate Hoffman in the now famous 23rd Congressional district of New York, Palin has demonstrated guts, leadership, political instincts, and a connection with real America that continue to dwarf those traits in almost everyone inside the Beltway. Oh, and BTW — she is a major reason that the now-famous special election of NY 23 is now famous.

All of which makes NY 23 one of three elections next week that will contain significant lessons to be learned for the 2010 midterms. Significant as the lessons are, however, they are somewhat nuanced — and if the conservative base and the GOP leadership do not reach the same conclusions from the results, the mega opportunity of 2010 will be impaired, if not wasted.

Along with NY 23, next week brings us governors' races in Virginia and New Jersey. As it stands now, Republican Bob McDonnell should win by an enormous margin in Virginia, and Republican Chris Christie will run very close to — and may beat — Jon Corzine in New Jersey. Hoffman has a real chance to win NY 23. If McDonnell wins and Christie even comes close, the lessons for 2010 hold.

The Virginia lesson here is simple. This normally red state turned blue for Obama, but now they are trending back red — as in red-faced embarrassment for buying into "hope and change," and angry red over Obama "fundamentally changing" the country. McDonnell is up on Creigh Deeds by 10 to 18 points, and Deeds and the White House have come just short of conceding already.

To lose, McDonnell would have to be caught on tape

lighting a cigarette, handing out bonuses to AIG executives, and using racial/gender slurs as he orders a scotch and other more personal favors from a pre teen ACORN approved sex slave. McDonnell is further aided by ads with Obama, praising Obama of course, yet "paid for by the Deeds for Governor Committee."

The lesson is this: red states like Virginia that turned blue in 2008 are moving back. The Obama-nation is not selling in these parts, and all you have to do in these areas is be a conservative and run like one. Period. That was not tried in 2008, by the way. The lessons from Jersey are not that difficult either. First, run as a smaller government conservative and you might make history even in this bluest of blue states. Incumbent Jon Corzine, a mega-wealthy Wall Street Democrat, has 25 million more dollars to spend than Christie, and there are 700,000 more registered Democrats than Republicans in New Jersey. Not only that, but there is a third party candidate in the race siphoning voters from Christie as well.

Even against this array of disadvantages, Christie has a 50-50 chance. How? By standing his ground and running against an unabashed liberal. In fact, were it not for the third-party candidate, Christie would be cake walking to victory. This is a key message for third-party advocates. Go third party and you will end up with more very liberal Democrats. The third party in Jersey may end up electing their *least* favorite choice of Corzine. That is Corzine's only hope. This is a *key* lesson.

And that brings us to NY 23...where no, this is *not* a race that disproves the Third Party assumption just made about New Jersey. The race between Doug Hoffman, ultra-liberal Republican Dede Scozzafava, and Democrat Bill Owens is extraordinary for a number of reasons. It's an off-year election in a single district where the "third-party" candidate is actually a Republican, who should have been the GOP candidate in the first place.

Doug Hoffman wanted the GOP nomination and likely would have won it in a primary, since he clearly is the base's choice. However, the local party tapped Scozzafava instead under somewhat murky circumstances - although everything was done in accordance with normal procedures for such an election. The problem is Dede is liberal, even for a Democrat.

All of which makes NY 23 a deliciously interesting laboratory opportunity for canny conservative Republicans...you know, like Hoffman and Sarah Palin. And here is the payoff lesson, as spoken by Hoffman himself:

"I think this is a battle for the heart and soul of the Republican Party and for the values and ideals that we — we say we stand for...basically, it comes down to two liberals in the race. And I'm the common-sense conservative Reagan Republican in the race. I think, if the Republican Party ever wants to get back into the majority and they want to get strong again, they have to stick to their ideals."

In other words, the third-party candidate Hoffman is referring to Republicans as "we" and calling himself the only true Republican in the race. In his mind, his candidacy is a road map for the Republican Party's success, even though he is running outside of it. That is not to disparage third parties per se, but only to point out that Hoffman is not making a third-party statement here. He is making an anti-establishment statement however, and the same can be said of his superstar endorser, Sarah Palin. In her endorsement announcement, she said:

"Republicans and conservatives around the country are sending an important message to the Republican establishment in their outstanding grassroots support for Doug Hoffman: no more politics as usual."

Palin went on to quote Ronald Reagan, who said that "blurring the lines" is not the way to rebuild the Republican Party. She too is attempting to rebuild the party by endorsing its defeat *in this specific election.*

And the same can be said for Dick Armey, Fred Thompson, The Club for Growth, Concerned Women for America, and others who have publicly supported Hoffman. (I would add that Tim Pawlenty showed his leadership mettle compared to Palin's by coming late to the Hoffman endorsement party.)

And really, this is the lesson of all three races regardless of their outcomes. If Hoffman comes close, or wins against long odds, as a third party — and if Christie comes close or wins in far-left Jersey — and if McDonnell wins big in a state Obama carried a year ago — the lessons are the same. Republicans will do very well to send their liberal cohorts "their own way" and revitalize the party Reagan-style.

Another lesson is that the very first public figure to fully invest in this theory was that hick ex-governor from Alaska. She rolled the dice, swung for the fences, thought outside the box and she took a chance based on her instincts. And guess what? Just like when she resigned her governorship, her decision is coming up aces. Again. Maybe our establishment geniuses can explain how someone so stupid can keep making so many wise decisions.

The conservative base is not surprised in the least. But the DC-Manhattan-corridor pundits and party hacks, who are still miffed by her resignation, have no idea what is going on with her endorsement of Hoffman, nor how it is playing in flyover country. And they will likely misread the tealeaves of these election results. Again.

The lessons drawn from November 3rd will have a critical influence on the development of the 2010 and 2012 elections. We cannot afford another polite RINO disaster, or another Perot Party disaster. Obama and his big government statists are moving way too fast.

We later found out that the 2010 and 2012 campaigns were developed in totally different fashions, and it's safe to say we suffered that feared "polite disaster" in 2012. Meanwhile, the NY 23 race was illustrating that the quaint idiom "all politics is local" was no longer applicable. This unhappy situation was far more than just a benign political shift — it was a shift away from the very founding precepts of our country. The article below is about much more than NY 23 because NY 23 was itself about a lot more than just NY 23. And that's the problem.

NY 23: Perhaps Not All Politics Are Local
American Thinker, November 1, 2009

That we all know — let alone care — about the goings-on in New York's 23rd Congressional District speaks volumes about how far away from our founding principles we have drifted. We should not know or care about NY 23 under our founding model, but make no mistake: we do know. We do care. We have drifted a long way.

At stake is the same principle debated in the movie "The Patriot."

Loosely based on the real life of South Carolina's Francis Marion, known as the "Swamp Fox," the film's debate was over whether the colonists should "trade one tyrant 5,000 miles away - for 5,000 tyrants one mile away." While Mel Gibson sounded pithy delivering that line, the ridiculous theory behind it was unearthed, and the colonists did decide to rid themselves of the "one tyrant 5,000 miles away," and with the Swamp Fox's help.

The result was not tyranny. Limited and local power cannot be such, by definition.

The idea — quaint as it sounds now — is that any problem you might have with a tiny government could be solved by simply sitting down with some local citizen legislator and working it out. Think Mayberry, where you could hash anything out with Andy, Barney, and the mayor at Floyd's Barbershop.

If that didn't work, you could simply run for office in a fair fight in a couple years. The incumbent would probably have tired of government "service" by then anyway. What a process! What a country!

The Feds? Oh, they were just a few guys to handle the Barbary Pirates and such. The idea was that you could live your life and never have to see, let alone deal with, anyone from a strong centralized government if you chose not to. You sent them a few bucks to fund the military each year and everything was fine. Thus the once-true cliché: all politics are local.

Now, however, we have to send money over the internet to a nice geeky accountant, (Hoffman) in a place we've never been, and hope like hell he can win a race decided by voters we will never meet.

Why? Because if he wins, it just might put a damper on the designs of a radical liberal from San Francisco, and a community organizer from Chicago, who are trying to "fundamentally transform" the nation birthed by the Swamp Fox and other patriots. Nobody outside of upstate New York *should have to know or care* what happens in that Congressional district...yet we do.

And no one in Texas or Florida or South Carolina should live in fear of whatever whacko is sent to Congress from the shadows of Berkeley, or from the machine politics of Chicago. Yet we do know, we do care, and in fact we live in fear of these people — and for good reason.

They consider all money as theirs, and they want to control every aspect of our lives — and they have made significant inroads towards doing just that in a few months. They are debating a piece of legislation (ObamaCare) that might in fact push the pendulum of government control past a point of no return. Most of the key people who are pushing this health care legislation are extreme liberals from parts of the country that will never fail to reelect them. The vast majority of the people they will affect, however, have no say in whether or not they get reelected.

This allows them to stay in the halls of power for so long that they accumulate power over years and years of simply being in Washington. *Thus, the longer they are isolated from reality, the more power they have to change reality. This is a scenario that guarantees a lot of problems.*

And this is exactly what our Founding Fathers did not want. King George was 5,000 miles away geographically, and even farther apart experientially from the colonies. Our country was founded precisely because the British model was deemed so unworkable and evil that it demanded we spill blood and treasure to stop it. "Don't Tread on Me" and "No Taxation Without Representation" were among the cries.

And yet now "our representatives" are debating so-called health care legislation that tells the IRS to decide what we're thinking when we spend our money, and tax it accordingly. Do we ask for an audit - or a séance? Does Carnac the Magnificent work for the IRS now?

How can this be? We have drifted into having about 325 tyrants in Washington, and they are opposed by about 225 scared folks who all too often go along to get along with the tyrants because they have been there too long too.

Consider: Barney Frank and Charlie Rangel can heap

oppressive taxation on hundreds of millions of us, yet we have no say in their "representation" status. In Rangel's case, he casually avoids living under those same tax rules, which runs slightly afoul of the "Don't Tread on Me" concept. Yet we can't do anything about it, or about Frank or Pelosi or Rangel or Waters or Waxman. Reid may get what's coming to him next year, but he can do much damage outside Nevada in the meantime. Obama is there for another three years, or maybe seven. All of that is very maddening, frustrating, and disheartening.

But right now, what we can do is get involved in New York 23, as many have. Newt Gingrich may have let history pass him by as he blithely deferred to the "local party officials" in a colossal gesture of group think, but we don't have to make the same mistake. For some inexplicable reason, it escaped Newt that government is so big and so powerful that New York 23 will affect all of us. Thus, it is our duty as citizens to get involved with NY 23. Rarely does a single district carry so much meaning. It is our patriotic duty to help the one person running in NY 23 who does *not* want NY 23 to ever to matter to us again.

Doug Hoffman's history indicates he might be that one person. Palin and Fred Thompson agreed before it was cool to be pro-Hoffman, and time will tell if that is true or not. But obviously a Hoffman victory will send a message to those who are doing all they can to increase tyranny...a fact that make us all citizens of New York 23 this week regardless of our zip codes.

Nonetheless, the Democrats were already using "all politics is local" as their prophylactic spin. They feared the worst in all three races and were desperate to protect their precious boy President. Their spin was nonsense; people were observably voting against Obama and using Deeds and Corzine as surrogates. These voters were a little like the secession petitions after the 2012 elections. It was a chance to vote against Obama once again. For all of the "he's so personally popular" garbage, people certainly do love to vote against the guy over and over and over.

Election Night 2009 brought a lot of good news, but not in NY 23. That inspired another preposterous Democrat spin, that a tiny district in upstate New York was a national election while two vast, statewide elections were merely local struggles. Yes, that really was the daffy liberal interpretation.

FORGET THE 2-1 SPIN; IT WAS A ROUT
American Thinker, November 4, 2009

The Democrats did not lose a 2-1 squeaker last night. They lost two monumental races, saw an overall evaporation of 25 basis points of support — and lost by nearly 500,000 cumulative votes in the three high-profile elections.

Or put another way, Republicans won two races decided by millions of voters — and Democrats won a small race dominated by party operatives. In addition, the GOP made some historic gains in Pennsylvania, Michigan, and Washington State special elections to boot.

In the context of Bob McDonnell's immense win in Virginia and Chris Christie's surprisingly comfortable win in New Jersey of all places, the fact that Bill Owens scraped up enough votes to win NY-23 is a testament to the superior political insider maneuvering of the Democrats over the Republicans. So you mean the GOP party apparatus stinks? Well yes, but I think we knew that already.

What we did not know was just how overwhelming the anti-Democrat tide would be among voters. In the three talked-about races, it was a blowout of something like 55%-42% overall, and this in precincts that voted for Obama 56%-44% just a year ago. The raw totals will end up a tad fewer than 2.4 million GOP votes to 1.9 million for the Democrats in round numbers.

So don't buy into any 2-1 split-decision analysis. It was a stunning reversal of a full quarter of the electorate in one year's time.

For the record, Barack Obama "voted present" by not even watching the election returns — let alone commenting — as his party suffered the massive 25% reversal. (Okay, I don't believe the reports that he didn't watch, but who could begrudge him a little fib considering the magnitude of the actual loss?)

The stunning stat of the night might be this: that McDonnell beat Creigh Deeds by a literally one thousand times the margin he did in 2005. Or it might be that Christie overcame a 700,000 party voter disadvantage to win a race with about two million total voters. Or it may be that all this happened with zero references to "reaching across the aisle" or mavericks or compassionate conservatism.

So what does all this mean?

It means Barack Obama, Nancy Pelosi, Harry Reid and "big tent" politics just suffered a huge electoral defeat. Likely the same can be said of whatever this week's Obama-Baucus-Bogus-Consumer-Ponzi-Care bill is being passed around these days. To quote CNBC analyst Jerry Bowyer, the 1,900-page health care bill is "now pulp." He made that call before 8 p.m. Eastern.

None of this will be in the White House spin — but at the risk of offending the sensibilities of the suddenly decorum-focused Pelosi — any attempt by the Democrats to candy-coat or minimize what happened last night is nothing less than a bunker-mentality fantasy.

Here is the breakdown race by race:

VIRGINIA: The result could be the name of a Star Wars Droid: R 60 D 40.

Virginians voted loud and clear to reject Obama and his party as McDonnell routed Deeds by almost 19 points. For those scoring at home, that's a 26-point swing towards Republicans — or away from Democrats — in precisely one year. The last time McDonnell ran against Deeds for Attorney General in 2005, McDonnell won by only 323 votes statewide. That was the closest race in Virginia's history. Last night, he won by over 3twenty,000 votes.

And there is much evidence that what mattered was the party symbol, not the candidate's name. Actually, the symbol that mattered was the D — and Virginians voted against that D. Some are saying that the key was a very disciplined and down-the-middle campaign by McDonnell against a poor Deeds campaign. Maybe. But that does not explain why all the down ballot races almost exactly mirrored that of the Governor's race.

Post election surveys indicated that voters were thinking about national issues, and beating the Obama agenda, by an overwhelming majority. In short, this was D versus R, or at least anti-D.

And you can bet that three so-called "blue dog" Democrats in Congress are taking a look at the tallies. According to Michael Barone, McDonnell won the three districts where freshman blue dog Democrats live by 62%-38%, 61%-39%, and 55%-45%. I think ObamaCare might have just lost three blue dogs in the Commonwealth.

NEW JERSEY: This win carries a lot of weight!

In Democrat stronghold New Jersey, the revulsion and rejection factor of Democrats continued in a major way. While Christie was given a chance according to recent polling, in historical context, this is a stunner. In a state where Obama carried 59% of the vote in 2008, incumbent Democrat Jon Corzine struggled to reach 44%. Corzine publicly hitched his wagon to the Obama White House, and whether or not the White House likes it, they are in the mire of this incredible defeat.

Corzine had twice as much money, a lot more Democrats to mobilize, multiple Obama appearances, and a third-party candidate handpicked to mess up Christie — and yet he still lost. Even reality challenged Juan Williams admitted this loss "was big" for the Democrats. Sure Corzine is wealthy, corrupt, and a tax-raiser, but that never stopped Democrats from winning in New Jersey before. Almost all of Democrats are all of those things in the Garden State.

NEW YORK 23: The Obama White House machine was far superior here to an awful local Republican Party.

Without a doubt, Hoffman's loss takes a bit of sheen off the night. Having said that, a single race involving roughly a hundred thousand voters in odd circumstances is not the equal of the multi-million vote governors' races. Don't let the Obama spin fool you with all the talk about the GOP losing a district they had held since the Civil War. Obama carried that district by 5 points in 2008. Moreover, he tapped the Republican House Member from this district for a minor cabinet post, for the express purpose of hoping the Dems could win an open seat. That was good tactical politics.

When local Republicans anointed the extremely liberal Dede Scozzafava without a primary, they were asking for trouble. You can call that awful tactical politics. Scozzafava's endorsement of Owens validated conservative activists, and those like Sarah Palin and Fred Thompson, in backing Hoffman. That an inexperienced candidate — with much of the official local GOP machinery pouting on the sidelines — lost to a suddenly very well-funded Obama-machine candidate is really no surprise. For all the national hoopla about Hoffman, the on-the-ground reality is that the Obama hacks beat the GOP hacks in the game of turnout and tactics. Is anyone surprised that the local Republican operatives would be outplayed?

In short, the night showed that the Tea Party movement and the palpable bubbling up of a conservative ascendancy is real. It would seem to indicate that a repeat of '93-'94 (fueled by Hillary Care) is at least possible in 2009-2010 (fueled by ObamaCare and all other symptoms of malignant government). Certainly last night was even better by any statistical measure than this same election night was in 1993, when the GOP also swept Democrats out of state houses in Jersey and Virginia. And it needs to be. Our Republic is in more danger than we were in 1993 — by any statistical measure. We won bigger, but it was necessary that we did. And that's the proper spin of election night 2009.

This was indeed an awful night for Obama and all liberals, and also a very accurate dry run for the 2010 mid terms. It was not, however, the death knell for ObamaCare, though it should have been, nor was it a harbinger for 2012, which it also should have been.

Two days after the electoral shellacking, real tragedy struck when a Jihadist Major in the U.S. Army killed fourteen soldiers at Fort Hood. Predictably, the liberal spin machine was out immediately to make sure that no one made the rash assumption that someone named Nidal Hasan, who was shouting Allahu Akbar as he shot Americans, was any sort of terrorist, by God. The media and other liberals seemed not to care at all about the soldiers who were killed. They were obsessed with the optics. Their spin was the formulaic warning against a rush to judgment, a warning they only issue in situations that call for a rush to judgment.

Contrast this with how the left reacted to the Gabby Giffords shooting, which was a rush to call it Palin's fault; or the Aurora incident, where they rushed to the judgment that it was the Tea Party's fault; or the Newtown killings, which were instantly the fault of the NRA, not to mention the fault of an "assault rifle" that remained in the shooter's trunk. The constant is that liberals don't seem to give a damn about the victims; they only care about finding a narrative they can exploit. This always includes a rush to judge law-abiding American conservatives, while never contemplating Islamic Jihadists, serial criminals, or perhaps the flawed liberal laws that make all of these disasters more likely.

The other constant is that these killers all recognize vulnerability, thanks to liberal gun policies. Hasan knew full well that the Fort Hood soldiers were irrationally not allowed to carry ammo, just as the strange Mr. Lanza knew an elementary school would be 'gun free.' There are never mass shootings where law-abiding citizens might be packing, witch is something to think about. In fact, the country is doing a lot of thinking about that right now.

Meanwhile, after the Fort Hood shooting, Obama, General George Casey, and the entire media bubble thoroughly disgraced themselves by their continued rush to non-judgment about the shooter, even in light of overwhelming evidence. Everyone instantly knew what had happened, and there was unspoken national embarrassment that our boy President and his toy General could not handle the truth.

The Fort Hood assault was another of those events that clearly delineates the real country from the Washington-NYC bubble elites. It was like one of those no-score little league games where everyone knows the score, but no one in charge will admit it. Obama and Casey were like clueless no-score league parents, walking around congratulating themselves on how enlightened they are by not to rushing to judgment with something as mean spirited as, you know, an accurate score. All the kids in the dugout - the soldiers – *certainly* knew the score. It was 14-0 in favor of the Jihadists. Obama, Casey, and our media came off looking ignorant and strangled by political correctness. You might think this could have been worked into a Romney narrative related to terrorism and bin Laden at some point, in which case you aren't an establishment consultant.

Naturally, many months later, the whole tragic affair was cleansed by the official investigations. While no one was held responsible, everyone congratulated everyone else on taking responsibility. (This is exactly what will happen with Benghazi, by the way.) Back in the real world, the soldiers are still dead, as is the Libyan Ambassador.

In December, there was another fruitless jobs summit, where Obama and a bunch of other people who have never created a job got together to talk about creating jobs. Of course, jobs were not really Obama's concern in the first place. ObamaCare was job one. Nothing will fundamentally change the country like a government take-over of one sixth of the entire economy, with the added benefit of being able to tell people what they can and cannot do. Again, Reagan warned over fifty years ago that the liberals' best chance of destroying the nation was through the back door of medicine, and Palin correctly discerned the unavoidable death panel aspect to ObamaCare three years ago. The GOPe has yet to catch up to either one.

But even in Massachusetts, many voters were starting to figure out the truth about ObamaCare. As a result the idea of the Democrats losing the Kennedy seat started to surface. Could 2010 start worse than 2009 ended?

Early 2010: Who Is the New Guy, That Number 41?

Well, yes, Scott Brown did indeed defeat Martha Coakley, running openly as number 41, as in the 41st vote in the Senate against ObamaCare. (Not to be confused with Client Number 9, Democrat Eliot Spitzer). This was the perfect capstone for Obama's first year, and quite a gift on the very anniversary of him taking office. It was a stunner that was built upon the multiple body blows the liberal President had absorbed, and it clearly rattled Team Obama. I just can't help shamelessly mentioning that Rush read every single word of this analysis on-air the next day.

What Has Brown Done for Us?

January 20, 2010

I bet they can hear this cheering all the way in Washington, D.C. It's just the beginning...when there's trouble (for Democrats) in Massachusetts, there's trouble everywhere. Rest assured they know it.

-from Scott Brown's opening statement last night

What has Brown done for us? He just administered a stunning "Tea Party Republican" thrashing to the "Kennedy Liberal Democrats" in Massachusetts — with ObamaCare front and center as the core issue at hand. That's what. Forget any other spin you hear — that is what just happened. *That Brown did not stress the party or the term "tea party" does not matter.* His issues were right off of the tea parties' posters and out of the official Reagan platform manual.

Sure, Martha Coakley ran a horrible campaign. But Democrats win safe seats with horrible campaigns all the time. Brown ran a great campaign, but good candidates lose uphill campaigns all the time in places like Massachusetts. And no, MSNBC, this was not a Tip O'Neil "all politics are local" referendum on potholes and such. *Thanks to big government liberals, no politics are local anymore.* Not even an obscure Congressional district known as NY-23.

This is because every single seat may now hold the key to Washington's ability to reach into the homes, wallets and lives of every American for any reason they deem necessary. And *that's* what this was about, with health care as the key issue but only one of many concerns about intrusive government. This was without a doubt another crest in the wave that started when Rick Santelli put CNBC and the term "tea party" on the map in February 2009 — an anti-big government rant that went multimedia viral thanks to the Rush Limbaugh Show and red "end of the world" headlines on the Drudge Report. It built with April 15 tea parties around the country and through the town halls of August and September.

It even survived the misguided effort to dub a pro-union thug song called "Shuttin Dee-troit Down" as the official anthem.

It was palpable. And this wave continued to rise in November as Republicans — yes, Republicans — rolled to stunning wins in New Jersey and Virginia. This wave was obvious to anyone and everyone not occupying office in Washington and certain pundit chairs in the D.C.-Manhattan corridor. The message was consistent. Washington was trying to "fundamentally change" America, and beyond their notice, Americans were waking up to what that means and were not shouting "no" — but "hell no!"

And no more resounding "hell no" can be remembered in decades than the one given in the Bay State last night. This is Massachusetts! Even McGovern won Massachusetts! Obama won Massachusetts by 26 points in '08. Last night, Coakley — and Obama — lost that same population by roughly 6 points. In round numbers, that's means a third of the state shifted. Simply seismic!

Brown may have won the "people's seat," but moreover, the Democrats have just lost "the Kennedy seat." Yet it is still not clear how they would answer the question: "Can you hear us now?"

Obama's 365 days

A year ago today, Barack Obama was all too anxious to

accept his victory and read deep meaning into it. Today, it appears he is not even willing to acknowledge his incredible defeat of last night, let alone learn from this illuminating moment. This is especially true as it relates to his legislative agenda. Regardless, Scott Brown has done a *lot* for us. And by "us," I mean America. Stopping health care now and exposing the obvious socialist power-grab of the Democrats are both tremendous gifts.

No RINO win

This was also *not* a win for the "reach across the aisle" establishment RINO Republicans or the David Brooks Republicans. Brown ran at every rally as the "41st vote to stop health care reform" and in no way was looking for an Olympia Snow-style accommodation. He was not, in the words of Bob Dole, trying to figure out a way "to pass a bill." And certainly, after being cooped up in a pickup truck for two hundred thousand miles, he does not have a "pant crease" sufficiently crisp to win over Brooks.

His final points last night were a Reagan-esque litany of low taxes, national defense, and national pride. Chants of "U-S-A" broke out several times. The Kennedy name was praised, but the only Kennedy ideas that were praised were the fiscally conservative ones of JFK. There was no remorse over "unfettered capitalism" anywhere to be heard. (Are you taking notes, Senator McCain?)

The only thing that might appeal to Teddy was the tongue-in-cheek implication by Brown that his two comely daughters might be available. Other than that, it was a show of belief in limited government and a hard line against terrorists. The best line was that American tax dollars "should be used for weapons to fight terrorists, not lawyers to represent terrorists." The crowd's roar at that was tremendous. This was not exactly McCain pussy footing around about water boarding.

Make no mistake about it: Last night was a fabulous victory for the ideas of the tea party movement and the core beliefs of the conservative base voter. Those ideas thrashed the ideas of liberal Kennedy-Obama policies. Period. Apply the "duck test." It matters not for the moment that Brown did not stress those terms — or that far too many GOP officeholders have not gotten it often enough. As Brown said late in his speech:

"Across this country — to all those folks who are listening, if you're covering me — we are united by basic convictions that only need to be clearly stated to win a majority — and if anyone doubts that in this next election season that's about to begin — well, let them take a look at what happened here in Massachusetts. Because what happened here in Mass can happen all over America."

Scott Brown, we were listening. We saw what happened in Massachusetts. And we definitely do hear you now!

Except the Obama administration chose not to hear. To admit the lessons of Massachusetts would be to admit defeat on ObamaCare, and that wasn't going to happen under any circumstances. Scott Brown's inability to learn the very lessons he taught is another tutorial altogether. He fully abandoned his message two years later, which led to the embarrassing loss to Elizabeth Warren.

There is instruction beyond that, however. It was obvious that Brown's win plus those of Christie, McDonnell and even Chambliss unnerved the Administration. Their reaction to Brown's rebuke is a demonstration of who these people really are. And by these people, I mean elected Democrats and their enablers in the media. Who they are now mostly is David Axelrod. Compared to Axelrod's escapades, the mind-numbing use of focus groups and phony polls by James Carville and George Stephanopoulos during the Clinton years is child's play. Axelrod does not merely use deception. He *IS* deception.

Before becoming Obama's guru, Ax got wealthy fabricating and executing phony grass roots uprisings for hire, purposefully called AstroTurf campaigns. It is an accepted fact that he's the father of this industry. More than just dishonest, AstroTurf campaigns are non-existent movements, propped up by phony polls, pushed by phony front groups, with the purposeful use of non-existent straw men as enemies. They are enigmas of vaporous and fabricated stipulations, wrapped in lies, and propagated by liars. They are the Obama Campaign and the Obama White House, in other words.

There's little doubt that Axelrod's fingerprints are on the hard left media's psy-ops war on the GOP. Perhaps few authors would include a Daily Kos poll from 2010 in a work about 2012, but this sham survey, as part of a coordinated counterfeit media campaign, is so indicative of how the GOPe is easily manipulated by our political enemies. This is fundamental to why Republicans lose.

DESPERATE TIMES AND LEFT-WING PSY-OPS
American Thinker, February 4, 2010

Fresh off getting thumped in Virginia, New Jersey, and most recently Massachusetts, the left is now in a full-fledged panic, and they're doing all they can to blur the obvious instructional moment: that the GOP can win by boldly going way to the right of the Democrats.

The Daily Kos recently released an odd poll of Republican voters — and now *The Politico* and other liberal organizations are trying to use the results to churn waters that are actually relatively calm. The GOP had better not bite.

The fact that the GOP wins by going boldly right of Democrats is something liberals have known since at least 1980. This explains their never-ending, disingenuous PR campaign to keep Republicans *in mortal fear of upsetting those precious moderates* by doing something rash — you know, like reading the 10th Amendment to the Constitution.

Yes, these would be the very same independents that rejected the "honorable campaign" of John McCain by 9 points. These are also the very same independents that came roaring back to the fold for Scott Brown. The McCain message that we have "nothing to fear from an Obama presidency" was not exactly what we heard from Brown. No. Brown fearlessly taunted Obama for insulting his pickup truck, and jabbed harshly at any and all liberals who want to give Miranda rights and ACLU lawyers to terrorists. This was the same Brown who chided the entire Kennedy machine for turning its back on that great supply-side economist, John F. Kennedy.

Scott Brown might not quite occupy the Jesse Helms perch on the far right, but he did draw significant doctrinal distinctions between himself and the entire Democratic Party, and the result is that he now occupies Teddy Kennedy's well-worn seat. Brown won moderates and independents by comfortable margins, the same way Reagan did in 1980 and the way Newt Gingrich did in 1994. He spoke passionately about what he believed and why — and *he attracted moderates. He did NOT pretend to be one of them.* Brown exposed sharp differences between himself and all ideas liberal — and the independents agreed with Brown.

You might say that Brown found the electoral middle — and damned if they weren't on the right the whole time. They just needed someone to proclaim in a clear fashion what that means and to contrast it with the left. Many in the liberal media know this, and it scares the heck out of them. What Brown knows — as well as the leftists at the *Daily Kos* — is that if these convictions can win in Massachusetts, they really can win everywhere. *But to win everywhere, they have to be tried everywhere...and THIS is the problem.*

And that's where the *Daily Kos* poll comes in. It was dreamed up, executed, and reported for the express purpose of scaring the GOP establishment out of using campaigns stressing these very basic convictions. Seriously, would there be any benign reason why the *Daily Kos* would pay for a poll of Republican voters? They are using the preferred liberal methods of creating straw men and changing the subject. The questions were childishly worded on purpose.

Do you believe Barack Obama wants the terrorists to win?

Do you believe ACORN stole the 2008 election?

Do you believe Barack Obama is a racist who hates white people?

These questions make it impossible to register displeasure with Obama without sounding juvenile. I can only wonder if the erudite David Brooks will have the mental dexterity to see through this brilliantly diabolical plot. I rather doubt it.

Another less than subtle subtext was that all conservatives are bumpkins of faith consumed by the following:

Should public school students be taught the book of Genesis?

Should women work outside the home?

Are marriages equal partnerships?

The idea was to hitch a scarlet letter of craziness and extremism to the Tea Party and social conservative movements. Nobody at the Tea Parties made any of this an issue, as there were no posters proclaiming "*bring the women home*" or "*keep 'em barefoot and pregnant.*" This is just naked political psychological warfare. Robert Menendez, the head of the Democrat Senatorial Campaign Committee, has stated that he wants to drive a wedge between the GOP and the Tea Party, and you can rest assured that this *Daily Kos* poll is such an attempt. And *The Politico* — a competitor of the *Daily Kos* who should be eager to point out that site's frivolity — instead jumps right in and sums up the poll results this way:

"The poll of 2,000 Republicans...paints a picture of a base that's angry, disaffected and acutely hostile to President Barack Obama. 39% of Republicans polled think Obama should be impeached, 36% say he wasn't born in the United States and one in four say they aren't even sure he's a U.S. citizen. Another 63% labeled the president a socialist."

The intended net result is to paint conservatives as infantile, religious zealots who are simply mad as hell and consumed with Obama's birthplace and a plethora of cultural issues. Why? To keep the GOP's party apparatus scared of and embarrassed over their own base voter. The idea is to make it plain to the suits inside the Beltway that the party must not get too cozy with these crazies, lest they never win another election. But consider their convoluted logic:

"*If Republicans want to leverage Scott Brown's Massachusetts victory into a November electoral avalanche, they'll need to keep their base riled up — but not too riled up. The party's greatest challenge, operatives and elected officials in both parties say, is keeping the conservative base energized without overshooting the mainstream and driving away the moderate "Brown independents" they'll need to take back Congress.*"

Moderate Brown independents? You mean those who

wanted lower taxes, less government, more business, no ObamaCare, and harsher treatment of terrorists? Those Brown independents sound a lot like Reagan, or Palin, or Tea Party conservatives to me. Yet the intellectual disconnect drones on:

"This shows a huge vulnerability for Republicans," says Jeff Pollock, a veteran pollster and Democratic strategist working for Sen. Arlen Specter (D-Pa). "Independents, who are particularly disinclined toward any kind of partisan rhetoric, are going to be turned off when they hear Republicans say stuff like this..." Pollock said.

That's plain silliness, and it comes from a consultant working for Arlen Specter, who is the poster boy with all that is wrong with Republicans going moderate. This one kooky poll shows a major vulnerability for the GOP? Really?

I say just the opposite. Brown's win shows that the right basic convictions need only to be clearly stated in order to win. State clearly that you believe in limited government and lower taxes. Be proud of the free-market system, be proud of the military, and be ready to treat enemies of this nation as they should be treated. And be proud to stand in the way of ObamaCare.

That is the message that the Republican Party must take from Massachusetts as well as New Jersey and Virginia. If the Beltway strategists for the collaborator Arlen Specter, as well as The Politico and The Daily Kos, want to believe that the GOP is all in a dither over the birther movement and keeping women at home, then let them have at it. They will pay the price in November of 2010.

But for the record — I do believe Obama is a socialist, because, well, he is. So call me crazy, but perhaps you should first check with Van Jones or Jeremiah Wright.

Looking back at this attempt to deceive the country demonstrates why it is important to look at years, and not months, in trying to understand what happened in 2012. In fact, the entire year of 2010 was a turning point, a time when the country was waking up to a government that was encircling them in a death spiral of rules, regulations, taxes and debt. Moreover, in 2010 the Obama team knew that this shift had their guy and their pet legislative initiative in deep trouble. There are reasons for this awakening, and reasons it went dormant again in Romney's campaign, and they are related.

Into the Spring and Summer of 2010

Given Axelrod and Obama's obsession with their grand plan, the next few months were dominated by the eventual down and dirty passage of ObamaCare, punctuated on the right by the continued fight for the heart and soul of the Republican voter. (As a note, I refuse to call it "The Patient Protection and Affordable Care Act" since it is not affordable, and hasn't got a damned thing to do with care, and the only patients/ patience involved will be the long waits to see a doctor.)

ObamaCare may yet destroy our country, and whether it does or not will depend largely on how the combat for messaging control of the GOP turns out.

Naturally, with such a struggle going on, several different factions were trying to define the Tea Party, the Republican Party in general, and whether or not a third party was the way to go for disaffected Republicans and conservatives. This battle was joined with a major rally in Nashville and continued into the annual CPAC Convention.

Palin and Glenn Beck were both having a significant impact during this time, and while they are often thought of as similar in message, there are actually some major differences between the two. Beck is brilliant at times, and yet, at other times, he is an enigma. To be sure, his expositions of Marxists inside the Obama regime were spectacular, yet his flirtation with the idea that both parties are *equally* at fault was unsettling — and simply not correct. Palin, along with talkers like Rush and Levin, concur that both parties are at fault, but they have a significant quibble with the "equally" argument, as do I. Given Beck's understanding of Marxism and history, it is puzzling for him to say so.

At any rate, these were the discussions going when Palin headlined a Tea Party event in Nashville. The emphasis of this entire convention was to delineate the differences between Bush and his GOPe and conservatives, and to serve as a reminder of what conservatism really means. You can bet Jeb was just as irrelevant as any of the rest of them, too. As you read what was said in February 2010, keep in mind how voters still blame Bush for the economy, not to mention Obama's Inaugural focus on Reagan. Also notice how Palin was schooling the GOPe about the left's psychological operations, demonstrating once again that she is not nearly as ditzy as they think she is.

REAGAN, BUSH AND THE TEA PARTY ZEITGEIST
American Thinker, February 8, 2010

While Barack Obama is busy blaming everything on George W. Bush, his existence was hardly acknowledged in Nashville at the Tea Party convention. In fact, Sarah Palin's "back to the future" vision for America skipped right over all the Bush years and went back to the principles of Ronald Reagan. That was perfectly appropriate for the Tea Party convention. It is the zeitgeist of the movement.

The "kinder, gentler, compassionate conservatism" of Bushes 41 and 43 brought deeply flawed big-spending concepts that have become confusing distractions. Those twelve years of drift — surrounding Newt Gingrich's forcing Bill Clinton to govern from the right for six years — have allowed liberals to blur issues and blame the failure of big government on conservatism. Ironic isn't it?

As a result, too many independents fell for the spin and assumed that the Republican brand forever meant the undefined Bush mush, instead of the Reagan revolution. This confusion, and a certain teleprompter, led folks to conclude that Obama was a reasonable, articulate, and super-intelligent post-partisan and post-racial pragmatist.

The Tea Party movement is precisely about reversing all of that nonsense. Thus, in this context, Bush Republicanism must be ignored and replaced. Talk of a third party must be swatted aside. The imminent threat is the liberal agenda, period. Palin and others clearly tied the movement and the future of the country to an embrace of the Constitution and the principles of Reagan. There is a conservative ascendancy within the GOP, and the former governor made it clear that the movement is about ideas, not about self-indulgent would-be leaders. (Snip)

While dismissing loyalty to party for party's sake, Palin's vision of the future is clearly one where limited-government proponents win primaries leading up to the midterms of 2010. With a clear rejection of the "both parties are equally bad" dogma, she is referring to *Republican* primaries.

Let's be honest: No limited-government types are likely to win Democrat primaries, and no third-party movement — or fifty-third-party movement — is going to remove Nancy Pelosi from the Speaker's office. Learn it, live it, love it. It was no accident that the most repeated name of the evening was Reagan. (snip)

Liberal Populism versus Conservative Populism

While populism is generally about protecting the good little guy from the big bad guy, definitions of the "bad guy" vary between liberals and conservatives. Since the media and some gutless corporate CEOs are all too willing to obfuscate the differences, it is critical that conservatives clarify. Conservatives believe in a pro-free market type of populism. In our world, the bad guy is big government, along with any business that cuts a market-perverting deal with government. Think Goldman Sachs, GM and GE.

It is important not to confuse this point with the liberal populist message, which is anti-business and promotes government as the pristine and impartial protector of the people from big powerful business interests. This inevitably leads to inside deals, which must be covered up with populist demagoguery.

Consider the health care debate.

Liberals said that objections to ObamaCare were just a ginned up fabrication of big insurance and Big Pharma — all the while cutting back room deals with big insurance and Big Pharma. That's liberal populist demagoguery and crony capitalism at work simultaneously! It's the worst of all worlds.

The Idea from the Start

Moreover, the very genesis of the Tea Party movement is based on the principle of fighting this. (Snip) ...And now, in just under a year, the movement has advanced to the point where it is considered the most dynamic and powerful political movement in the country today. While some Tea Party goers focus on important single issues like TARP, immigration, AIG bonuses or even NAFTA, they are in the minority. Not everyone holds passions consistent with the Santelli inspiration, but it is beyond debate that the essence of the movement is conservative, pro-business, pro-self-reliance, and most of all, anti-big government.

And with this maturation of the movement and its new place in the spotlight, more message coherence is going to be needed. It cannot be all things to all people forever, though some of that universality was instrumental in the early large crowds. Palin understands that this is a 'leaderless-by-design' movement, and this movement is all about the Constitution, and the most recent successful manifestation of this thinking was the Reagan Revolution. Palin instinctively reached that conclusion and made that clear.

This movement was also part of Scott Brown's victory, even if Brown avoided the terms "Tea Party" and "Palin" for tactical reasons in liberal Massachusetts. This did not escape her, as she spoke several times of Brown's win as part of the war against the "Obama-Pelosi-Reid agenda," a war Brown surely has enlisted himself in. Come to think of it, the "war against the Obama-Pelosi-Reid agenda" is a pretty good definition of the Tea Party.

Piggybacking on Brown, Palin deftly added to the movement revulsion to the childish political correctness that is infecting our efforts in the war on terror. As Palin quoted from Reagan, the only position acceptable is "we win, they lose."

Palin's multiple references to Reagan and his principles point out yet again how much more tethered to the truth and reality she is than so many of her detractors in the GOP establishment. While the GOPe has buried their collective heads in the sand and pretended they had nothing to do with the Bush and McCain disasters, or that Todd Akin is the problem, Obama has been busy undoing Reagan's impact on the country. This is what "fundamental transformation" has always meant to Obama, something he confessed during his second Inaugural address. While this has escaped the wizards of the GOPe, the unrefined hick from Alaska had this figured out years ago. She must just be lucky.

A couple weeks after Palin's big speech in Nashville, the internal conservative conflict raged on with the annual CPAC

Convention. At CPAC 2008, Romney, who had just dropped out of the race against John McCain, gave the kind of speech that might have won him the nomination (or the 2012 Presidency, for that matter) had he campaigned the way he spoke. Then with the ashes of McCain's mushy defeat still around us in February of 2009, Rush electrified CPAC with an off the cuff, passionate treatise on what conservatives believe and why we indeed have America's best interest at heart by "wanting Obama to fail."

Thus, as CPAC 2010 rolled around, there was anticipation surrounding Beck's address. For reasons we mentioned above, Beck had become one of the leaders of the anti Obama and anti-liberal (progressive) movement with his daily Fox show. Beck would spend about fifty-five minutes systematically exposing Obama appointees like Van Jones, Anita Dunn and Cass Sunstein, after which he would mystifyingly close his show by insisting our problems had nothing to do "with R's and D's." Sometimes he would even add that it's "not about left and right." This disconnect, and not jealousy, is what caused tension between Beck and other conservative talkers.

Nonetheless, he was right in the middle of the GOP civil war as a player, relevant to both 2010 and today. He was having a tremendous positive impact on the GOP, yet he couldn't bring himself to say so. "I have not heard people in the Republican Party admit yet that they have a problem" he said at CPAC, echoing words said many times on his show, adding "I haven't seen the come-to-Jesus moment from Republicans yet." I'm not sure what Beck was looking for as a sign precisely, considering there had been "come to Jesus moments" all over the place since right after Obama's election — moments Beck could rightfully share credit for.

What caught my attention was the undeniable third party subtext imbedded in his comments and tone. What else could "not about R's and D's" mean, exactly? Let me clarify that my inclination against a third party had (and still has) nothing to do with excusing the inexcusable behavior of "the

R's," because I do not excuse it. The Party establishment's intellectual corruption is what this book is about, after all. My doubts have more to do with timing and with human nature than anything else. Any new party would be staffed by humans who are subject to the same flawed human nature the current GOP party hacks are. This is why there are over fifty "third parties," with no real impact. Besides, at this point in 2010, there were a lot of great conservatives who were emerging as Republicans in the mid terms. Since these mid terms were a last chance election, 2010 was not the time to experiment.

WORSE THAN AWFUL
American Thinker, February 25, 2010

The debate over third parties and Republicans comes down to this: evil versus awful. That's it. Your next Congress and your next president will be from either the evil party or the awful party. Whatever perfect virginal parties are out there, and not yet formed, will not develop in time to save the republic.

Besides, no one in politics is perfect, and virgins are equally rare.

Threatened with the loss of liberty from the "fundamental change" on the way from the Obama crowd, none of us on the *right should luxuriate in irrelevant and phony purity*. There's a reason they call government "making sausage." No one who has ever actually been in the sausage factory can remain pure. You can do that only if you remain irrelevant. Irrelevance will not stop the evil of a government takeover of our society.

Irrelevance is cathartic. It feels good. It is liberating. It is still irrelevant. A progressive Republican may sometimes be awful, but it is not the same thing as a progressive Democrat. (Please see the 2009 health care vote for some recent compelling evidence.) These differences have a real impact on everybody's freedom.

Newbies on the right may assume that they are the first Americans to ever have this anti-Washington outrage, but that is simply not the case. This self importance is somewhat analogous to Obama thinking that American history started at his birth and American greatness started at his inauguration.

Consider that it was precisely the conservatives *within the Republican Party* who sounded the loudest alarms against Obama. And by "within the Republican Party," I include party officials, elected officials, media figures and voters who readily identify themselves as Republicans. These are all people "within the Republican party." It is always important to distinguish the differences between establishment Republicans and other Republicans. It is a mistake to judge the entire national party by the establishment hacks like Michael Steele and his staff. Most folks who insist on doing this cannot name another person who ever held this job. It is not relevant. It is a glorified fundraising job.

And it's no secret that McCain and others like David Brooks and Colin Powell were blind to Obama in varying degrees. But so were so many independents and moderates and unaffiliated voters who have suddenly become enlightened. As flawed as many Republicans are — and I have written extensively on how flawed many of them are — the folks who *were* right about Obama are the not-so-flawed Republicans. The very folks who rightly warned of a government run by the terrible trifecta of Obama-Reid-Pelosi were mostly the same folks who warned of the dangers of having folks like McCain represent the party. Alot of Republicans are bad guys to be sure, but most of the good guys are other Republicans.

And what did those prescient Republicans get for being right? They were ridiculed and lampooned by the Beltway pundits, pollsters, and strategists, who said that making this clarion call was a huge mistake. The independents and neophytes rejected this warning by the Republican right and voted in droves for Obama. Others "disgusted with both parties" stayed home. And guess what: Obama, Reid and Pelosi now govern every single one of them. How did that equal disgust with both parties work out for them?

Not well. After a year, many have decided they do not like it. They have decided now to join the outrage over the liberal takeover of the nation. Welcome. We've been waiting for you.

History and perspective are critical here. They teach us that today's choice is between the awful Republican Party and the evil Democratic Party. Awful can be rehabilitated, starting with the good that is in the party, and it has happened twice in the last thirty years. Evil is evil, period. There is a difference, and one should never harp on the awfulness of the Republican progressives without praising the Republican conservatives. Moreover, it is critical that you contrast the evil left as the only other option, and perfection is not on the ballot. I didn't create the situation of evil versus awful, but I do recognize it. Facts are stubborn things.

History always teaches us this too: that under Reagan, the GOP was barely in control of the conservatives, yet magnificent and long-lasting good was done for us and freedom everywhere. Today, it's barely under the control of the moderates. The needed change is not that difficult. Regardless, we must make it, because the GOP is the only thing between us and a socialist state. I'm not asking you to like that fact, simply to recognize it.

Scott Brown's cloture vote was awful. If he votes for the actual bill, that would be more awful. Call it that. I'll join you. No, I'll beat you to it. Together we can try and purge this capitulation and shift more influence to the Wests and the DeMints and the Palins and Levins and many, many other greats in the awful party.

But don't forget that Martha Coakely or Ted Kennedy would have matched Brown's awful cloture vote and gone him one better with a vote for evil ObamaCare. Take your choice. Awful or evil. It's all you have currently.

The desire to throw up ones' hands and leave the GOP is fully understandable, and there is admittedly something cathartic about it. While I won't drone on now about the usual electoral realities you've heard before, I will suggest that third parties are like virgins: once consummation has taken place, they are no longer pure. The thrill will be gone, and they too will be infested with turf protecting bureaucrats and politicians. After all, who else would be attracted to that line of work? That's why I say this is a problem of human nature, not party labels.

Down in Texas, the wing of the GOP that Beck despised was just about to feel the wrath of a "come to Jesus" moment in a Republican primary, as the Bush Rove team was working for Senator Kay Bailey Hutchinson in her bid for Governor against Rick Perry. KBH is very much an establishment Senator, and is another Exhibit A for precisely what is wrong with the GOPe. This is why her loss was deliciously satisfying, not to mention imminently clarifying with the elections of 2010 now close at hand. Rove, the man that so many donors trusted with their money – and again with our futures in 2012 — was badly thumped in his own state as late as 2010. I guess no one noticed Rove's failure in Texas. Oh wait, I did.

Like Saxby Chambliss' win in Georgia in early December of 2008, this Texas result is profoundly educational, with ramifications for 2012, and yet so few people ever talk about either one.

TEXAS-SIZED LESSON: THE
NEW TONE ERA IS OVER

American Thinker, March 5, 2010

While the ever-helpful Jurassic media is trying to force-feed conservatives and Republicans groupthink analysis of Rick Perry's thumping of Kay Bailey Hutchison (KBH), the GOP had better heed the main lesson: The "new tone" era is over.

Consider: The political team and concepts that dominated the Lone Star State just ten years ago, and subsequently engineered two presidential elections, just got whipped in what amounts to an intramural contest in their own state. KBH's incompetent primary campaign was itself a caricature of the senior Senator — and it was precisely that caricature that her opponents wanted to portray. Perry and erstwhile Tea Party candidate Debra Medina did not have to do much but get out of the way, and let the KBH campaign prove that the senior Senator and her top advisers were indeed all creatures of Washington, and hopelessly out of touch.

And for some reason, Hutchison, along with advisers Karl Rove and Karen Hughes, thought that the best way to counter this was to bring in George Bush 41, George Bush 43, and James Baker to campaign. What, were John McCain, Bob Dole, and Olympia Snowe too busy to come? Oh, and to top it off, the Hutchison campaign ads featured endorsements from the traditional liberal newspapers. I wonder if that was Rove's idea? Conversely, Perry brought in Sarah Palin to campaign for him and proudly addressed numerous tea party rallies.

Predictably, the results were disastrous for Hutchison. Perry defeated her 52%-31%, with Medina getting 17% of the vote. It was actually worse than it looks for Hutchison, however. Ideologically, Medina and the tea party movement are much closer to Perry, thus the net result is that the KBH campaign was on the wrong side of a better than two-to-one landslide. Yep, a three-term sitting Senator, who had never before lost a statewide race, just got more than doubled up in an intramural contest!

How did this happen to the once-all-powerful Texas machine of Bush, Rove, Hughes, et al? How did this happen to the 'architect?'

I submit that for all of the micro-management brilliance of Karl Rove in engineering nationwide campaigns precinct by precinct, there was certain tone-deafness to the deeper yearning of the electorate.

(Snip)

Perhaps this Texas massacre simply exposed a blind spot that has been prevalent in Rove since 2000, if not longer. Election history matters and there are lessons here critical for conservatives and the GOP to learn for 2010. And this includes questioning assumptions made about whom the real political geniuses are who the right candidates are, and what the right messages are to take forward. The folks running the KBH campaign decided that her big message was, in effect that she "can work with people." Does this sound familiar (McCain)?

(Snip)

And this is the type of message that KBH brought into the campaign with Perry, who on emotional and philosophical issues like the Tenth Amendment, President Obama's liberalism, and even secession, is not at all interested in playing nice or working with people or forging a new tone. While the KBH style is just another tired iteration of John McCain's "reaching across the aisle," Perry's style is closer to "*Don't mess with Texas!*" The KBH campaign was the classic inside-the-Beltway RINO effort fueled, by groupthink assumptions. Perry, though certainly hip-deep in the Texas party establishment, is not of the Washington establishment, and he heralded a pro-tea party, pro-Tenth Amendment, anti-big government, and anti-Obama message.

While certainly there were a lot of Texas-only nuances in this campaign that we did not address here, the message concerning the 2010-midterm elections is clear. It's the message of those tea parties of the spring — and the town hall meetings of the late summer and fall.

It's the message of Virginia, New Jersey, and Massachusetts. It is a conservative message of less government, less taxation, less regulation, and more freedom. It is a message about soundly defeating anyone who would stand in the way of that message, and not of "working with them."

KBH was reportedly upset about McCain's pick of Palin for the number-two spot on the ticket, a spot she wanted and thought she deserved. Moreover, she actually thought that her message of a willingness and ability to work inside Washington in a bipartisan way was the message the people were craving. She was still drinking the McCain "reach-across" Kool-Aid as of this week. So was Rove!

Well, they were both dead wrong on all counts. And it's very satisfying that their own beloved Texans, along with Palin, were the ones to deliver the message to these two. The new tone, which came home to roost with Obama's election in November of 2008, is now officially dead. KBH had better heed the message, as should Rove, or any Republican who wants to be on the right side of history in 2010.

Even as I look back on it, it still astonishes me that KBH thought an extension of the McCain campaign would be what

Texans were clamoring for. Moreover, Rove and his team agreed, demonstrating their own abhorrent tone deafness. Rove was badly out of touch with his home state in late 2010 and was just as badly out of touch with the national electorate in 2012.

A quick aside about Senators like KBH and the constant conservative commentary about RINOs (Republicans in Name Only): there's some merit to understanding moderates on a geographical curve, at least with respects to how damaging they are. KBH, along with fellow Texan John Cornyn, McCain of Arizona, Lindsay Graham of South Carolina, Chambliss from Georgia, Mitch McConnell from Kentucky and other moderates from solidly red states, are probably more destructive to conservatism than people like Scott Brown from Massachusetts. This is not a by any stretch a defense of blue state Brown; it's an indictment of red state moderates by comparison.

Our biggest problems in Congress are the result of moderates and squishes being elected from solidly conservative states. Doing so really damages the philosophical make-up of the Congress, and that make-up dictates the tenor of our national discussion. Getting Ron Johnson from blue Wisconsin is a bonus, but we need more people like Jim DeMint and Ted Cruz from solid red states, not a bunch of Lindsay Grahams. This is just another reason Senator Hutchinson's crushing defeat was so encouraging, even if this particular race was for Governor.

* * *

Meanwhile, Obama and the Democrats had learned very little during their long slog to foist ObamaCare on a nation that had clearly rejected it, perhaps intentionally. As the ObamaCare vote was coming down to the wire in March, Obama was still confident of his ability to sell the idea, if only his magnificence could be seen on TV just one more time. He agreed to defend his position on Fox News, and with Brit Hume out of the anchor chair, it's safe to say that Obama thought he was in for an easy time with young Bret Baier. Not so much, it turns out. At the time, this interview was considered a newsworthy development in the ObamaCare fight. It also exposed some breathtaking groupthink from conservative pundits.

BRET BAIER: 1; PRESIDENT OBAMA: 0
American Thinker, March 18, 2010

Don't you just love it when a young student hammers the arrogant professor in a debate? That was the distinct feel of last night's "Special Report" program, where Bret Baier interviewed President Obama. For the record, Mr. Baier is the victorious young student in this analogy.

Certainly this wasn't what the White House had in mind when President Obama agreed to sit down and chat with the heretofore-unknown Fox anchor. Where are Anita Dunn and the war on Fox News when you need them?

And with all due respect to Brit Hume and Charles Krauthammer, who refused to acknowledge on air what we all saw, that their colleague bested the President, Baier clearly had Obama fumbling around, stuttering, and totally flustered. Like some other young and studious-looking white guys, Paul Ryan and Eric Cantor, Baier used annoying and inconvenient facts to unveil the childish and petulant Obama - the Obama a fawning Jurassic media has never bothered to investigate.

The best example of this was when Obama tried to play an unseemly game of "top this" with Baier over concerned Americans' e-mails:

BAIER: Let me insert this. We asked our viewers to e-mail in suggested questions. More than 18,000 people took time to e-mail us questions. These are regular people from all over the country. Lee Johnson, from Spring Valley, California: "If the bill is so good for all of us, why all the intimidation, arm twisting, seedy deals, and parliamentary trickery necessary to pass a bill, when you have an overwhelming majority in both houses and the presidency?"

Sandy Moody in Chesterfield, Missouri: "If the health care bill is so wonderful, why do you have to bribe Congress to pass it?"

OBAMA: *Bret, I get 40,000 letters or e-mails a day.*

BAIER: I know.

OBAMA: *I could read the exact same e-mail —*

BAIER: These are people. It's not just Washington punditry.

OBAMA: *I've got the exact same e-mails, that I could show you, that talk about why haven't we done something to make sure that I, a small businessperson, am getting as good a deal as members of Congress are getting, and don't have my insurance rates jacked up 40 %? Why is it that I, a mother with a child with a preexisting condition, still can't get insurance?*

So the issue that I'm concerned about is whether not we're fixing a broken system.

The funny part is that Baier was coming at Obama with a variation of the favored tactic that the president and other Democrats continue to use *ad nauseum*: quoting e-mail anecdotes as a way to make a point. It clearly got under Obama's skin, revealed by his quick jump to a graceless phrase like 'jacked up.' The "I get forty thousand letters or e-mails a day" retort from the president was sensationally sophomoric in tone also. Like a number-one seed in the NCAA's playing a tougher than expected number sixteen seed, Obama was clearly caught off-guard by the high level of the competition in this interview.

Evidence that he was off balance could be found in the fact that he avoided answering almost all of Baier's questions, and resorted to burying himself in the worn-out clichés of this entire debate, as this early exchange demonstrates:

BAIER: You have said at least four times in the past two weeks: "the United States Congress owes the American people a final up-or-down vote on health care." So do you support the use of this Slaughter rule? The deem and pass rule, so that Democrats avoid a straight up or down vote on the Senate bill?

OBAMA: *Here's what I think is going to happen and what should happen. You now have a proposal from me that will be in legislation, that has the toughest insurance reforms in history, makes sure that people are able to get insurance even if they've got preexisting conditions, makes sure that we are reducing costs for families and small businesses, by allowing them to buy into a pool, the same kind of pool that members of Congress have.*

We know that this is going to reduce the deficit by over a trillion dollars. So you've got a good package, in terms of substance. I don't spend a lot of time worrying about what the procedural rules are in the House or the Senate.

(BAIER TRIES TO REDIRECT— CROSS TALK)

OBAMA: *What I can tell you is that the vote that's taken in the House will be a vote for health care reform. And if people vote yes, whatever form that takes, that is going to be a vote for health care reform. And I don't think we should pretend otherwise.*

(AGAIN, BAIER TRIES TO GET OBAMA BACK TO THE QUESTION, LEADING TO CROSS TALK)

OBAMA: *Bret, let me finish. If they don't, if they vote against, then they're going to be voting against health* *care reform and they're going to be voting in favor of the status quo. So Washington gets very concerned about these procedural issues in Congress. This is always an issue that's — whether Republicans are in charge or Democrats in charge — when Republicans are in charge, Democrats constantly complain that the majority was not giving them an opportunity, et cetera. What the American people care about is the fact that their premiums are going up 25, 40, 60 %, and I'm going to do something about it.*

The "Bret, let me finish" statement had the same feel as the "John [McCain], the campaign's over" moment of the health care summit. It was a juvenile, "I'm going to take my ball and go home" remark. Another key moment was when Baier pressed the president with an "in your face" question on the Slaughter Rule and the president's call for "courage." In this case, the president's answer had nothing to do with the question.

BAIER: Monday in Ohio, you called for courage in the health care debate. At the same time, House Speaker Pelosi was saying this to reporters about the deem and pass rule: "I like it, this scenario, because people don't have to vote on the Senate bill." Is that the kind of courage that you're talking about?

OBAMA: *Well, here's what's taking place - we both know what's going on. You've got a Senate bill that was passed, that had provisions that needed to be changed. Right? People were concerned about, for example, the fix that only fixed Nebraska, and didn't fix the rest of the states. Now, a lot of the members of the House legitimately say, we want to vote on a package, as the president has proposed, that has those fixes embedded in it. Now that may mean they have to sequence the votes. But the ultimate vote they're taking is on whether or not they believe in the proposal that I put forward, to make sure that insurance reform is fixed, to make sure the deficits are reduced, and premiums go* *down, and small businesses are helped. That's what they're concerned about.*

Frankly, I'm not sure what the president was stammering about in that answer, but since he brought up the provisions that singles states out, Baier pushed for clarifications on which fixes were still in and which ones were out — and Obama could not give clear answers on those. This snippet is illustrative:

OBAMA:... *this notion that this has been not transparent, that people don't know what's in the bill, everybody knows what's in the bill. I sat for seven hours with —*

BAIER: Mr. President, you couldn't tell me what the special deals are that are in or not today.

OBAMA: *I just told you what was in and what was not in.*

BAIER: Is Connecticut in?

OBAMA: *Connecticut — what are you specifically referring to?*

BAIER: The $100 million for the hospital? Is Montana in for the asbestos program? Is — you know, listen, there are people — this is real money, people are worried about this stuff.

OBAMA: *And as I said before, this — the final provisions are going to be posted for many days before this thing passes, but —*

BAIER: Let me get to some of the specifics on substance, not process.

OBAMA: The only thing —

(BAIER, TRYING TO REDIRECT, LEADING

TO CROSSTALK)

BAIER: (INAUDIBLE)

OBAMA: — *the only thing I want to say, just to close up, is that when you talk about one-sixth of the economy, this is one-sixth of the economy that right now is a huge drag on the economy.*

Liberal Fox Contributor A.B. Stoddard was correct when she said that Baier "had the president off-guard" and that "he [Obama] was at his worst" in the interview. While I am not sure exactly what interview Hume and Krauthammer — two pundits nearing the end of brilliant careers — were talking about, the interview all of America saw was a clear defeat for President Obama and his health care plan. The fact that Obama agreed to appear on Fox News likely means that his party is in trouble on the vote count, and it also meant he likely thought Baier, a man lost in the deep shadows of Fox's other stars, would be easy fodder.

As it turns out, Baier was anything but easy fodder. This debate was easy to score. Baier: 1 Obama: 0.

We saw previews of the Obama we would see in the debates, at times low energy and flat, at other times defensive and petulant. He's been pampered and protected his entire life, and Baier exposed him. This interview also demonstrated why the elections of 2009 and 2010 were as much anti-Washington as they were anti Obama. There is no explanation for Hume and Krauthammer claiming that Obama won that exchange other than having a predetermined Washingtonian template going in that he was going to win it. He clearly lost, yet they insisted otherwise. There's no answer from Krauthammer yet on whether Obama's use of "jacked up" disqualifies the "elegant" label so often applied by Dr. K over the years.

At any rate, the take away is that the arrogant Democrats were going to ram ObamaCare through regardless, and the

GOPe would marvel in awe of their power. On March 23rd, ObamaCare was signed into law. The odious ceremony, with Nancy Pelosi and her oversized gavel prancing across Washington, is an image that few conservatives will forget. Here were the Democrats, pulling every despicable trick in the legislative book — and some that weren't even in the book yet — to pass nation-altering legislation along party line votes, and their response was to spike the football.

Yep, nice guys, just in over their heads, right?

After signing ObamaCare in the spring, our young President was about to run headlong into some tough realities in the summer. The anger over ObamaCare had not even started to subside when another critical event happened on April 10th: the Horizon BP blow out.

An event like this was an amazing opportunity to educate the public on the realities of energy, not to mention overbearing bureaucracies and the inadequacies of academia nuts. Energy impacts every single person every single day, and it should be an electoral slam-dunk that always works for our side. Energy is critical to overall economic health, and every election about the economy is by definition about energy, though it is rarely couched in those terms. Energy is not an issue, or even THE issue. Energy is EVERY issue.

WHEN PROFESSOR OBAMA
MEETS DIRTY REALITY
American Thinker May 28, 2010

Just plug the damned hole! That, more or less, is the leadership and direction we are getting from our president as we grapple with the oil spill in the Gulf. What else should we expect from a socialist theoretician who has never actually accomplished anything in his life?

I guess we could expect him to take credit with his daughters if it works.

This is what happens when an academic finds himself in the position of actually having to get something done. Nothing written on a blackboard or recited from a textbook or lectured from a podium will plug the leak miles deep off Louisiana. Nothing in Barack Obama's background full of lectures and textbooks makes him fit for any job where actually getting things done is important.

Like many activities that impact our existence, drilling for oil is damned hard, damned risky, and damned expensive, and it involves a lot of hard physical work and technical know-how. The same can be said of making automobiles, building houses, or manufacturing the heavy equipment that makes all of these activities possible. The problem is, academics unfamiliar with such work and know-how believe their tenured cushiness and "think-how" is enough.

I guess if you can Google something, you can convince yourself that you can actually do it.

The only ingredients that academic theoreticians add to the equations of necessary hard jobs are the ridiculous rules and regulations that make them even harder and more expensive and riskier. The oil spill in the Gulf is not the result of failed enterprise. It is the result of government-mandated difficulty. In his press conference, Obama mentioned that this was a difficult project because the oil is spilling a mile under the ocean floor. You don't say! Whose fault is that? Is this where BP really wanted to drill in the first place???

Academic liberals and their friends in high places have placed such incredible difficulties in front of domestic oil producers via regulation and legislation that it is stretching the limits of what man is capable of doing just to get the stuff out of the ground. There is much easier oil to get in ANWR in Alaska, as well as the oil shale and tar sands in the west, not to mention the calmer and shallower waters all over the place off our coastlines — yet the liberals have blocked production in all of those areas. So down, down, down BP and everyone else must go. As long as they are American or British, that is.

It's enough to demand that Obama power Air Force One with solar energy, or just shut up about BP and the oil industry. The only oil we are now allowed to go for is doggoned near impossible to get to. Nothing — and I mean nothing — is easy to do many thousands of feet under the surface of the water.

So now President Obama, who has always aligned himself with the environmental movement that has pushed our drilling efforts into the extraordinarily dangerous deep waters, is becoming ironically victimized by that very difficulty. Try as he might to blame BP or the oil industry as a whole, or even the fact that we all need oil, the national finger of blame is slowly rotating right back to him, and his administration's laissez-faire response for the first month following the disaster.

The professor has not a clue what to do. This stuff is hard. Really? You mean if drilling several miles deep below the water and mud on the bottom of the ocean is hard — then repairing a screw-up in the same location is hard to do, too?

Yes, it's hard. Very hard. And as such, perhaps it would have been appropriate for the liberal academic theoreticians and environmentalists to consider this when demanding that oil exploration and recovery be done only in places man is hardly equipped to go. Obama himself described the environment at the leak as one where "man is unable to go." Yes, he really said that, and the irony totally escaped him, bless his little academic heart.

Perhaps the world of the classroom is such a comfy and reality-isolated environment that liberal theoreticians never stop and think about such real world difficulties ahead of time. Ensconced in world-class campus buildings that liberal academics could never build, their neat little worldview remains uninterrupted by reality. No doubt, the reality of the energy and the pollution and the carbon footprint involved in building college and university buildings never crosses their tiny little minds as they cash their paychecks and preach against everything that makes their ivory towers — not to mention their paychecks — possible.

And almost everything that makes those things possible is related to oil and energy production and consumption. It's one thing to see teens and twenty-somethings who share the Appalachian State University campus with my daughter walk around in their liberal daze, totally unaware of what built this campus in the Carolina mountains — while they hold their cars together with anti-capitalist and anti-business bumper stickers. It's quite another to have a President, who ran a messiah-complex presidential campaign, still be such an intellectual child — and one hell-bent on running everything nonetheless.

And it's appropriate that now the president is about to have his reputation further tarnished by the very difficulties he and other liberals have placed on the energy-producing sector of our economy. Now the professor child is upset about a spill in his little utopian sandbox. The child is whining and pointing fingers and demanding that someone fix it. It is eating into his playtime for shooting hoops and playing golf, and it is so much messier than theoretical issues.

The problem is that the child has no clue how the sandbox was built or how the pristine sand got there. He has no clue what built the house in front of it or how the lawn around it gets mowed. He really has no clue where the money comes from to make all of it possible. But sadly, the child has the keys to his little kingdom.

And liberal academic children have had way too much power for far too long. Academic children thought every American should own a home regardless of his or her ability to pay a loan, so they made difficult rules for the lending industry. They thought Americans should want, and Detroit should build, little green cars - so they made life difficult on the popular and profitable SUV models. They thought unionized government employees should be able to retire early, and have unlimited health care benefits, so they wrote these into contracts that are now ruining state budgets.

And now this. The idea that we must go miles deep to find our oil is more liberal theoretician environmental groupthink. The problem is this very idea is now boomeranging back and devastating our environment, and a good chunk of the Gulf economy with it. And the liberal academic theoretician is finding out that solving these very real problems is very hard indeed. Everything is when you're thousands of feet down.

Or maybe not. Hey, just plug the damned hole.

Frankly, had the Romney Campaign and the Rove directed Super PACs poured some of their dollars into a message similar to that column, there is no way Obama would have been re-elected. With his odd little Energy Secretary, Steven Chu, a devastating energy focus could have been done with humor very easily. Then again, our headquarters is only slightly more familiar with energy reality than Obama.

The stunner of all exit poll results from 2012 was that an astounding 73% favor more domestic oil production. That over a third of them still pulled the lever for Obama is testament to how phlegmatic the Romney Campaign was on energy. As mistakes go, the fumble on energy only ranks behind the miscalculation on unemployment and the "inherited" economy by the Romney camp. Energy, unemployment and the economy are all joined at the hip anyway, not that the economic illiterates in the media, or the Romney Campaign, have ever noticed this particular truth.

Obama shouldn't be able to get elected to county council, let alone the Oval Office, in a country where three out of four people want more domestic oil produced. And yet, with an androgynous establishment that remains traumatized from the days when we had "oil men in the White House" (cue ominous music), the GOP was unable to capitalize.

In July, more truth and reality were trampled as the Democrats showed the ultimate in chutzpah by passing financial regulatory reform known as Dodd-Frank. This was either an Orwellian stroke of genius or unbelievable economic ignorance. Consider: the bill that was touted as the salvation for our banking system and the economy was named in honor of the two men most responsible for the destroying them in the first place. Dodd and Frank? Are you serious? It took a number of months for people to understand how satirically awful this bill is, and the GOPe has not yet figured out how powerful of a topic it could be. Dodd is part of the club and Frank is gay, so we can't criticize either of them, apparently. We "must not assign blame," you know.

The late summer of 2010 may also be known as the Muslim Summer, not to be confused with the Arab Spring. In August of 2010, the Pew Research Center came out with a poll showing that 20% of the nation believed Obama was Muslim, and the percentage believing Obama to be Christian had plunged to 34% from the 50% who believed it when he took office. Just like the Daily Kos poll after Scott Brown's win, this was clearly psy-ops conducted and publicized in order to reintroduce the narrative of how ignorant and mean spirited conservatives are, especially religious conservatives. It was aimed squarely at the GOPe, playing on the paralyzing fear they have of anything that is even remotely racial or religious in nature.

This article followed a lot of public discourse over the

Ground Zero Mosque, and gave respondents a chance to blow off some steam over the issue.

LET ME TRANSLATE: WE DON'T BELIEVE HIM — OR YOU.

American Thinker, August 22, 2010

Memo to the ruling class media: We are not ignorant or stupid. We've not forgotten Jeremiah Wright. It's not that we don't "know" what faith Obama subscribes to — it's more that we don't believe him. Or you. Sorry. Not buying. Besides, sometimes we just like to tweak you with our poll answers, and use any poll as an excuse to "vote against Obama" in any way, shape, or form.

Frankly, it has been equal parts comedy and insult to watch the ruling-class media haplessly wrestle with the reality that millions of Americans believe Obama to be a Muslim. They are so clueless.

As if we needed any more proof — this is simply another positive dose that the ruling-class media and the country are divided by a cosmic gulf of philosophy, reality, and experiences. And they are just beside themselves that a country can be obsessed with Obama's supposedly Christian pastor in the spring and summer of 2008, and yet can totally forget about all that in the summer of 2010, and call Obama a Muslim.

They so miss the point. We have forgotten *none of that Jeremiah Wright stuff*. In fact, apparently now more Americans are deciding to look into all of this, and process it in light of Obama's actions.

So allow me to help the media out on this thorny, confusing issue:

We know you claim him to be a Christian. We know Obama

has at times claimed to be a Christian. We know Jeremiah Wright's Trinity Church claims to be some kind of Christian denomination. We simply doubt any of that is true. And the more we watch all of you, the less we are inclined to believe any of it. (And by "we," I mean folks who would respond "Muslim" or "not sure" to your poll questions.)

We also know Obama's father was a Muslim, and we know his stepfather was a Muslim. We know that under Sharia Law, he *is* a Muslim, and that much of the Muslim world regards him as a Muslim. We know his mother was an atheist. We also know Obama sent a bureaucrat out to claim that NASA's top mission was Muslim outreach. We know he skipped the Boy Scouts' 100th Anniversary bash, and we know he's had a couple Freudian slips pertaining to his faith. We heard him called the Islamic call to prayer the most beautiful sound on earth, an assessment that seems odd for any Christian.

We know that in light of all of this, some sycophantic White House spokesperson has the gall to say how "obvious" Obama's Christianity is. Depends on what the meaning of "obvious" is, I guess.

There's more. So much more:

We know Jeremiah Wright rejects America's founding principles — which are consistent with what we call Christianity — and many of us believe our founding principles were divinely inspired. Moreover, we know that Obama is on board with Wright on this — at least to the point of claiming that our Constitution is flawed in how it grants individual rights and liberty. We happen to think that rights Obama wants to curtail come from our Creator.

We know Obama has appointed proud and unabashed Marxists into his government. We happen to know that Marxism is by definition anti-Christian. We know he has confiscated the wealth of others to redistribute to his union thug friends under false pretenses. We know he turned his back on Iranian protesters in favor of an Islamic regime. We know he publicly defers to folks like Chávez and Saudi royalty more than he does Texas and Arkansas governors. On and on we could go here.

So what is so blamed obvious?

The only thing obvious here is that if Obama is a Christian, he is absolutely awful at walking out his faith. Or, as might be said at any basic tent revival, he done "backslid." (Does anyone in the media even have any idea what I'm talking about?)

In other words, we are paying attention to what is real, and to what you are reporting — and the two are not syncing up.

Answering a Poll

Another dynamic here is how the average person contemplates poll answers. I know that in the isolated, sanitized, academic world of the ruling class — you tend to look at every poll answer as an equal entity. You tend to look at every answer as a window into the soul and understanding of each responder — and you assume each responder has given equal thought to your little poll. You overestimate your importance in our lives. You assume we take you and your little poll seriously.

We don't. Frankly, we just like to mess with your head sometimes. Had Time or the Pew Research group polled me, I'm sure I would have said "Muslim." Do I really believe he is a Muslim? I frankly hadn't given it a lot of thought until now — but I know he's not a Christian under any definition with which I am familiar.

I know he's a Marxist, and I know he hates America, and I know he is at the very least sympathetic to Muslims.

He has a Muslim-sounding name, by the way, in case you hadn't noticed. Further, I know that for all of your bashing of George Bush and Sarah Palin over their overt Christianity, it will tick you off if I say I don't believe Obama to be a Christian. Yes, we love to tick you off! That right there is enough for us to tell a pollster Obama is not a Christian. And for all of your protestations that there's nothing wrong with being a Muslim, you will panic if we think your guy is one. I know you better than you know us, and it is indeed fun to pull on your chain.

So to register my displeasure with Obama's "Christianity" and to simply irritate you, I would have answered "he's a Muslim" to your precious poll. It's my way of voting against Obama before November 2010, and November 2012.

And certainly I am not alone in this thinking.

I have to admit, I felt a lot better after getting that one off my chest, and honestly enjoyed reading it again, too. The sad state of the GOPe is that the fear that grips them completely negates any ability to think rationally. No doubt Axelrod laughs his droopy fanny off at Republican strategists, susceptible as they are to the most transparent of tactics.

The bigger problem on issues like this is that the concept of reality is lost, and in this case the entire Muslim world laughed their fannies off at all of us, Republican or Democrat, liberal or conservative. This Mosque was outrageously insulting, especially in light of Jihad and its attendant symbolism, and therefore a great opening for Republicans. It is analogous to us building a B-29 Museum in downtown Hiroshima. I wonder what the liberals and the establishment would think of *that?*

7

THE DESTRUCTION IS HALTED... FOR A WHILE

As summer turned to fall, the final primaries for the 2010 mid terms were at hand, and the shoot out for the soul of the Party was even more intense and heated than before. While all of this was going on, the Jurassic media was pretending that the GOP was falling apart and headed for defeat. They clearly didn't believe this, as they were in full-fledged panic mode right before the voting. Strangely, the GOP establishment seemed almost as unhappy about the prospects of a big Republican win as did the Democrats.

Before the actual mid terms took place, the GOPe had their candidates challenged in numerous primaries, including Delaware, where Christine O'Donnell shocked ultra liberal Mike Castle. The establishment was not happy, and this highlights the reality problem the establishment has concerning the ruling class, and those under their thumb.

DELAWARE CROSSES THE WASHINGTON
American Thinker, September 15, 2010

Establishment Washington got yet another whipping last night, as "the unelectable" Christine O'Donnell — supported by Sarah Palin and the Tea Parties – rallied to beat well-connected liberal Mike Castle convincingly in Delaware's Republican primary for Senate. Castle, we were told by the powers that be, was the only electable Republican, and his loss is already being mourned by "Beltway conservatives" like Karl Rove and Dana Perino, not to mention the National Republican Senatorial Committee, which has announced that O'Donnell will have to finance her campaign on her own. [Editor's note: the NRSC reversed that decision 24 hours later).

Well, fine. The last time Republican voters agreed with the Beltway pundits (and the Democrats) and awarded a nomination to "the most electable Republican" we got John McCain. Remind me again how did that work out exactly?

Thankfully, Delaware's voters ignored their party apparatus, actually held a true Republican primary, and chose the person who most closely represents what the Republican base voter believes in. This is what party primaries used to be for, and is what they should still be held for. It is simply unforgivable for Republican apparatchiks to choose sides in a primary — yet they do — and they are so often disastrous picks. Can you say Arlen Specter? Charlie Crist?

So while there's no guarantee of success in November for O'Donnell, she joins a list of "unelectable Republicans" past and present like Ronald Reagan, Jesse Helms, Rand Paul, Scott Brown, Sharron Angle, Chris Christie, and Marco Rubio, to name a few. Their stories are varied, but all were deemed "unelectable" by the party insiders, and they were all considered too conservative.

O'Donnell's story of last night was simply a continuation of their stories in this very unusual 2009-2010 election cycle. All faced establishment candidates and long odds — and yet all won by being unabashedly conservative. All read the tea leaves of the national mood much better than government insiders and political pros.

(Snip)

...It's possible that O'Donnell can do the same in the general election in a tiny state like Delaware, where face-to-face politics is the rule...(snip)

Perhaps electorates cannot change fast among very large populations, but understanding the dynamics of small voting populations is one of the ways Tea Party groups are showing superior sophistication to the political pros. Small-population Delaware, Nevada, and Alaska have just as many Senators as do New York and California, and these are prime places to take a stand for principled conservatism with unknown candidates. The Tea Party has shown strategic savvy in this regard.

Yet the siren call of name recognition, inside connections, and perceived electability endures among the formulaic party pros.

Never mind that Mike Castle simply joins other moderate and respectable "electable Republicans" on the ash heap of history like McCain, Crist, Bob Dole, Arlen Specter, latter-day Jack Kemp, and Lisa Murkowski. All were establishment favorites who have, for varying reasons and in varying ways, brought shame and defeat upon that very establishment's party. Some even became official enemies of the party, proving that conservative doubts about them were justified all along.

But the Beltway arrogance is not deterred.

The long knives of establishment Washington — including the blades of Rove and Perino — were already slashing into O'Donnell last night. They mumbled about her personal problems, her inexperience, and her unclear financial background as reasons she cannot win the general election.

Well let me clue these comfortable Beltway mavens in on something: many of us country-class peons out here - not on the government dole - have had problems like O'Donnell's because of the burden of supporting the government dole, not to mention the rash of bureaucrats at every conceivable level of government. It is becoming damned near impossible to negotiate a life outside the Beltway without some problems. That's exactly what the Tea Party movement and all of these elections are about.

We are sick of it!

In fact, the Delaware seat up for grabs is "the Joe Biden seat," a seat that for decades has included the perk of a private AMTRAK car every morning and every night for Biden. Whatever O'Donnell's personal and financial problems are, they may have something to do with the fact that the taxpayers weren't subsidizing her every whim the way they have Biden's and Castle's for decades.

It is too early to know if Delaware's voters will look at O'Donnell's candidacy that way in the general election — but we do already know this: Washington insiders' views of electability are deeply flawed, and Washington has never been so isolated from the rest of the country. If elected, O'Donnell nor Miller nor Angle nor Rubio will be a threat to "work with" the Obama agenda or, worse yet, jump parties.

The voters instinctively know this. That's why they are voting for these people. And that's the takeaway from the amazing victory last night for Christine O'Donnell.

In fact, the establishment was so irked over Delaware that Rove and other GOPe figures continued their hissy for days. We have touched on some of the following themes before, but they remain relevant as long as Rove and our current crop of consultants remain relevant.

THE ARCHITECT HAS NO CLOTHES

American Thinker, September 16, 2010

Frightening as the image might be to ponder, "the architect" Karl Rove was stripped bare for all to see on Fox News' Hannity show Tuesday night, thanks to his odd response to Christine O'Donnell's win in Delaware.

Rove demonstrated to all what I have believed since 2000: that he is a political operative with little or no evidence of a philosophical soul. Voters, equally soulless in his mind — are mere commodities to deal with, and precincts are the way these commodities are organized. They are to be bought and sold with the micromanaging of a trade deal here, or a pro-life direct mail piece there, orchestrated by the ruling elitists in Washington.

One gets the feeling that he could have worked equally as happily for a Democrat simply by changing a few words on certain ads to certain districts.

Consider:

When Bush was in office, Rove predictably started out on a plan to form what he called "a permanent Republican majority" that would be constructed with a mushy new tone, a "can't we all just get along" mentality. The strategy would dictate that no one would ever return fire on political opponents — while having a "flexibly philosophy," to which Rove would adapt policy as issues came and went in certain parts of the country.

There was by design no coherent message of constitutional conservatism, which is what most of Bush's voters thought they were voting for. How and why Rove thought this could work is beyond me. What he thought it would accomplish, even if it were possible, is an even more salient question. It could not work, and it did not work.

So I have to ask:

What will a Senate majority full of Olympia Snowes and John McCains and Lindsey Grahams get you? Easy. You get Barack Obama, Nancy Pelosi, and Harry Reid in power. This is exactly the legacy of the Bush presidency, and Rove was right there at the levers of power the entire way. Truth be told, Rove's biggest architectural accomplishment is aiding the creation of an electorate that would vote for someone like Obama. By doing his part as senior advisor to the president to define conservatism down, he sullied the reputation and disoriented the understanding of what it means to be conservative to millions of half-informed voters nationwide.

(Snip)

The Reagan revolution was built on a right-brained type A concept of big ideas and big dreams — and all of them based on our Constitution and the American dream. The same can be said for Newt Gingrich's Contract with America election of 1994. No one worried about ginning up certain precincts here and there with flexible philosophies, because there was a wave of consistent philosophical truth that made renting individual precincts irrelevant. And that is how you win, a dynamic that escapes the mind of Karl Rove.

Rove was not the only establishment consultant exposed by the O'Donnell affair, either. Some other party handlers joined in, including Mike Murphy, who more or less said he was taking his ball and going home.

Murphy's public pout accurately portrayed the arrogance of the party operatives and pundits, especially his "do the math" snarl. A quick study of the "math" proves that Republicans win more "independent" votes and more total elections when they articulate conservatism, or when the Democrats expose themselves as far left lunatics, giving doctrinal clarity. While

GOP consultants want non-ideological and non-threatening campaigns, Republicans only win with daring ideological campaigns. The one-sided discussion I have with Murphy below is exactly the discussion going on today.

DO THE (THIRTY-YEAR) MATH: THE CONSULTANTS ARE WRONG

American Thinker, September 17, 2010

So the inside-the-Beltway political pros are all in a tizzy that their omnipotence is being questioned by the great unwashed in the Tea Party movement.

In reaction to the Christine O'Donnell win, and the part that Sarah Palin and Jim DeMint played in it, veteran consultant Mark Murphy sniped that he, too, was a conservative — but that he "could do the math." Murphy's contention is that conservatives like Palin and DeMint are not smart enough to "do the math." You know, that math that tells us a win for liberal Mike Castle in Delaware is really what conservatives need.

Tea Party-type conservatives, according to Murphy, are not smart enough to figure out the professional math, and he has polls and focus groups and formulaic opinions that say so. He says we must leave the political math to the pros.

History says the pro's political math is flawed. I'll take history over focus groups any time.

There have been three great elections for Republicans in modern history — '80, '84 and '94 — and all three were the result of a wave of conservatism. There have been five awful elections - '92, '96, '98, '06 and '08 — and all the result of purposeful moderation from the pros.

The rest have fallen somewhere in between, with

Republican success mainly the result of the Democrats doing us a favor by swerving way to the left. In short, the three-decade trend is clear. Republicans do well when they run more conservatively, and they can also succeed if the Democrats let their liberalism show in the campaign. But when the waters are muddied, it is always a disaster for Republicans.

So, Mr. Murphy, get out your calculator and lets "do the political math."

The years 1980 and '84 were two of the great election results for Republicans, with the solid and unabashed conservatism of Ronald Reagan leading the way. In 1980, Reagan administered a whipping to an incumbent, and in '84, he won 49 states as the incumbent. The only effort to reach the independents was to invite them to join the GOP on the solid right.

The year 1988 delivered a somewhat successful election, as the nation thought that Bush 41 would be a continuation of Reagan — helped by the fact that Mike Dukakis bragged about his ACLU membership. We didn't fully understand a "kinder and gentler" Bush Republican party yet.

1992: By now, we fully understood "kinder and gentler." This was magnified by the fact that Ross Perot siphoned off some conservatives. Clinton won the only way Democrats can — the opposite of how Republican win — by appearing moderate. Incumbent Bush got only 38% of the vote. This was the classic establishment campaign disaster.

1994: The third fabulous election for Republicans — was the result of the very conservative Contract with America in contrast to Clinton's most liberal policy, failed Hillary Care. Again, the appeal to independents was to join the Contract with America on the right, not to pretend that we were in the middle.

1996: Dole-Kemp, that moderate disaster of a ticket, gets soundly defeated by a Lewinsky-weakened Clinton. And who can forget Jack Kemp's fawning "thank you Al" moment? Thank *you*, Jack....not.

1998: There was only one really conservative campaign in the nation: that of Jesse Ventura who ran way right of both other candidates in Minnesota. (He governed as a moderate and left in disgrace four years later).

2000: Bush-Cheney eked out an electoral win over Gore-Lieberman. Bush ran as somewhat conservative, and got some cover from Gore's obvious liberalism. The "new tone" is born as a result of the close election.

2002: The far-left Wellstone Memorial allows for Republicans to have success while running an only somewhat conservative campaign.

2004: Far left Kerry-Edwards again gave just enough cover to the moderately conservative campaign of Bush 43.

2006: Moderate disaster, set up by Dennis Hastert, and Bush's faltering conservatism. Two establishment scandals didn't help either.

2008: McCain. Oh, let's "reach across the aisle." Enough said.

Now, Mr. Murphy, how is your math holding up? But hold on, it gets worse for your mathematical case.

When Republicans have had moderates win elections, it has often set the stage for future disasters of even greater magnitude. To name a few: Charlie Crist, Arlen Specter, and Jumpin' Jim Jeffords. So, Mr. Murphy, since it's safe to bet that all three of these guys had the backing of the establishment Republican strategists before they started jumpin' out of the party, I must ask how the pro's math is working out for you now?

But wait, it gets even worse still.

In fact, the existence of the power base of Obama, Reid, and Pelosi is the direct result of directionless moderate Republicans giving the appearance of being "the party in power." The truth is that Bush got in trouble when he signed legislation put forth by Democrats, with the help of the moderate and liberal Republicans. To the American voter, all such damage accrues to the "party in power."

Because Bush was in the White House and the GOP had the House and the Senate, all of the blame went to the GOP. Ironic isn't it? Most of the bad stuff was actually Democrat legislation. These were things supported by the likes of McCain, Snowe, Graham, Collins, Hagel, Hayes, and Castle — and on and on.

And yet, because of how our system works, the party that is the only home of conservatism got thrown out for being too liberal. And they got thrown out by the most radically liberal group in our history. This is the math that these Beltway left-brain number crunchers never crunch.

Mr. Murphy, can I get you a drink?

The problem is this: the consultants are too busy being thermometers instead of thermostats. They take the temperature, and then figure out a way that their candidate clients can match that temperature. It never occurs to them that their candidate might actually take a stand and invite the independents to join them. Reagan did this twice. Gingrich did in 1994. They were more like thermostats. They set the terms of the debate, and invited everyone to share in the wonders of this country as defined by Constitution-based conservatism.

They never changed to match what they perceived the

beliefs of the moderates to be. And that's the reality that
the consultant nation just cannot wrap their heads around.
Inside the Beltway, it is just so pervasive a thought pattern
that none of the pros can think outside that tiny little box.
But history is clear — and so is the math. Conservatism
works, every time it's tried. Mr. Murphy, it's so easy that
even a political hack can do it. Or, maybe not.

This history of campaigns is indeed clear, as is the unhappy
history of the GOP when they have numerical majorities, but
not philosophical or functional control of the government.
The latter is often the result of the former, which we saw
during Bush's tenure. Technically, Republicans controlled
the branches, but there was never conservative control at any
point, though the assumption was that everything going wrong
was a conservative screw up. This is why electing people like
Castle and McCain is always a long-term problem. It can end
up no other way.

As the 2010 election neared, in an odd self-destructive
manner, it seemed more important to Beltway insiders that the
Tea Party fail than anything else — including actually winning
the Senate. As breathtaking as this may seem, this was actually
was proven shortly after the election. More on that, and the
losses of Joe Miller, Sharron Angle, and O'Donnell later.

Another dynamic was the hunt for exactly which planet
Nancy Pelosi lives on. Wealthy, powerful, and isolated, the
Speaker exists in a realm where she reaps the fruits of an
economic system she neither understands nor appreciates, and
she has power over people she neither likes nor comprehends.
She was predicting victory for her party to the very end,
seemingly oblivious to the fact that her very existence was one
of the main factors in her party's impending doom. Pelosi and
her grotesque gavel were symbolic, and in many House races
the main issue was to remove her as Speaker.

In Nevada, Harry Reid seemed to be headed for certain
defeat. Angle had ridden the Tea Party to victory in the

primary over Sue Lowden and Danny Tarkanian, and her uphill fight against the most powerful man in the Senate captured everyone's imagination. Many think Tarkanian, who is not part of the DC establishment, would have better handled the "nuances" of Las Vegas voter turn out. But for some reason, he lost as much support after Lowden's "take a chicken to the doctor" comment as Lowden did, and Angle vaulted from third to first. Vegas politics... you gotta love it.

In Wisconsin, another liberal icon, Russ Feingold, of McCain-Feingold fame, was in trouble. Businessman Ron Johnson was running a refreshingly honest campaign that was well funded because, well, Johnson is well funded. He "built it" himself, by the way. Johnson v. Feingold dovetailed with the governor's race in the same state, where a "nice young man from accounting" named Scott Walker seemed to have a shot. Yes, the People's Republic of Wisconsin was under conservative siege.

And in Florida, turncoat Crist (who could have seen *that* coming?) was running a classic John McCain campaign, as an Independent. Unable to accept the fact that Republican voters had rejected his Obama loving style, he was convinced that his perpetual tan, GQ style, and absolute lack of core beliefs would put him over the top. At the time, Marco Rubio was in no danger of losing to Democrat Kendrick Meek or to Crist. So desperate were the racially sensitive Democrats to beat the non-white Rubio, they dispatched Bill Clinton to try and talk Meek into dropping out in favor of the white guy (Crist) at the last minute.

The Rubio contest was about much more than just the crucial Senate seat. In this case, the liberals' fear of Rubio is the same as their fear of Justice Clarence Thomas during his 1991 confirmation hearings. The left simply cannot afford to have their entire racist template destroyed by a black or brown American rising through conservatism or the Republican Party. This would threaten their 90% plus death grip on minority votes, not to mention screwing up a couple of perfectly good narratives. So Clinton was dispatched to Florida to be to Rubio what Anita Hill was to Thomas: a desperate foil.

As an aside, it was the character assassination of Thomas, featuring Hill in the starring role, that enlightened a self-described "hippy dippy party boy" named Andrew Breitbart. Breitbart was crucial to conservative successes of 2009, 2010 and 2011, and his main message is one I happen to agree with: that we must aggressively counter all phony liberal narratives, especially the race card. Breitbart understood something else that few in the establishment do, "FOR REVOLUTIONARY MARXISTS, there is an inextricable link between racism and capitalism." That quote is from SocialistWorker.org, and demonstrates that the charge of racism is indeed a vital weapon in the left's attempted theft of the country, and not some isolated issue to be avoided at all costs. RIP Andrew, you've educated and inspired an army.

(As an historical footnote, some 80% of the public believed Clarence Thomas over Anita Hill during the hearings, yet years later the public was split 50-50. Oh well, just another fraudulent liberal narrative that improved with age.)

Meanwhile, sensing a tsunami coming their way while living in denial at the same time, liberals were acting batty as the 2010 election drew close. The Clinton/Meeks caper wasn't the only act of desperation they tried. They went to the old playbook and tried to paint the Republicans as a bunch of Bible thumping authoritarians, even though the Republican agenda consisted of reigning in spending, cutting taxes and regulations, and stopping ObamaCare. Democrats even tried to make an issue out of masturbation (yes, they really did) and witchcraft. To hear the Democrats and their buddies in the media, you would think Jerry Falwell was running in all 435 districts and all 33 Senate races on a Puritanical platform that would imprison anyone caught doing anything other than the heterosexual missionary position with anyone other than their first wife.

And when the liberals were not obsessing over self-gratification or the Bible, they were telling voters not to "give the keys back to the folks that got us into this mess in the first place." This line is repeated ad nauseam and always for the purpose of blaming Bush, the other Bush, Republicans, Reagan, tax cuts and free enterprise for all our economic problems. Yes, Reagan too, as we now realize he is Obama's ultimate target.

This argument could be the fulcrum on which our future balances, and while Obama would win twice on this fiction as neither McCain nor Romney contested it, his car key appeal was a clunker in 2010. The smaller but higher information electorate understood that free markets and Constitutional conservatism were not to blame. Not every voter could point to specific liberal policies on everything from energy to mortgages as the root causes of the bad economy, but at least there was the realization that the answer was not Obama's turbo charged leap into socialism. The car had to be turned around instead.

It was self-evident that a big set of keys were to be taken away from the Democrats, the House keys. Realizing this inevitability right before the election, the only thing for the media to do was downplay the election's significance. With pundits suddenly upping projections of Democrat losses to fifty or sixty seats, damage control and desperation were paramount. Now mind you, this was just weeks after the media assured everybody that the Republican Party was committing suicide by Tea Party.

The Washington Post, Politico and others ran undeniably coordinated stories about how the elections "didn't really matter" because "nothing was going to change" in Washington. Depressing the vote was all the Democrats have been able to rely on in the past two cycles. That it worked in 2012 and failed in 2010 sheds light on why conservatives usually do better in the non-Presidential election cycles.

In off years, smaller and more informed electorates will focus on ideas instead of candidates, while Presidential campaigns often subrogate ideas to the cult of personality, captivating a larger and less informed electorates. The personal image of the nominee dominates all messaging, so major mistakes are made as any idea uncomfortable to the personal handlers are necessarily jettisoned. These close confidants have their jobs as the result of sycophantic loyalty in the first place, and any familiarity they may have with the ideas that make an election important is purely incidental.

As if we needed proof of this, Campaign Manager Matt Rhodes assured Mitt - after the loss - that he would "rather lose with you than win with anyone else." With the future of the nation at stake, Rhodes could only have uttered such a pitiable statement by being consumed with a person and totally devoid of any ideas. Obviously, to Rhodes, a relationship with Mitt is more important than the whole damned country. Liberals are also aware that such a personality war is to their advantage. Obama Campaign chief David Plouffe admitted that their base "doesn't exist without belief in the candidate" and "it was all because of him (Obama)." Jim Messina concurred, adding "the best grassroots campaign in history" was totally dependent on voters who "have their own relationship" with Obama. Perhaps such relationships are built on free Obama phones.

Since 2010 was a non-Presidential year, ideas were front and center and the messaging was sharp and clear. With the establishment largely irrelevant, reality took center stage again, and Conservatives and America won in an epic blow out. While it took a couple of weeks for everything to be finalized, in the end the GOP took sixty-three House Seats and six Senate seats. Perhaps more significantly, there were over seven hudred GOP pick-ups nationwide in state legislative bodies, plus a lot of Governors, and now those assemblies and executives are doing some great things.

Unlike typical wave elections, however, the Democrats actually won most of the extremely close contests. In other words, these astonishing results were just a few thousand votes from being much more one-sided, as we still had 'the margin of ACORN' to deal with. Naturally, in light of ACORN, the Franken/Coleman race in 2008, and George Soros' "Attorney General Project," many suspect that a few GOP wins were stolen. For some strange reason, Nevada comes to mind. Harry Reid managed to sneak through in what was one of the more dubious results outside of a banana republic, no offense to banana republics intended.

TSUNAMI-LITE

American Thinker, November 3, 2012

In every monstrous storm, there are a few ratty old buildings that somehow remain standing in the calm afterward. Such is the case with 2010. Nevadans were so angry at Harry Reid that they punished his son with a resounding defeat — but could not bring themselves to let go of the perceived perks their state gets by having the number-one seat in the Senate, so they returned ole Harry. Dammit!

On the other hand, anything that irritates Chuck Schumer can't be all bad.

For some strange reason, three big states — California, New York, and Illinois — decided to continue their governor-assisted economic suicide. Those are a few of the head-scratching paradoxes staining an otherwise-historic wave election, validating the notion of conservative ascendancy across the land. (More on those later.)

It was a tsunami-lite that dramatically shifted the power in the House of Representatives and many state houses and legislatures. These power shifts will have ramifications in the lives of people everywhere, and will also have impact on the 2012 election, which we are told will begin today.

This was ascendancy so dramatic that it washed the "Obama Senate Seat" away from the Democrats in deep-blue Illinois, and handed the GOP the majority of the governorships and state legislatures nationwide. While the national thrashing is what most will talk about, the carnage on state Democrat organizations was even more impressive. (Snip)

Sure, the Tea Party movement may have had stumbles in Nevada and Delaware, but they had big wins in Florida and Kentucky in the Senate, numerous governorships, and a ton of House seats. And in the case of Florida and Kentucky, ousting powerful establishment Republicans in primaries set up the Tea Party victories.

And in the House, longtime Democrat committee chairmen fell like bowling pins, and sometimes by big margins to Tea Party Republicans. That there was no reinforcement of the national message by the GOP establishment probably caused them to leave 10 to twenty House seats on the table. To the extent there was a lucid message, you can thank the Tea Party movement and other non-establishment forces.

When Barack Obama said "I won" in 2009, he was referring to people voting for his "hope and change" without the foggiest notion of what it meant. Today, conservatives can say "we won" with the confidence that the 2010 electorate knew exactly what it means. Moderate Republicans had best say nothing.

Yes, I know Sarah Palin told Brett Baier that the Republicans should be willing to work with Obama in order to get things done for the country. The problem with her statement — as if she really believes it — is that small government cannot compromise with statism. That there were a few election results that seem to counter the conservative ascendency speaks to the fact that there is education to be continued and perhaps certain states beyond saving. And there might be some historic and illustrative moments attached to those that will speak to other campaigns.

Reid's sketchy pyrrhic victory in Nevada is crushing emotionally, but perhaps is a gift in disguise. Running against Reid and Nancy Pelosi surely boosted conservatives' chances nationwide, and now these two can continue to harm the Democrats — assuming Pelosi stays in the House with her demotion from Speaker. Moreover, the Republicans can now fight against the Obama-Reid agenda and not appear to be picking on the black guy. This will help comfort the squishy spines of the establishment.

California, Illinois and New York just gave the rest of the country explicit permission to tell them to go to hell when they come begging for bailouts of their bankrupt state budgets. By electing Brown, Quinn and Cuomo, voters in these states somehow decided that it made sense to allow government unions to swallow them whole. I say: have at it, and the rest of us will sit and watch and use your failures as informative moments for the next election cycle.

In the meantime, voters in North Carolina and West Virginia take the schizophrenia awards for somehow opting out of the Tea Party movement. The Robert Byrd seat from West Virginia, however, is now held by a blue dog so conservative that he ran slap over the ghost of Reagan in his last minute lurch to the right. With so many Democrats in the Senate up in two years, and Joe Manchin now in, the Democrats will suffer the awful fate of "controlling" the Senate while not having the philosophical majority. This is not bad news for conservatives particularly, as Pat Caddell called it "functional control" for the GOP.

And keep in mind; this is a GOP that now numbers Marco Rubio and Rand Paul among its new stars. This will change the tenor of the Senate debate if nothing else.

North Carolina oddly left three of its four blue dogs in

office while states like Virginia, Florida, Kansas and Pennsylvania swept theirs all away. Outliers like these made the difference between 65 House seats and perhaps 80-90. Those blue dogs will now have to explain their conservative campaigns as they caucus with what is now a very leftist radical minority Democrat House caucus.

These races were the cloud behind the very shiny silver lining last night, but again these could be gifts in disguise. Even with the big wins of last night, there is still low hanging fruit for conservatives in 2012. And that will help shape the very critical national debate that we will continue to have starting today.

The Angle loss was a stunner, especially since Scott Ashijan's phony Nevada Tea Party candidacy was mathematically insignificant. Some are convinced that the NRA endorsement put Reid over the top, which is interesting in light of recent events. The NRA is doing the right thing by jumping right in Obama's face and calling him out on his hypocrisy on gun control, however they are being willfully ignorant supporting Democrats under any circumstance. I'm aware that certain Democrats, like Reid, will "support" gun rights on a survey, but I also know that electing Democrats will *never* help the rights of gun owners in the long run. Besides, whenever the NRA gets bad press from the Democrat controlled media, it's Republicans and conservatives who share in it by assumed association. The NRA, whom I support, should be ashamed of ignoring these realities.

Outside of Reid's win, Miller's loss in the odd world of Alaska elections was perhaps the most disappointing. He was beaten in a dishonest and filthy campaign that owed as much to Lisa Murkowski and the GOPe as it did the Democrat Party.

What Alaska and Delaware proved is that the Rove led establishment would rather lose certain races and blame the Tea Party than try to win those races with Tea Party candidates. Conservatives often vent and say the "GOP deserves to get beat" when they act this way. True, they do deserve it, but it's you and I that pay the price of those defeats, not the GOPe per se. Personally, I don't think we deserve it.

In spite of all these tensions, the 2010 victory was critical and amazing. There was still some money left on the table, thought, and that table was to reset immediately for 2012.

Shortly after the election, unions re-emerged as a major issue. It became obvious that the left had no intention of interpreting the 2010 thrashings as a 'no,' since they never take no for an answer. The end of one campaign is merely the beginning of the next one when your life focus is on government, which it is for most unions today. They exist only to vote repeatedly for the great national larceny that is unfolding.

In Madison, Scott Walker was sworn in as Governor on January 3rd, 2011. By early February, the teachers unions in and around town had already started their sore loser campaign. All Walker had done was have the temerity to do what he promised he would do. It was obvious that the Wisconsin Democrats and liberals everywhere thought they could simply trot out the sacrosanct teachers, and Walker would be done. (As we would find out during the 2012 campaign, the liberal answer to every single question is to "hire more teachers, firefighters and cops.")

The role of unions in our economic problems, especially public sector unions, cannot possibly be over stated. They are a titanic disaster. Unfortunately, the issue of public sector unions was barely mentioned at all in the 2012 campaign, even though they are prominent among the problems governments and private companies face. Moreover, this issue is a major part of the conflict between the government and citizens, a conflict that no one can deny. There are some uncomfortable truths about public sector unions, and these truths must be confronted, even though it does rattle the cages of the GOPe to do so.

END PUBLIC SECTOR UNIONS...PERIOD
American Thinker, February twenty, 2011

It's about time. I've been waiting for this debate to mature for 15 years.

The contests in Wisconsin and New Jersey over public sector union benefits are merely financial precursors to a more substantial philosophical and fiscal war that has been on the horizon now for years, if not decades. When you acknowledge the coming hostilities, you realize that Governors Walker and Christie — courageously as they are behaving — are only nibbling around the edges of the real issue.

And the real issue is whether public sector unions should even be allowed to exist. Frankly, when even a modicum of common sense is infused into the equation, the answer is a resounding no. And the foundational reason is simple. There is no one at the bargaining table representing the folks who are actually going to pay whatever is negotiated.

Is it just me, or could something go wrong here?

Well let's see what could: California, New Jersey, Illinois, Michigan, Chicago, New York State, New York City, Wisconsin...on and on I could go including almost every city and state where government workers are unionized. Oh, and have you seen pictures of Detroit lately?

The problem is that our country has been lulled to sleep over decades of hearing that government workers are dedicated low paid public servants who trade good pay for security. And every time a union pay debate came up, it seemed only cops, fire fighters and teachers were mentioned. No one stopped to think that most government workers are actually bureaucratic charmers like those we see at the DMV, the IRS, and other government offices —

and not «heroic teachers» or crime fighters.

But as long as the private sector was humming along, there was no reason for reality to permeate that myth in most peoples' minds. But the reality is that government workers long ago passed private sector workers in pay and benefits, and now the compensation is more like 150%, or even double, factoring in all the benefits, including more vacation days than private sector workers enjoy. And the inestimable value of job security remains intact and strengthened — while all of us in the private sector deal daily with the risk-reward constraints of reality that are only getting riskier. Government bureaucrats are the very people making it riskier in the first place.

And along the way — with a public school teacher-educated population that understands nothing about economics — the sheer lunacy of the very concept of government unions has escaped almost everybody. It's almost as if the union teachers were lying to their students about economics on purpose. Some people actually hold to that theory.

Consider: Unions exist primarily for the function of collective bargaining, where the union bosses will negotiate on behalf of all the workers with the management of a company over pay and benefits and other conditions. This built-in adversarial relationship, along with the realities of a limited resource — known as operating revenue — does a pretty good job for the most part of keeping contracts in line.

The union bosses represent the workers. Management represents everybody else, including the stockholders, vendors, customers and potential customers of the company. In other words, management represents everyone whose interests are served by keeping payroll costs down. In the case of a government workforce, those whose interests are served by keeping costs down would include everyone who pays taxes and fees to said government. The universe of people represented by management is far larger than that represented by the union. However, public sector "collective bargaining" is a hoax, given that there are only chairs on one side of the bargaining table. There is no natural force working to keep payroll costs in line.

Quite often, the very politicians who are "negotiating" with the public unions are politicians who have been financed by those same unions. Under any circumstances and in any economy, it is simply a matter of time before these costs reach a tipping point. We are at that time. There is simply no more money to give to these public sector unions — period.

And that is why we are seeing what we are seeing in Madison this week, and it is why we have seen the emergence of Chris Christie as a national phenomenon. I am relieved that things are finally so bad — that they are good. And by good, I mean that folks now cannot help but pay attention to the issue of public sector unions. It's likely that the very existence of these unions has only been allowed to happen because it's the kind of issue an electorate is never forced to confront — until they are forced to confront it. And now they are. There is, as Charles Krauthammer said, a bit of an earthquake in the country. People are sensing that the nation is spinning off a cliff.

And it is, and public sector unions are the primary reason why. This conclusion is inescapable. And when you understand that, you understand that public sector unions cannot be allowed to exist. If they are, we will never turn back from the cliff.

At this point in early 2011, we had no idea just how far the unions and the Democrat apparatus would go in persecuting Walker. He and Christie represented fiscally sound Republicans in a fight against greedy, violent and infantile union thugs. Only the unserious would argue that the net impact of these union battles shouldn't have helped Republicans in 2012. And yet back at GOPe headquarters there was a consultant driven fear of insulting potential union voters, failing to understand that those who would be offended by the truth are *never* going to vote for Republicans anyway. Why is that concept so hard?

This was about the point in 2011 when the coming Presidential Primary season was coming into focus, and there were trial balloons floated and exploratory committees formed. Underlying this was the conservative base's continuing fight with the establishment, especially against the GOPe posture towards Obama and the antics of Speaker John Boehner.

One of the widespread misconceptions about this disdain for the establishment is the assumption that the only source of tension is their betrayal of conservative principles. That's certainly part of it, but their timidity when confronted by the media or by Democrats is just as central to this antipathy. If anyone doubts this, consider the splash Donald Trump made by firing a few shots across Obama's bow in the spring of 2011. His first salvo involved Obama's birth certificate, but once the battle was joined, Trump then lit into Obama on China, OPEC and jobs. All of this was incredibly refreshing. Trump let his anger at Obama show, and he eschewed any hint of robotic political speak. He was real, fearless, passionate, and in Obama's face. It was an astonishing contrast to the flaccid tone taken by the GOP's house eunuchs.

Talk radio and the political message boards exploded with visceral support for Trump, much of it from hard-core conservatives. He was such a sensation that Rush invited him on air for an extended interview, a rarity on that show. Support for the Donald was so deeply felt on some websites that any anti-Trump commentary was harshly rejected as typical party establishment turf protection. Of course, there is just one teeny tiny problem here. Trump is no conservative. Not even close.

All of which indicates that conservatives were yearning for

a fighter even more than someone who was philosophically sound. Christie's rise had also proven this, as many conservatives were enamored with him throughout 2010 and 2011. Trump, however, is more demonstrably liberal than Christie, and far more so than even squishes like McCain. Trump had the perfect public tone, but he's a doctrinal mess, as he proved with the following babble to Limbaugh about Paul Ryan and Medicare:

> **TRUMP:** But the Republicans shouldn't get too far out because they're already making plans to say, incorrectly, that the Medicare is gonna be terrible for the seniors, et cetera, et cetera. This is Obama's fight, and he should be leading it as the president. We shouldn't get too far out in front...but I will say, Rush, the Republicans have to be careful. And I'm a fan of Paul Ryan, but he shouldn't get too far out with some of these plans, because they're gonna belabor it. One thing with me: If I decide to run I am gonna cherish senior citizens. And the Democrats, and I know 'em all because as you know I come from New York and it's virtually a hundred percent virtual Democratic, right? He's (Ryan) doing a plan, he's done a plan, he's come out, and what the Democrats — and I see it more and more and I hear from them because, again, you know, living in New York that's what I see is Democrats all over the place — are going to do is say it's attack on Medicare. And Medicare to a lot of people means seniors, and that this is a very strong attack on Medicare. And I honestly think you have to go down the line in a bipartisan way. You have to go down with the Democrats. I don't think they should be too far out in front. Don't forget, we don't have the president yet. Hopefully we will have. We don't have. He's supposed to be leading this attack, not us. And they can do rejects, they can criticize his plan, but in my opinion...You know, there's an election in 2012, right?... The fact is, I think somebody that got along with the Democrats — and I do get along. Now, you know, that could change instantaneously. You understand that. But

the level of animosity...You know, in the old days "across
the aisle" wasn't the worst thing."

The interview with Rush was embarrassing, as Trump
rambled on incoherently and spilled the beans on a fatal
shortcoming, an inclination to reach across the aisle and work
with Democrats. Yes, it's true, while Trump was willing to
publicly fight Obama like few others were, his plan if elected
was to take bi-partisanship to a whole new level. He was
Lindsay Graham cross- dressing in Michael Savage drag.

This paradox is what makes the lesson of Trump of the
utmost importance. Voters were aching to get behind anyone
who had the willingness and capacity to run fearlessly straight
at Obama. The Republican establishment was not looking for
that, so after Trump took Obama down a couple of pegs, the
Romney Campaign made sure to re-establish Obama as a nice
guy, who simply, gosh darn it, inherited a terrible mess.

Meanwhile, away from Washington, there was more on the
minds of people than just electoral politics, and yet all of it was
related to politics. That's the problem with big government, as
by definition, every part of life becomes political inherently.
The main conservative argument is that what goes on outside
of government should dominate Washington, or at least be
free from it, while liberals believe Washington should rule
everything, if not confiscate it.

As such, it is relevant that elites ignored an event in the
spring of 2011 that touched a lot of people where they live:
the release of *Atlas Shrugged Part 1*. The producers of this
film understood better than anyone in the media or pundit
class that with Obama in office, interest was booming in Ayn
Rand's work.

One who didn't understand that mood was Speaker
Boehner, who missed a major dynamic playing out among a
critical Republican constituency, the entrepreneurial class.
Hell, he used to be part of the entrepreneurial class! When the
GOP loses touch with the entrepreneurial frame of mind, they

are inevitably doomed.

Thus, the following is about much more than a movie release. *Atlas Shrugged* demonstrates that, fifty years ago, an atheist Russian was more in touch with the theft of America today than the current Republican establishment is. If you believe, like our consultants, that campaigns come and go on temporary strategies and issues, then you'll not see the relevance of this piece. If you understand how decades of refusing to stand up for the truth is why we start every election cycle way behind, then you will. The movie's relevance to the left's contemporary attempts to confiscate the nation is almost scary, and Ayn Rand saw the GOP establishment coming years ago.

QUICK: SOMEONE TAKE BOEHNER TO *ATLAS SHRUGGED*
American Thinker, April 27, 2011

If you happen to be some Congressional bureaucrat on the staff of the Speaker of the House and you are reading this, please kidnap your boss and take him to the nearest theatre playing *Atlas Shrugged* Part 1. Why, you ask?

Because in the same week that unelected and unaccountable bureaucrats cost Shell Oil four billion dollars and ran them out of drilling off Alaska — and more bureaucrats began their attempt to cost Boeing over a billion dollars and South Carolina a thousand jobs — our namby-pamby Speaker of the House sided again with the wrong team.

So grab the Speaker and please go see *Atlas Shrugged today*. Do not wait. Do not walk. *Run*. Please go see it, and take Mr. Boehner some notes, before he becomes totally irrelevant and takes the free enterprise system down the drain with him.

Consider:

In a life-imitates-art period like few others I can remember, we have seen the following happen in the few days since the movie was released:

-Jesse Jackson Junior publicly blames the iPad for a loss of jobs. His incoherent babbling about economics is not worth repeating here.

The National Labor Relations Board (NLRB) sues Boeing to keep America's largest exporter from opening a plant in South Carolina that will create over a thousand new jobs, because the state is a non-union (Right to Work) state. By the way, Boeing has already built the plant and has added 2,000 union jobs in Seattle in the last couple of years to boot.

President Obama orders Attorney General Eric Holder to investigate oil companies and speculators (you and I know them as investors) over the rise of gasoline prices. Holder will not be investigating the EPA or any other bureaucrats who have halted or slowed down oil production, however.

Seven more oil rigs are run out of the Gulf of Mexico by government regulations and headed to Brazil — where crony capitalist extraordinaire George Soros will make a killing. Soros supports Obama. What are the odds?

What the juxtaposition of *Atlas Shrugged* and the events described above shows, if nothing else, is that we understand them more than they understand us. And by us, I mean freedom-loving supporters of the free enterprise system. By them, I mean liberal statists and socialists. And Ayn Rand, for all of her quirks, understood the free market, and how big government punishes success in the free market. She also saw crony capitalism coming down the pike with a scary prescience.

In short, in 1957 Rand understood the America of 2011 better than our current Speaker of the House does. This is inexcusable on the part of Boehner, who was elected to Congress in the early '90's as a small businessman. It's one thing for an elected Speaker to make poor political calculations and/or to negotiate weakly with the opposition. The unhappy nuances of the realities of the sausage process — which Boehner did not invent — can also be forgiven to a certain degree by thinking supporters.

But when a Republican Speaker, with a business background no less, flunks the very basics of Economics 101 on an issue as critical to our republic as energy production, it is a preeminent crime. It's bad enough for former Speaker Newt Gingrich to sit on a park bench and wax eloquent with Nancy Pelosi on manmade global warming. It's quite another when the sitting Speaker "goes Pelosi" on us at the very moment we need a clear voice in Congress on the realities of the market, and the realities of the self inflicted wounds, from our very own government.

The irony of Boehner's ignorance this week is that he and those like him were very clearly predicted by Rand in the mid 1950's. Without beating the analogy to death for those who haven't seen the film, Shell Oil almost perfectly fits the situation "Wyatt Oil" faced in the plot. Boeing is part "Taggart Transcontinental" and part "Reardon Steel." You could switch Colorado with South Carolina. There is no specific Boehner character, but he certainly fits the mold of a politician who just finished his visit from power broker "Wesley Mouch." True to this form, Boehner actually said the following this week to ABC News:

I don't think the big oil companies need to have the oil depletion allowances, but for small, independent oil-and-gas producers, if they didn't have this, there'd be even less exploration in America than there is today.

This is eerily reminiscent of the line where a government bureaucrat whines, "in an age of steel shortages, we can't have one company producing too much." That is classic liberal rationale if I've ever heard it. The idea was that fairness as defined by the government, is more important than production. Boehner stepped right into Rand's 54-year-old caricature. And nowhere in this statement is any evidence that Boehner is at all concerned that the EPA is forcing Shell to walk away from their four billion dollar investment in the waters off Alaska.

But he wasn't through stepping in it. He added:

We're in a time when the federal government's short on revenues. We need to control spending, but we need to have revenues to keep the government moving. And they ought to be paying their fair share.

Pay their fair share? There was a lot in *Atlas Shrugged* about the heavy hand of government propelled by "fairness." So what *is* their fair share? Who decides that? Are they not subject to tax laws now, or do they have the GE plan? Or the Tim Geithner plan? How about the Charlie Rangel plan? And if they pay more in taxes, how will that produce more oil and how will that help me at the pump?

So we have to ask just what's next Mr. Speaker? Will you side with the NLRB against the Boeing Corporation? Or the state of South Carolina? Where does your siding with government against private companies stop? What do you think about states› rights?

In short, Mr. Speaker, Ayn Rand saw you coming. She warned us about the likes of you. Go see yourself on the silver screen. She knew you in 1957 better than you know yourself. And if you don›t start to understand yourself today as well as she did 54 years ago, the power of your office means that we will all suffer from your ignorance.

Boehner was just a young boy when Rand wrote the book, and yet he is clearly one of the political stooges she predicted, as are a lot of the GOPe folks.

As mentioned above, the National Labor Relations Board's lawsuit against Boeing was a critical event. There is no issue, outside of maybe the Keystone Pipeline, which so clearly demonstrates the total incompetence and anti-business attitudes of Obama and his party. Nothing can be said by even the most cynical of spin masters that can put lipstick on this union pig.

This is precisely the kind of issue that can potentially focus minds of low and mis-information voters who are not involved otherwise. For that to happen, however, candidates and their campaigns must explain them in context. The Romney campaign decided it was only important as a localized "South Carolina jobs" issue. It was so much more than that. The Boeing fight clarified so much about why we are right and liberals are wrong, and how the nation is being stolen in front of our eyes. Obtuse niche thinking is what happens when you obsess over focus group responses while ignoring the larger realities outside your window. No doubt the fear of offending union goons was at play here, as well.

* * *

The month of May came along, however, and a major event blew everything else out of the news cycle. *Obama was re-elected!!!*

Well, that was not exactly what happened, but that was the media spin after Seal Team Six killed Osama bin Laden. Many of us never bought into that notion, and yet the Jurassic media was almost universal in this assessment, as was the establishment. As you read the following description below, contrast this analysis with how Romney-Ryan handled the bin Laden issue.

OBL's Death a Victory for the Adults

American Thinker, May 3, 2011

The children are celebrating and taking credit for the death of Osama bin Laden, but make no mistake, this is a win for the adults. This will give Obama a short-term boost in the polls, but I suspect that after a few days or weeks of liberal celebration, reality will start to sink in for more and more Americans.

Now by adults, I mean folks mature enough to understand that the world is a mean place ruled by the aggressive use of power, and that the only way to stop evil from ruling is for the good guys to use more power and to use it more aggressively. And by children, I mean the overgrown juveniles who refuse to understand this reality as it is and who like to think the Muslim world adored us until Bush-Cheney and Rumsfeld came to power. Long before Election Day of 2012, this will become evident. Because when you drill down, the death of bin Laden has nothing to do with the core beliefs of this President or the entire liberal movement.

The death of bin Laden has nothing to do with closing Guantanamo Bay. It has nothing to do with trying Khalid Sheik Muhammad in New York City. It has nothing to do with avoiding collateral damage at our own soldiers' peril, and it has nothing to do with Patti Murray's gushing about bin Laden's day care centers. We did not kill bin Laden by trying to understand why they hate us so much, and we did not do it by allowing Jamie Gorelick to keep our CIA and FBI and Special Forces from talking to each other.

We were not successful because we allow gays in the military or because we set lower standards for certain groups so as not to hurt their self-esteem. We did not kill him because we unionized TSA agents thereby memorializing their right to grope us without fear of losing their jobs. Killing bin Laden was not the result of Teddy Kennedy sanctimoniously railing against Abu Ghraib, nor was it the result of Cindy Sheehan's hatred of George W. Bush. The protestations by liberals — including John McCain — against water boarding, and other forms of enhanced interrogation techniques had nothing to do with this either.

Code Pink was not involved, and this strike had nothing to do with Obama's doctrine of "courageous restraint." This operation did not involve the UN, and it was not multi-lateral. And for sure, the supposed worldwide peace and respect the mere election of Barack Obama was going to bring the United States had nothing to do with it either. In fact, as I add it up, there is not one single scintilla of liberal thought or policy that had anything to do with the successful operation by Seal Team Six.

In fact, under Obama's government shutdown program, Seal Team Six team members would not have been paid.

When you get right down to it, the successful taking out of bin Laden is a stunning defeat of everything childish about liberal foreign policy and national defense. That all of this happened while a liberal kid was in the White House reminds us of the cliché of the rich kid who "was born on third base but acts like he hit the triple." And make no mistake about it; with the repeated mention of the "I" word in the Sunday night address, Obama wants us all to think he pulled the trigger.

So let's look at what really happened.

First, it is educative that candidate Obama campaigned against the idea of even killing bin Laden. Now he's taking credit for masterminding the entire op, and the military hating leftists are now ready to call him the return of Patton. I thought leftists hated Patton! But let's look at some background. What really happened is that the Intel trail ultimately culminating in Sunday's events started in 2007 at Guantanamo Bay. The first key piece of Intel was the identification of the couriers who kept bin Laden informed. Perhaps we'll never know for sure if water boarding led to this first nugget of information, but you can bet that whatever it was, it falls under the very adult notion of "enhanced interrogation" techniques. In other words, Obama is the beneficiary of tactics he campaigned against — that were performed at a location he promised to close down.

The credit belongs the adults who put in place these interrogation techniques, and who decided they would take place at Gitmo. That would be Bush, Cheney, and Rumsfeld. Three adults. And this intelligence nugget led to a four-year chain of events that ended this past weekend with what must have been a real life Jason Bourne scene. But the guys who did this, the Joint Special Operations Command, have been operating in the Afghan-Pakistani theatre for ten years. Sunday night was merely the result of ten years of hard and dangerous work started by — the adults. This all started "on Bush's watch."

To sum it up, everything we as conservatives believe about our country's defense, the War on Terror, interrogation, special ops / black ops, Gitmo, and the realities of the world was validated. Our ideas won. Our tactics won. An enemy we never hesitated to call out was killed.

Everything liberals believe about the same was defeated. They are trying to take credit for a win in a war they never acknowledged, thanks to tactics they openly hate. With a childish liberal in the White House, that may not be evident to much of the country at the moment. But I predict it will be. Facts are facts. The adults won. The kids were along for the ride kicking and screaming. Americans' curiosity with how this all went down will bring this to light.

Leon Panetta's recent admission that waterboarding was central to the gathering of intel that led to the killing of bin Laden validates that entire article. Then again, most of us assumed as much instantly, and that makes it all the more inexcusable that Romney-Ryan blew this one. To lose on this particular issue is imbecilic in light of the realities described above. So why did Romney-Ryan meekly congratulate Obama on the death of Osama and then try to change the subject as quickly as possible?

They did so because the real credit, such that it should go to any elected official, goes to Bush-Cheney. Team Romney apparently figured it was better to let Obama have this one than to risk any association with Bush or with torture. In the simplistic analysis of the Campaign, the decision was made to ignore the facts, ignore Seal Team 6, and ignore all of the special operatives who set the table for this operation over a ten-year period. Just PUHLEEZE don't make us mention Bush or Cheney!

Okay.

It's understood that Bush left office with abysmal approval ratings, and the name Bush is now radioactive. But whose fault is that in the first place? That would be the architect and Senior Policy Advisor, Karl Rove. How's that for painful irony?

Adding insult to injury, we now know that boy Barack held back on this operation twice literally on orders from the shadow president Valerie Jarrett, and really deserves no more credit than your typical Occupy hippie living in a decommissioned school bus near Zuccotti Park. This was an astounding operation, and it was the culmination of ten years of treacherous work and yes, *water boarding*. Get over it. Community organizer Obama, Assemblyman Obama, and Senator Obama was against every bit of it every step of the way. Until, that is, he could benefit from it. Again, it's amazing how these liberals can find the flag in certain situations.

8

GOP PRIMARY SEASON—THE EARLY DAYS TUTORIAL

The end of bin Laden fell right on top of the beginning of the Republican nomination season. To be sure, the sparring between prospective candidates was a long and informative process, and a lot of definitive campaigning took place well before the first votes were taken in Iowa. Nonetheless, Team Romney later isolated their General election campaign from this entire exercise as if it never even happened, which is the thorny result of nominating a man isolated from the very reasons your party exists in the first place. A number of historical columns will be used in this section to authentically recount the mood of the season.

The Very Early Days

The first debate, albeit an unofficial event, was held in Charleston in early May, 2011. Romney, who was already pretending he was the presumptive nominee, skipped it.

But wham, out of nowhere came this Herman Cain guy. The charismatic businessman from Georgia dominated this first event and was proclaimed the clear winner by almost the entire obligatory Luntz focus group. Moreover, the focus groupies said they were prepared to vote for Cain immediately.

This was astonishing considering only two of them had even heard of Cain prior to that evening. (More amazing is how the establishment will pick and choose which focus groups they pay attention to.) Many who watched on cable, as well as the conservative talk radio universe, shared the focus group's assessment.

I should mention that four months earlier I had published "The Top Ten Reasons to Support Herman Cain for President," a column that had gone viral and provided talk show host Neal Boortz, a good friend of Cain's, material for his show. From my perspective, a Cain candidacy was not just about Cain, it was about the country, the truth, and how to take it to Obama. Among the reasons to support Cain was the race card being taken off the table, his real world experience, and his willingness to ignore the consultant class and get under the skin of the establishment. My theory was that, regardless of where Cain's candidacy ended up, all of these were good lessons for the GOP to learn. This is precisely why I wanted his campaign to last. He could help treat the establishment's RDD.

While not well known, Cain had been a favorite at Tea Party and other rallies for months leading up to the 2010 mid terms, and he understood the defining mood of the moment. Support for Cain was not wide, but it was deep; there was respect for his message and ability, even among those who did not support him due to the long odds against success. As such, the Charleston debate kicked off an amazing three weeks for Cain, culminating in his official candidacy announcement. There are lessons in the movement that led to his early success, and those lessons are critical to understand to this day.

ROCK YOU LIKE A HERMAN-CAIN
American Thinker, May 22, 2011

In the shadow of the CNN complex and totally ignored by much of Atlanta's local drive-by media, Herman Cain officially divulged a very poorly kept secret Saturday: that he is running for the Republican nomination for President. And in case anyone is not sure exactly what Mr. Cain›s intentions are, he clearly said that he is running with only one thing in mind — which is to finish number one.

So while that idea may seem fanciful to the pundits and the mainstream media (and Beltway bubbled conservatives like Charles Krauthammer), the impressive size and staggering energy of the 15 thousand folks at Olympic Centennial Park gave the rally the feel of a winning movement. As an observer of political rallies and campaigns off and on since 1980 — and a sometimes operative since 1992 — I do not reach that conclusion lightly. Frankly, I've rarely been to a political event that had this energy. It had sort of the same feel as the televised introduction of Sarah Palin in September of 2008, and also reminded me of a Reagan rally I attended in 1980.

It is no coincidence that others have compared the feel of Cain events to Palin and Reagan events also. They have that same unmistakable energy, and Cain has an "it" factor that is apparent. He is a happy but intense warrior like Reagan, and can even pull off the cowboy hat look. (Memo to Mitch Daniels, please don't try this at home).

Moreover, we should not separate what took place Saturday from the knowledge that Cain has routed the current and expected GOP fields in several Iowa Caucus polls, and has been second and first in respective Zogby Polls. Gallup, in a survey that managed to find Republican voters who hadn't heard of either Palin or Mitt Romney, showed Cain with a low name recognition, but higher favorables than any other announced or expected candidate.

Knowing this, the atmosphere was super charged with the passion and newness of an insurgent campaign, plus the confidence gained by a remarkable few weeks. This period started with the South Carolina debate "win," included confirmations from Donald Trump and Mike Huckabee that they were not running, and ended with Newt Gingrich imploding about four times in 72 hours. The Cain campaign advanced six months in those 22 days.

Cain has meticulously chosen a team and implemented a plan that is extraordinarily well conceived. With the same focus and planning that one would expect from a CEO with business turnaround experience, he has launched a campaign from nothing that now has some twentyo thousand internet based volunteers, and a donor base growing by leaps and bounds. Cain handpicked his Internet guru for the campaign that put this plan in place, but also earned a computer science degree himself. Cain was a techie before techie was cool, one of the many impressive things about his resume that gets lost in all of the "pizza man" jazz. At 65, he has a very modern campaign structure around the Internet and social networking. (snip)

When you couple this with the fact that Cain became a Tea Party favorite with his many speeches over the last two years, these are the makings of a brush fire ground up campaign. Thus, when the announcement rally drew larger than expected crowds, and the atmosphere was electric, I was not surprised, because there is simply more to the Cain Train than most people realize. There was a festive atmosphere and a lot of cheering, but those cheers came from many cheeks moist with tears that a Cain candidacy is actually what real hope and change should feel like for America.

I am confident that were there operatives involved with the Romney or Gingrich or Pawlenty campaigns in attendance, they were busy tapping out frantic emails or texts to their headquarters. In spite of the heat, there was a combination of white country music performers, black clergy, and a super charged Tea Party, yet independent, audience that created a scene any political veteran would recognize instantly as having the "scent of a winner." It's hard to describe, but you know it when you are around it. And you also know it's contagious.

Certainly, anything can happen in politics and with a fledgling campaign, the next 22 days might be as bad for Cain as the last 22 have been good. But in 2012, there isn't the need for a massive TV advertising budget, and certainly the elections of 2006, 08 and 2010 have shown us that highly paid "Republican strategists" are not only unnecessary, but usually a detriment and a waste of money.

But the main reason I think Cain's candidacy will continue to develop is Cain, combined with the times we are in. Herman Cain is a meticulous CEO whose life story is the essence of the American dream. His campaign, like his life, will be the sum of his focused planning plus his irrepressible personality and persona. He has a connection with voters that is incontrovertible, and for some reason, he just looks and sounds exactly like a man with his experiences should sound. And having stared stage 4 cancer in the eye and beaten it, he is fearless — and his "give a damn" is broke.

All of which makes him refreshing and honest. You get the idea that a Cain-Obama debate would be the wise grandfather taking the arrogant, silly whippersnapper to the woodshed. That thought alone will likely bring supporters Cain›s way, and keep his campaign relevant for a long time to come.

There were also a couple of funny motifs feeding into the momentum for Cain, including "Honkeys for Herman," and "Crackers for Cain." While an uptight liberal or a domesticated Beltway consultant would not understand, these were very effective and non-offensive ways for white voters to get the message across of just who in the race was the real black man.

It was all in good fun, and Cain embraced it. Anything that will make the liberals' heads explode is a good thing, as it rallies supporters while having the potential to set off a few light bulbs among the low information crowd. This just doesn't register with our consultants, who run fearfully from exploding heads. Cain's bad twenty-two days would come, but not for months. In the meantime, he tapped into something palpable.

Debates dominated the early campaign season, and trapped by a certain conventional wisdom of how to go about things, they were morphing into an intramural death match. Fueling these tensions were any number of inane gotcha questions, which only served to lead discussions away from the real problem, which was Obama. A tough primary season is good, but I don't agree with the dogma that it should be about destroying each other with gotchas.

The primary process should have been about two things and two things only: who had the best vision for beating Obama, and who would quickly undo the damage once that is done. It shouldn't have been Perry versus Mitt versus Cain versus Newt versus Bachmann and so on. It should have been Perry versus Obama, and Mitt versus Obama, and Newt versus Obama, etcetera, allowing us to visualize whom we needed to run against Obama. This is a subtle difference perhaps, but important.

And in the aftermath of what was universally considered a rather odd debate on Fox in August, this discussion of assumptions reached a tipping point. Another tipping point, about a particular candidate no one was taking seriously, was also on the horizon.

DEBATE'S BIGGEST LOSER? CHRIS WALLACE AND FOX
American Thinker, August 13, 2011

While there seems to be some debate over who won the Republican debate in Ames, Iowa, there seems to be consensus on who lost: Fox News in general and Chris Wallace specifically. In the mind of many conservatives, the Fox questioners did their best MSNBC impersonations by peppering the candidates with mostly meaningless irrelevancies. Folks are asking what good are tough questions if they are meaningless? Uh, none.

Which brings up another question: what is the point of a debate anyway? Or an interview for that matter? The point should be to shed light on who might make a good President. But that›s not what motivates the media in these events. The typical debate or interview question is all about the interviewer trying to make him or herself look good by putting the candidate in an awkward situation. The media, and many Americans have been lulled to sleep under the ridiculous assumption that debates and interviews should be all about who can navigate the awkward moment the best. They should not be, at least not primarily.

Now let me hastily add that handling awkward situations *is part of the skill set* necessary in any leader, but only a small part. Leaders, including Presidents, are normally in control of situations. This is especially true in the early days of their administration when they have a wave of support and often a somewhat compliant Congress. What we need from our questioners is to shed more light on the vision a candidate has for the country, and how he/she will implement that vision while they *are in control.*

Our economy is dead because of the policies Obama, Harry Reid and Nancy Pelosi implemented while they were *firmly in control.* Osama Bin Laden is dead because of decisions made by Bush and Cheney while they were *firmly in control* — even thought it took years for those decisions to bear fruit. The point is this: what a President will do while in control has exponentially more impact than how a President reacts to an awkward question

(when a journalist is in control.)

Vetting this control dynamic is especially helpful during the primary process. Primary voters in a party out of power are aching for the person who best understands what is wrong with the party in power, and who can best lead a turn around of the problems that party has created. They are not served by a self-absorbed Chris Wallace, asking a question in August, based on a question Wallace himself asked in May. (The obsession the Fox team had with their prior interviews was surreal.)

And memo to the normally reasonable Byron York: that question about Michelle Bachmann and her husband and the Biblical passage of marital submission? Really? Will anyone ask a question about Constitutional submission?

Apparently shedding relevant light is not the media template. To media mavens, such questions would seem like softball questions and reflect poorly on the journalist. Well fine. Presidential debates are not about the journalists' reputations, or at least they shouldn't be.

Perhaps it is time to rethink some debate assumptions, at least from the party standpoint during the primary process. The Jurassic media is really not a necessary ingredient in this process in this day of the new media and the social media. Engaged primary voters, who are the entire ballgame at this juncture, are easily able to follow the candidates through talk radio and the internet — including the social media.

In other words, there are not many Republican primary voters in the country who care what Wallace thinks. After last night, many will not be particularly interested in what Bret Baier or Byron York think either. Neither the candidates nor the voters need these people, and if they are not going to add anything to the process, they should be jettisoned.

Why not have folks like say, Mark Levin and Andrew Breitbart (this column was written prior to Andrew's untimely death) and Rush Limbaugh ask the questions? Admit it, that would be a fun night, and at the end of two hours, you would have a great idea on which candidate or candidates would be Barack Obama's worst nightmare, and who would be the free enterprise system's dream come true.

And isn't that the point of the primary process? I say it is. It is time for some outside the box thinking. RNC are you listening? (Wait, don›t answer that).

Actually, there was one clear winner last night — and it was the man who has run the absolute worst campaign up to this point, Newt Gingrich. He scored huge points when he substantively humiliated Wallace over the "gotcha" questions. Whether or not Gingrich was just frustrated, or whether he was prescient enough to know and understand that our misguided media own much of the blame for the mass elections of incompetents, is unclear.

The fact remains that he nailed an absolute hot button with frustrated voters when he shamed Wallace. Herman Cain also scored big when he was incredulous that any thinking adult actually wondered if Cain were serious about an alligator and moat comment weeks earlier, and Mitt Romney scored when he refused to accept a questioner's premise and stated he would "not eat President Obama's dog food."

The lesson is clear. The mainstream media — and Fox is getting more and more mainstream every day — is not the friend of the Republican primary voter. Any candidate who will show his or her mettle by calling them out for their ridiculous practices will score big. As it should be.

This debate was a harbinger for two different dynamics

that were to emerge soon in the GOP fight. An anonymous message board commenter identified both at the time: "The author is absolutely correct. When a friend asked me Friday what I thought about the debate, my response was, 'Well, I thought I liked Chris Wallace but now I think he's a jerk. And I used to dislike Newt Gingrich, but now I can't remember why.'"

This comment was typical of many, as the debate signaled the beginning of the first surge for Newt, happening at the very moment his candidacy seemed doomed. Poll numbers would not reflect this surge for weeks, but the green shoots of resurgence were growing with each debate.

Newt had been buried by a number of problems right out of the gate, not to mention his well documented inconsistent past. His comment about Ryan's Medicare plan served to remind voters of his unfortunate chat with Nancy Pelosi "on the couch" over global warming, and many voters were still struggling over his ill conceived dalliance into the New York 23 race months earlier.

What is significant about this performance is that it signaled the return of the "good Newt." His conflict with "bad Newt" is more than just a skirmish inside the considerable mind of Mr. Gingrich. It is a microcosm of the debate between the establishment wing of the GOP and the majority of the GOP base electorate. The good Newt articulates what the Tea Party conservative Reagan base believes with devastating acumen. The bad Newt is the unreliable establishment groupthink Newt, eaten up with establishment reality deficit disorder, albeit without the support of the establishment, as it turns out. This schizophrenia is an integral part of how the 2012 election turned out.

Also noticeable was the cooling between conservatives and Fox News, which continued to percolate. The base started to regard Fox as part of the Romney Campaign and the GOP establishment, if not another extension of the Jurassic Media.

Shortly after that Fox debate, Rick Perry's long awaited

entrance into the race sucked all of the oxygen out of the field. His candidacy also heated up speculation about what Palin would do, as she and Perry were considered political allies. At any rate, Perry immediately jumped to the head of the polls in the "non-Romney" semi-final. As the successful long time governor of a gargantuan and economically powerful state, Perry had just enough dangerously confrontational views to make him appealing to the non-establishment types. With his great hair and ability to pull off the hat and boot look, he came straight out of central casting if you're looking for a big time southern politician or an oil magnate. With Obama in office and gas prices where they were, many people were looking for both.

Without a doubt, he could have assembled a well-run and well-financed campaign. After governing Texas for a decade and thrashing KBH in the last election, there was no doubt about his credentials, and the Texas economy would contrast nicely with America's under Obama. Perry was also socially conservative, but not threateningly so. Yes, the idea of Perry, going toe-to-toe with Obama, was exciting. His poll numbers were way up in the 30's simply on the basis of his announcement. There was just one problem. The idea of Perry and the reality of Perry didn't match up.

It took two, maybe three debates, but the thrill of Perry was quickly gone. The death knell was his "heartless" comment about immigration, but his cause was badly damaged before that, due in part to a run in he had with Michelle Bachmann. Bachmann had peaked at the now meaningless Ames Straw Poll event, which is nothing but an over-hyped fundraiser for the Iowa Republican Party. (Interestingly enough, the Iowa Governor admitted as much weeks before this book was released.)

It was obvious that Bachmann resented Perry's quick rise to the top among voters she had worked so long and hard to win. In early September, she and Perry got into a profoundly absurd spat in a CNN debate with Wolf Blitzer over the

HPV controversy. Setting aside Perry's nanny state decision regarding these vaccinations for a second, Bachmann destroyed her own candidacy with a catty, over the top attack. After scoring some valid points about interventionist government and crony capitalism, she then tried to paint Perry as the next iteration of Joseph Mengele conducting Nazi style experiments on young Texas girls. It was painful.

Perry was wounded, but Bachmann even more so, all to the delight of Blitzer and others in the media. With Obama and liberals destroying the country, media figures loved Republican on Republican crime, especially on tangential issues like this one. In effect, both Perry and Bachmann were done as real competitors for the "non-Mitt" nomination.

So where would the non-Mitt voters go now that Perry and Bachmann had lost their shine? Newt was gaining support, but few were ready to turn to him yet, given his past. Tim Pawlenty was long gone, and Palin was still on the sidelines.

So who then? Well shucky-ducky, as Herman Cain likes to say, suddenly people started jumping back on the Cain train, figuring it might have legs after all. Many of Cain's early naysayers had assumed he would be long gone by now, and since he was still around, some of them jumped aboard. He took the lead in most polls.

As I maintained from the start, elements of the Cain message and his support are fundamental above and beyond Cain. One fundamental was a consistent rejection of Romney by three of four voters. Cain continued to be the happy warrior, attacking only Obama and liberalism in the debates and in public statements. He was convinced that the "citizen's Tea Party movement," as he called it, had changed everything. Romney seemed to look at the Tea Party and the conservative base as obstacles, and he didn't mind assaulting other Republicans at all.

In fact, Romney's campaign and the GOPe thought all of this was a waste of time and money, simply delaying the inevitable Romney nomination. And the Romney-Ryan

Campaign that ran against Obama certainly was unattached to the entire Republican Primary process. It's as if that campaign wanted to rid themselves of all of these true believers and just cajole or fool enough independents into the booth where they would not be offended by anyone who actually gives a damn about anything.

A lot of things would happen before Romney could rid himself of all of the true believers, however. In early October — no surprise by this time -- Palin announced that she would not be running. This crushed a lot of her supporters, many of whom had convinced themselves that she would rush in and save the party and the country with a late Republican or third party run.

The former Alaska Governor is far more practical than many of her hardest core followers. Palin was focused on saving the country and not focused on the election of any person per se, including Palin. This is quite a contrast to the childish obsessions over personalities typical of establishment handlers.

She made all of this clear in her official announcement release and a same-day interview with Mark Levin. The choice of Levin's show was no accident, as "the great one" worked in the Reagan Administration and, like Palin, has a feel for the role Reagan still plays, including his existence inside the head of Obama. All of this is kind of funny, as many establishment figures have insisted for years that the "era of Reagan is over," and yet from Obama's second Inaugural we can conclude that Reagan is still his primary target.

In explaining her decision to Levin, Palin's insights were very relevant to the 2012 election, the GOP civil war, and the government siege. It was evident that she understood the fundamental problems facing the country better than the elites in Washington, and as a result, had a superior emphasis and message.

"We need to continue to actively and aggressively help those who will stop the fundamental transformation of our nation," said Palin, and insisted that we must "instead seek the restoration of our greatness, our goodness and our constitutional republic based on the rule of law." In other words, job one was to help anyone who was in the position to remove the current occupant of the White House, because that occupant was destroying our greatness, our goodness, and our Constitution. Palin was aware that nothing else mattered if this was not done, and she didn't say anything about what a nice guy that occupant was. Part of this 'nothing else matters' assertion was that a third party run by her or anyone would be cataclysmic by guaranteeing another four years of Obama.

Palin accurately targeted the most devastating parts of this fundamental transformation, adding that it's imperative to "drive the discussion for freedom and free markets in the race for President, where our candidates must embrace immediate action toward energy independence through domestic resource developments of conventional energy sources."

Palin was correctly explaining that energy and the economy are linked and that both are necessary to the very notion of liberty. This was a refreshing perspective compared to that of political handlers, who live on a planet where these are somehow separate concepts. You know, a planet where "jobs voters" and "energy voters" and "freedom voters" are unrelated and must be pandered to with different messages.

Palin continued to connect the dots, insisting that we must focus on stopping "onerous regulations that kill American industry" and added that "our candidates must always push to minimize government to strengthen the economy and the private sector." In context, she was including the IRS, the NRLB, the EPA and ObamaCare among the institutions that are stealing the country from the private sector producers, thereby diminishing everyone's liberty. Her entire political non-candidacy was based on a perfect big picture analysis of the threat that Obama is to America. It was far more than just an "economy stupid" message; it was a message that recognized what's important about the secular role of government, even to Christians who contemplate their political decisions in prayer. And that role is to allow for maximum liberty by staying limited, which she correctly defined as the opposite of Obama's fundamental transformation.

Even months later, I am struck by her insistence that all of the jockeying inside the Republican Party only matters in light of rescuing the country by stopping Obama and the liberal agenda. Obviously I agree, as that is the main thesis of this book. Contrast this with our masterminds in the GOPe, who act like fancy little eunuchs regarding the cult of Obama, a myth they helped create in the first place. Tell me who the smart ones are? Again, we face the inherent problem that people, and not ideas, hire consultants, so consultants are obsessed with people, and normally devoid of ideas.

Secondly, I was struck by her instinctive emphasis on energy, one of the main areas where the establishment has a perpetual reality problem. There has never been a healthy economy in world history without reasonable market based energy prices, and no one truly enjoys liberty under the weight of spiking energy prices either. While many issues need to be addressed, energy is in a class by itself. As discussed around the time of the BP oil spill, and it cannot be repeated often enough, energy is not an issue and isn't merely *the* issue. Energy is every issue.

Obama is so wrong on energy, and his policies, not to mention his peculiar Energy Secretary, are reason enough to vote against every Democrat in every race. Moreover, any talk of an economic or housing recovery that doesn't start with domestic energy production is a waste of time. There is no easier way for the left to steal the country than to use punitive energy regulation to destroy the economy, and with it our freedoms.

And yet, with the exception of a short window of time in Newt's campaign and a late effort from an energy PAC spearheaded by Scott Nobles, there was no emphasis on it. This makes two general elections in a row where this opportunity was flat missed. Perhaps we have too many consultants living

the limousine or Seinfeld lifestyle in DC or Manhattan, causing
them to miss energy's impact on, well, everything. To them,
energy is just a "sector," with its own special interests, but
of no particular importance outside of that sector's interests.
Reality Deficit Disorder!

Frankly, I'm a little miffed there isn't more Tea Party
emphasis on energy. Given its relationship to freedom, jobs,
debts and deficits, it really should be the perfect Tea Party issue,
especially since everything stopping our energy production is
the result of a bureaucracy gone wild, the fundamental Tea
Party emphasis. The energy industry is partly to blame too,
as most of their own marketing would lead us to believe that
they too hate oil and are sorry it's what they produce. Their
message should be, *"You need it, we have it, and since it was
damned tough to get, we deserve a profit. If you think this is easy,
feel free to join us or invest in us. That's called free enterprise.
Now, go buy some gas and don't bitch to us about the price. Bitch to
government, because they're making more off this stuff than we are,
and they didn't do a damned thing to help get it!"*

Can you imagine if an oil company ran a promotion like
that while keeping their prices competitive at the same time?
Someone might actually learn something. Also, just a thought:
I wonder how much overlap there is between energy ad/PR
execs and the GOP consultant class. They fight their respective
PR wars in the same self-loathing way.

Anyhoo, rant over, even though it *is* on topic.

Palin's non-candidacy set off a flurry of speculation about
her supporters, and had Perry and Bachmann not imploded,
they would have been positioned to pick some up. That left
Cain, Newt and Rick Santorum, and a case could be made for
all three. Santorum was nowhere to be found in the polls at
this point, while Cain had the most momentum. Few voters
were ready to jump in behind Newt, although he was quietly
picking up steam. Cain, however, picked up a lot of them and
stayed ahead in most polls.

While all of this was going on, something else emerged

that seemed to work in Cain's favor, and should have worked to the advantage of all Republicans in 2012, including Mitt Romney. It was the mother of all real life object lessons about America's future.

WALL STREET MOBS PLAY INTO HERMAN CAIN'S HANDS
October 13, 2011

If anyone needed more evidence that the stars seem aligned for Herman Cain's campaign, consider the logically challenged Occupy Wall Street protestors. The intellectual bankruptcy and childish behavior of the protesters provide a jaw-dropping contrast to Cain, whose "only in America" success story gives breath to his pro-liberty and pro-America message, not to mention his Tea Party-type supporters.

This striking comparison gives Cain a boost simply by its existence. The very nature of the gatherings — the "Occupy" mobs versus the Tea Party rallies — give us a glimpse into our collective choice of futures.

Imagine: if our nation was filled with OWS protesters, there would be no civil society, no economy, and no opportunity — except for the chance of a power-grab by totalitarians. Trash, feces, and bitterness would dominate the landscape. Property would be something that you take from others, and government bureaucrats would be the main purveyors of that theft.

The mob's understanding of reality is so stunted that the iPhones and blankets and food, and even the condoms they depend on, are products of a free-market capitalist system they want to demolish. These are intellectual children — and a society must have intellectual adults in charge, or it will fail.

On the other hand, if our nation were filled with Tea Party followers, the country would be clean, prosperous, and polite. There would be significant emphasis on leaving the country better for the next generation. Opportunity would be there for those who would but pursue it. Property would be something you have the chance to earn and keep. Government would be limited, and certainly not central to our lives — indeed, government would protect us from the likes of the mobs. From what I can tell, no one would mistake a police car for a port-a-potty.

As it stands now — politically speaking — our country is at a tipping point, with the forces aligned with the protesters on one end of the spectrum and those simpatico with the vision of the Tea Party on the other. As stated by Mark Levin earlier this week, if "the libs are not defeated," then this (the protests) is what America at large will become in ten years. Ten years may be a generous assessment.

So why does this play into Herman Cain's hands in particular?

There are several reasons, but I'll preface them with the concession that the protests are good news for all conservatives simply by giving everyone a glimpse of the socialist dream world. These images and the support given to the movement by Barack Obama, Nancy Pelosi, and Harry Reid should be great news for every GOP candidate in November of 2012. I just refuse to believe that this is the America that a majority of voters want.

Cain specifically gains from this, though, due to the fact that he has shown the confidence in the last couple of days to call it as he sees it. Everyone else in the field is staying silent or repeating shallow bromides given them by handlers. Cain is saying what many are feeling.

But this is more than just an empty PR strategy advantage for Cain. His very life puts the lie to the protesters message (such as it can be deciphered). He instinctively speaks from the point of view of all of us who want but our fair shot at the American dream. His anger is righteously aimed at those who would destroy that dream with their ignorance of it. He realizes that a government growing in size, scope and reach is the hammer that these liberals will use to destroy the dream. This is Tea Party 101.

And Cain's candidacy is a more or less a creation of — or a reaction to — the citizen's Tea Party movement. This is what launched the idea and formed the foundation of the crazy notion that he should run for president. This is who Cain is, and he is by definition the opposite of OWS. Michele Bachmann, Rick Perry, Rick Santorum, Newt Gingrich, and even Ron Paul all share a bit of the Tea Party zeitgeist. But Cain is the essence of it, coming as he has from the world of free enterprise.

Moreover, Cain's business career is one of Main Street more than Wall Street. So while Mitt Romney has an amazing business career as a credential, his business career was also a Wall Street career. The problem is that Wall Street has become more and more of a crony capitalist institution over the years, and shares little with the entrepreneurial spirit of "building a better mousetrap." Thus, there is a sliver of anger at Wall Street the Tea Party perspective too. (snip)

For all of his brilliance, and his understanding of the times we are in, Newt's history of dalliance with political correctness is why he is probably not the man for this point in history. Cain, meanwhile, was living the private-sector American dream, beating cancer, and publicly speaking out against the dangers of liberalism. He instantly knew to get on the Tea Party train. This is why many in the Tea Party are now on the Cain Train.

Who knows how long Cain's crest will last? What's for certain, though, is that for the time being the "Occupy" mobs are only going to make the Cain Train more crowded.

I think it's safe to say in retrospect that Mitt's campaign remained discomfited by the comparison of Bain Capital to OWS. Frankly, the comparison should have been pursued. Mitt's career at Bain was all about tough choices demanded by a grown up world, while OWS was about selfish demands and never growing up. The image of a typical OWS encampment allows us a peek at the future, which is a powerful object lesson by itself. The fear of even having this discussion with the voters is one reason we are not happy with the GOPe. They would rather change the subject to something trite like "jobs and Ohio" without realizing that a communist movement central to the Democrat universe *is* about "jobs and Ohio."

For the time being, the Cain train did indeed stay crowded, right on through October and into November. Allegations of sexual improprieties surfaced against Cain as a cruel Halloween joke on the 31st, but it took a few weeks for that story to prove its legs. These allegations originated from the building where David Axelrod lives, which surely is a mere coincidence.

Newt Yes, Newt No, Newt Yes

The GOP nomination process was about to enter a new phase in November, a phase where we saw, among other things, the fall of Cain, then the rise, the fall, and the re-rise of Newt.

In early November, the "Florida Tea Party Convention" was held in Daytona, and, as it happens, I gave a keynote and also moderated the candidate's forum with Cain, Santorum, Bachmann and Gingrich. The straw poll from Daytona mirrored much of what was going on around the country as Cain polled 50% to Newt's 37%. This was interesting because this particular Tea Party event had more of a social-issue flavor than most, and yet Santorum and Bachmann were buried by support for Cain and Newt. Everyone there seemed to like Santorum and

Bachmann, but few thought they had the ability to lead.

Not long after that, the allegations were really slowing the Cain Train down. He would not withdraw until December 3rd, but by mid November it seemed fatal to his campaign. Such a fledgling effort, awash with the assumed purity of an outsider, simply could not survive these charges, true or not. Ironically, this was probably the first time that never having held office really hurt Cain. If you've been in politics for a while, and your alleged foibles are well known, you are immune to a degree. You know, like, say, Newt.

Newt's support was almost totally from people who had indeed written him off due to his past slippages in both policy and fidelity, yet who had given him a second look due to his message and tone, primarily in the debates. He was called a Churchill figure by some — flawed, frumpy, overweight, gruff, flawed, and brilliant. Did I mention flawed? At any rate, in mid to late November, Newt completed his come from behind story by catapulting into the lead in most of the national polls.

WHY NEWT'S SURGE WILL CONTINUE
November 17, 2011

Newt Gingrich's stumble out of the campaign gate — causing him to lose his top advisors to Rick Perry — might well be the best thing that has ever happened to his political career. That, along with his debate performances and a handful of other circumstances, explains why the former speaker of the House is now surging in the polls and why it is likely to continue.

And yes — those are the words of one who has written Newt off for good on more than one occasion, and for what surely seemed like good reasons.

But those reasons seem long past now, as the former speaker has proven himself a far superior advocate to anyone else running of what it is that animates us on the conservative side.

And it is this ability — *combined with our yearning for someone with this ability in light of the inarticulate Bush-McCain years* — that has convinced many to take a second, third, fourth, or fifth look at a man many of us had given up on. Yes, we know that Newt has not always acted like a conservative, and yes, he tends toward being an incessant government tinkerer. Yes, some of those marital issues are troubling, as was NY-23 and the David Gregory/Paul Ryan thing, and most of all...the Pelosi global warming thing. Yes, we get all that. No argument here on those points.

Yet, even so, the idea of Gingrich versus Obama on a stage more significant than even the single Presidential contest, is increasingly compelling. Admit it: you were giving Newt a second look long before you dared say so out loud, or post it on a message board. And this has nothing to do with how Gingrich has pummeled his Republican opposition because he has not done so. Not a whiff of it.

Quite the contrary, in fact. No other candidate, except Cain, has been nearly as openly enthusiastic about the entire GOP field as has Gingrich. Many times he has prefaced an answer with a statement to the effect that any of the folks on the stage would be far superior to the person we have now in the White House. After which he would go on and explain why this is so - and do it better than any of those others could explain it. Moreover, unlike Bachmann and Huntsman, he slammed the media when the Herman Cain harassment stories first broke, and refused to join in the self-important "charges are serious and must be answered" meme, no doubt written by the political hacks working for the other candidates.

All along, Gingrich, along with Cain, aimed fire at Obama specifically and liberalism in general. Newt has not so much as fired a shot across the bow of the other Republicans, let alone fired a direct hit. Interestingly, it is Cain and Gingrich who have surged. It is obvious that GOP voters are interested in only a vision for beating Obama and for governing the country after this is accomplished. They are manifestly not interested in the attacks that Rick Perry, Michele Bachmann, Rick Santorum, and Mitt Romney have leveled at each other. Since this started, Bachmann and Perry have bottomed out while Santorum has stayed on the bottom, and Romney has held firm at his +/-25% share of party support.(Snip)

All the while, Gingrich and Cain were ignoring the nonsense and keeping their eyes on the ball. And the voters have responded by leaving the Perry, Bachmann, and Palin camps and gravitating towards the two Georgia natives. And as recently as two weeks ago, it seemed as if Cain were the man for the times and would keep most of that support. He is the man of the free market/Tea Party with an exemplar American life story and a gift for oratory. Gingrich, even with this bump, seemed sentenced by his "personal baggage" and political missteps to be a supporting actor to the Cain story.

The last couple weeks have been very telling, however. Cain has struggled from the not only the harassment charges per se, but perhaps from the mental and physical fatigue that ensued. By comparison, Newt has faced all of this before. We all knew the stuff we wouldn't like months ago. That's why we didn't like him months ago, and why he stayed in the low to mid-single digits for lo these many months. The change is this; in every debate he has reminded us why we used to like him. He has also reminded us why we don't like the media, and reminded us why we like all of the GOP candidates in comparison to Obama.

In fact, since only Ron Paul looks worse in a suit, Newt is subconsciously reminding us that a "crisp crease" and metrosexual "cool" are really not as sexy as a command of every single issue, and an ability to lace that knowledge with some pepper when needed. By contrast, we are also reminded why we have dreaded every presidential debate since Reagan-Mondale. We haven't had a *yes!* moment in these things since Reagan, and we desperately need one.

But it goes deeper than just those moments. The campaign debates of 2012 will be definitive moments in our national conversation, and I think many instinctively know this. We will have on display some spokesperson for conservatism debating Obama and the Occupy America vision, and it will impact perhaps every race in 2012. And many are now saying out loud what they've been whispering for months. The debate stage matters more than ever before — and on that stage, Newt is the best. The future of the Republic is at stake. And that is why Gingrich is in the top tier to stay.

As it turned out in, the Presidential debates were not definitive moments in our national conversation, nor were the two visions of America even debated. Instead, the debates were not part of any meaningful conversation at all because meaningful conversations are not what Mitt and his handlers wanted. The GOPe always fears the big philosophical conversation. I have no idea if Newt could have won, but I know for sure that with him as the nominee, the campaign would have been sharply ideological. Two clear visions would have been obvious, and the likeability bunk on either side would have been out the window. Perhaps Newt would have swung and missed, but Mitt was out on called strikes.

With Iowa approaching, Newt continued his surge into mid December and was generally seen to be leading the field by something like fourteen points. He was flat out threatening to make the rest of the field irrelevant at the time, which had Rove, Jennifer Rubin, Krauthammer, Will, and the rest of the establishment in a panic. These same people, who are nauseatingly deferent to the likes of Obama, Chuck Schumer and Harry Reid, were virtually accusing Newt of being Satan. Headquarters couldn't figure out what the hell was going on and acted like support for Newt was the strangest, most inexplicable phenomenon ever in any election cycle.

Frankly, I found it amusing — and very easy to explain. The rise of Newt and the establishment's reaction to it simply demonstrates their reality and truth problem.

NEWT'S RISE: IT'S THE PERSUASION, STUPID
December 12, 2011

While the entire elite insider structure of both parties in a full tizzy over the out-of -the crypt rise of Newt Gingrich — and the national pundit class totally vexed by it — allow me to unlock the deep dark mystery that has them all scratching their pointy little heads.

It's the persuasion, stupid.

Now before you slough that off as too simplistic of an analysis, keep in mind how rare true persuasion is these days in politics. And by true persuasion, I mean the ability to persuade voters to consider changing their minds to agree with the politician who is speaking.

Generally, the only persuasion we see today is the phony attempt to make voters think some politician agrees with them. This normally happens after some insubstantial political consultant has persuaded some soulless office seeker that this is the way to win the precious moderates and independent voters. Too many folks running for office are merely thermometers, hiring a consultant to take the electorates pulse and then attempting to reflect it. True leaders are like thermostats. They set the temperature and bring the electorate to them.

Now keep in mind that the keepers and beneficiaries of the status quo almost always reflexively attack anyone who even tries to do this. This was true of Gingrich back in the '90's when as a pugnacious minority leader he had the temerity to go hard after Bill and Hillary Clinton. His leadership and creativity led to The Contract with America revolution in the 1994 midterms. That election was conservative America's shining moment between Reagan's win in 1980 and the 2010 midterms.

And Reagan himself was the great communicator — which is to say, persuader - and that was the magic of Reagan. He never won a single moderate or independent vote by pretending to agree with their moderation. Instead, he persuaded the moderates and independents that he was right — or at least trustworthy enough — to deserve their support. The elites had a similar visceral hatred and fear of Reagan that they now have for Newt.

It was often said of Reagan "agree with him or not, at least you know where he stands." Has that ever been said of say, Mitt Romney? I didn't think so. (snip)

Then there's Marco Rubio — whose ability to speak on the greatness of the American dream reminded people of Reagan — who sent the elite insider structure of the Charlie Crist wing of the Republican Party into a self-immolating tantrum. Upon getting the Senate nomination, Rubio was considered such a threat by the entire Democrat elite structure that they sent Bill Clinton down to Florida to try and get Kendrick Meek to drop out of the race, in an attempt to coagulate the anti-Rubio vote. Rubio still scares them today, and for good reason.

Face it. The ability to persuade is rare, and the courage to try even more so. Few have both traits. In the culture of our politics, it is so much easier to join the go along to get along game. But those few who know how and why to persuade strike fear into the elites and always have.

Which brings us to the frustrated campaigns of Michele

Bachmann and Rick Santorum, and their supporters. They too are miffed by the rise of Gingrich, and openly feel jilted by conservatives who are supporting the former Speaker. Again, the key is persuasion. Bachmann and Santorum stake their claim to the conservative voter on some iteration of their being willing to "take the slings and arrows" for their beliefs. They both have the "courage" part down, admittedly. That's an admirable trait. But with all due respect, neither candidate has much ability to persuade anyone to do anything other than respect his or her principles. Ability matters, period. This is why many voters who are principally simpatico with Bachmann and Santorum, prefer Gingrich nonetheless.

Now such an observation might indicate the selling out or compromising of conservative principles, but that charge ignores the practical results of applied persuasion. Persuasion leads to accomplishment, and Newt Gingrich has accomplished more great things for conservatism than anyone else in the field, even though he is surely not as reliably conservative as some in the field are.

This is critical, because when you get down to it, it is far more practically important to all of us what our politicians accomplish for conservatism than how purely they believe it. Again, ability matters.

The Contract with America campaign itself was a stunning success for conservatism, as was the Welfare Reform pushed through by that same Congress. Ditto the Clinton balanced budget, also the result of that Congress. Behind all of those efforts was Minority Leader (and then) Speaker Gingrich. And all through those fights, Gingrich took most of the heat directed at the entire conservative movement.

To be fair, that intense criticism weighed heavily on Newt, and he and the "Contract" Congress did fizzle out after a few years. It was the first Republican Congress in 40 years, and the first in the new media era. The withering attacks could not have been understood beforehand. No doubt, the CWA opportunity was not maximized. And Newt deserves a lot of the blame for that. Again, no argument here on that count.

Moreover, the trauma of all of those attacks are certainly at the root of some of Newt's disturbing intellectual dalliances with pet causes of the left. He was beaten down by the media attacks on him in the '90's and was no doubt tired of being hated. Human nature is what it is.

Which brings us back to the power of persuasion and Newt. His rise is based on the fact that he has persuaded many that he now understands the problems facing our nation, and he understands the media's key role in those problems. He understands that while no one is perfect, all of the GOP candidates are far superior to the current occupant of the White House. He seems not to mind at all being hated by certain groups. In fact, he now seems to relish it. He is a master at deconstructing their reasons for hating him.

In other words, he has persuaded a lot of conservatives that he fully understands the battleground now and what is at stake. Whether or not he has persuaded you is your personal decision. And he certainly might step in something along the way to persuade people the other way down the road. But for now, the reason he is on top is simply too easy for the elite pundits to figure out. It's the persuasion, stupid.

Of course, Newt did step in something down the road that persuaded people to abandon him, and that is covered shortly. In the meantime he was very persuasive, and his anti-Obama, anti-liberal message was impeccable. He could weave elements of what seemed like an attack on a journalist seamlessly into a substantive conservative treatise. Someone described Newt in the Republican debates as a Rembrandt, schooling some paint-by-numbers students.

His meteoric revival had sparked the interest of some big donors, primarily casino owner Sheldon Adelson, and the Super PAC Winning Our Future (WOF) was gearing up. As a result of the convention in Daytona and other work, I was hired by WOF. Suddenly I was on the inside of a major Super PAC supporting a red-hot candidate. Very cool.

Or so I thought. It was not long before I found out just how intractable the consultant groupthink was, even in Super PACs. As was pointed out a couple of times earlier, there is a good Newt/bad Newt tussle within Newt himself, and this schizophrenia was evident in his campaign staff and inside WOF as well, with a mix of establishment types plus a few people like myself who dwell in that strange dimension known as reality.

To reiterate what Pat Caddell said, handlers "in the Republican consultant-lobbyist-establishment complex do not want to hear any views from outsiders because it threatens their racket." I will add that their regard for real life perspective was, shall we say, minimal. The following weeks would bear this out, as the primary campaign was entering one of its two dark periods.

9

WE STRIKE GOLD, THEN ABANDON THE MINE

In Iowa, the entire field was in a panic and *all six* targeted Newt with their ad buys. This was indicative of a number of things, not the least of which was the hooey about the crucial magic of the Iowa Caucus. You know the drill, every four years we are told endlessly how the wonderful folks of Iowa get to meet and know the candidates personally, thus making them immune to normal attack ads. Uh, okay.

Newt refused to return fire and insisted on staying "relentlessly positive," which is no doubt a banality from some focus group. Frankly, he should have stayed relentlessly negative, against Obama. His entire resurgence was based on that, along with explaining why conservatives are right and Obama and other liberals are wrong. It was working spectacularly, so I begged, cajoled, argued and debated others inside the PAC to run a sharp anti Obama campaign in the spirit of Newt's debate successes. I scripted aggressive ads featuring sound bytes of Newt and the cheering from the debates and backed those up with press releases. It was an obvious strategy, but others thought using debate clips was the strangest idea in campaign advertising history. The ideas were rejected.

Ignoring Obama and staying "relentlessly positive,"

Newt's poll numbers turned relentlessly negative in the face of the astonishing six to one assault. Iowans fell for the ads like delinquents fall for late night trial lawyer appeals, and Newt faded badly in the Caucus. Santorum was apparently where the Newt voters fled, and he came in second to Romney, or so we thought.

Since Romney was assured of winning New Hampshire, there was panic inside WOF and Newt's campaign — and much joy in establishment city. There was already the conventional wisdom going around that Mitt would have this thing sewn up by the end of New Hampshire, which had been the GOPe plan all along. You can interpret that as Romney wanting South Carolina to be irrelevant and Florida a fait Accompli. As an aside, this Iowa-New Hampshire kick-off must be changed if Republicans ever want to nominate a winner again.

During my years at the University of South Carolina, I had observed that the Palmetto State takes a certain pride in not caring what anyone else thinks about anything, especially when it comes to picking Republican Presidents -- including candidates rejected by Iowa and New Hampshire. So as bad as Iowa turned out, and as awful as New Hampshire looked, I held out some hope that, if Newt could just limp into the state with any pulse at all, there would be a small chance for a reversal.

Allow me to reiterate that while I was indeed invested in Newt's success, the driving focus for me was not Newt himself. It was Newt's message and tone that I was excited about. He was the only candidate at this time with the message and tone required to beat Obama, and campaigns should always be more about the message than the personality. My advice on Super PAC conference calls was to ignore Mitt and return to a message that would peel off some of the soft support for Santorum, Perry and Bachmann, as well as attract Cain and Palin backers who had not landed yet. Mitt had been stuck at around 25% for the longest time, so the best thing for Newt to do was to focus on getting the lion's share of the other 75%.

That 75% was there for the taking, too. Most of that was soft support or un-committed, while Mitt's 25% was firm. The way to do it was to run against Obama, which is what Newt excelled at, and which is what interested that 75% in the first place.

For some strange reason, Santorum could pile on Newt while getting credit for not attacking anyone. He was also praised for consistently standing up for conservative principles at all costs, even though his last Senate campaign was rife with "Rick can be a good liberal too" talking points drivel. In fact, outside of social issues, Santorum has not been particularly conservative, and he has even shown the willingness to be an establishment lackey, as demonstrated by his support for Arlen Specter.

It was almost as if saying anything about Santorum was "hitting the girl," so I warned the PAC that we had best make the case to his voters *gently* before his supported firmed. The Beltway consultants insisted that I was crazy, that we had nothing to worry about regarding Santorum, and that we must "hit back at Mitt." And they wondered why I kept bringing up that Obama fellow, anyway.

Apparently, many of these hacks know each other, at least in passing, and this was now personal between Newt's guys and Romney's guys. This included the campaign and PAC advisors on both sides. It didn't matter what would work regarding the nomination; all that mattered was 'beating the bastards' working for Mitt. It was personal, and the emotional response was to "hit back at Mitt," never stopping to ask the question, "What will this accomplish, exactly?"

Nonetheless, I thought I was making some slight headway with my "Obama is the problem" strategy until I was informed in January that WOF had purchased the film "The King of Bain, When Mitt Romney Came to Town." This left wing atrocity might as well have come from Michael Moore's darkest fantasy or the Politburo collection. It was the biggest piece of overly emotional, anti-business, propagandized liberal porn I've ever seen. Buying this trash was nothing more than a tantrum, a purely visceral response to "hit back" at Mitt, without contemplating that Newt has risen in the polls precisely because he had only hit Obama and other liberals.

I went ballistic and insisted that we were 'bat shit crazy to run to the left of Mitt' (a direct quote) and sarcastically asked, "Does anyone remember Barack what's-his-name?" I foretold the obvious, that this film and this strategy would bring a hell storm of derision down on us from Rush, Hannity, Levin, Beck, Savage and the entire right wing blogosphere. I knew Mitt was going to win New Hampshire anyway, and there is no way to win a Republican primary in South Carolina when the entire talk radio universe was against you. What were we doing?!

I lost that argument as well, so I suggested a "King of Bain" release effectively separating Wall Street from true Main Street free enterprise. Besides, I had made this very point just weeks earlier, in the column about OWS. The group flatly rejected that idea; their reasoning speaks volumes about the establishment's opinion of the rest of the country. They insisted it was too complicated; that no one would ever understand it; and besides, "all voters *need* to hear" is that Mitt fired people in an election year about jobs. Let that sink in for a second. Quick, someone tell Palin and other conservative rubes that this crony capitalism stuff is just too complex for non-elites to understand!

As angry as I was at Mitt and his horrific campaign team during this time period, I was insulted by the idea that shedding jobs at Bain disqualified Romney as a job creator. I was thinking, "Now wait a doggoned minute, since when does downsizing a business disqualify one as a job-creating President?" Besides, do we really want to reinforce the notion that a business owes jobs to workers? And doesn't our government need downsizing in the first place? I excused myself from further Bain related work and media inquiries that came my way were redirected to a guy named Rick Tyler.

Tyler's campaign season is an interesting study in consultant careering. He had succeeded Tony Blankley as Newt's Press Secretary in 1997 and was on Newt's original campaign staff in 2011. He left for greener pastures in Texas as part of Perry's team when Newt stumbled out of the gate. Without Tyler on the team, Newt then surged. Perry, with Tyler, fell from around 35% in the polls to 6%. Naturally, with Perry's campaign in shambles, Tyler bolted again and landed at Winning Our Future. So after failing twice in one season, Tyler still had a third paying gig. Welcome to the fail-upward world of Republican consulting.

Not only did he have the job with WOF, but, as a former Press Secretary for Newt, he had tremendous sway inside the PAC. He and I clashed regularly. Tyler, by the way, thinks very highly of Shepard Smith and Joe Scarborough, and conveyed to me that he honestly has no idea why conservative voters can't stand either of them. He nixed a press release making fun of Scarborough in response to Joe trashing Newt, insisting we "gain nothing by running against Joe Scarborough." Huh? What happened to this hit-back thing?

You'll find it interesting that Tyler ended up handling communications for Todd Akin, a campaign so dismal that neither the establishment nor outsiders wanted anything to do with it. That makes Tyler 0 for 4 in the 2012 cycle alone. You can bet he banked a lot of cash and will be employed again in 2014. This is the smarmy, dense, nepotistic inbred world of the Republican consultant class. Like liberals in government, they often fail their way up. Tyler insists he is not establishment, by the way, typical of many who are.

But I digress.

The Bain campaign was not only a spectacular failure for Newt in the GOP primary season, Axelrod credits it for giving Obama a running start on characterizing Mitt as a cold hearted SOB for the general election. This is the ultimate insult to Mr. Adelson, whose money largely funded this effort. Adelson's main concern from the start was defeating Obama, and yet there is evidence that the misuse of his money actually contributed to Obama's victory. It was establishment consultants who made those decisions, and it's a shame that a patriot like Adelson had his resources so badly misused. And yes, Adelson is a patriot; his lifestyle won't be altered regardless of what Obama does. Agree with him or not, any notion his support was motivated by greed is harebrained class envy. This concept escaped a certain lifetime government employee named McCain by the way, who felt the need to criticize Adelson publicly.

In the interim, Newt was getting crushed on talk radio, cable and across the right wing message board universe, as he should have been. For every dollar WOF spent on Bain, Newt probably received a hundred dollars in negative press. Heck, one Rush monologue is worth millions, and Rush spanked Newt for longer than one monologue over Bain. So did Levin, Beck and others, all of which was fully predictable and totally deserved. Naturally, Newt finished way down in the pack in New Hampshire, and Mitt cruised to the comfortable win as expected.

The other big news out of New Hampshire, though we didn't realize it at the time, was Stephanopoulos' question to Romney during a televised debate, asking about banning contraception. This had everybody vexed, since no one had ever mentioned contraception, let alone banning it, at any point. As we would find out later when Sandra Fluke became a household word, this was the first shot in the "war on women." Stephie was planting the seed, to be watered and fertilized later. Very well fertilized, I might add.

The small news out of New Hampshire was that Jon Huntsman dropped out of the race and endorsed Mitt. Both events were presumed.

South Carolina... Finally!

After New Hampshire, Newt's campaign and our PAC limped into South Carolina with but a faint pulse. Remember that Newt was only a few weeks removed from lapping the field. The others had acted shamefully, but Newt and his PAC had not reacted properly either. Thus, what happened in South Carolina is crucially instructive about the war inside the GOP, as well as the essence of the Washington/citizen divide.

Somehow Newt was still hanging close to Mitt in polls in the state, proving the contention that South Carolina rarely feels constrained by whatever Iowa and New Hampshire have to say. With two televised debates before the voting, there was a glimmer of hope. Newt was the one candidate who could turn things around with a single debate answer.

The debates were to be held on Monday and Thursday, ahead of a Saturday primary. As the Monday debate approached, none of us could have anticipated what was about to happen. The date, the setting, the drama — it was an amazing event. Talk about turning things around with one answer.

Newt and the '10 PM Question'
American Thinker, January 18, 2012

It's 10 pm. It's Martin Luther King Day. You're in the South. A packed auditorium is deathly quiet. A large national TV audience is watching. The electoral stakes are sky-high. You are sweating on behalf of your favorite candidate. Then an African-American journalist calls your guy's name — and asks a racially tinged "gotcha" question.

OH NO! Hit the mute button. Take a beer break. I can't bear to watch! Why *do we let liberals moderate* our *debates?!*

Well, it's not exactly "the 3 am phone call" from the 2008 race. It's really much scarier than that. It's the "10 pm question." And you can bet your bottom dollar it's coming to a General election debate near you. So the question the Republicans need to ask is this: who do you trust to handle "the 10 pm question"?

And let's be honest. We absolutely cringe at the thought

of most of our candidates — past and present — having to face such a scenario. We wouldn't want to hear George W. Bush stumble through that one, even with all the Karl Rove "new tone" compassionate conservatism he could muster. His dad might have handled it even worse.

We certainly wouldn't be too excited to see John McCain field it. That probably would result with McCain reaching across the aisle and endorsing Obama on the spot. We heard Jack Kemp totally flub a question not nearly this hard, in fact. How about Bob Dole? Dan Quayle? Yikes!

Oh, I suppose Mitt Romney would sound bite his way through it with some Massachusetts moderation without totally blowing the campaign. But poor Rick Santorum fell prey to political correctness in a much easier moment, bringing the ghost of MLK down on himself. And Ron Paul set a new standard for Republicans sounding like Democrats on issues of race in the last two debates.

No, there's only one Republican we would like to hear answer such a question, and boy did we ever hear it Monday night in the Myrtle Beach Republican Debate. Juan Williams — fired from NPR because he was too Islamo-phobic, yet not Fox-phobic enough — asked the 10 pm question. He thought he had a winner. Juan's flaw, however, is that he picked such a situation to call on Newt Gingrich. He wanted Newt to flail away trying to defend some of his previous statements through the typical liberal racist template. Juan, like his Fox cohort Megyn Kelly a few weeks ago, clearly thought he had Newt cornered. Newt cornered by a reporter? Yeah, right.

What followed was a four-and-a-half-minute exchange that led to unprecedented ovations for Newt that rocked the GOP nomination race. Frank Luntz said he'd "never seen anything like it" in twenty years of debates, and Rush Limbaugh played the clip over and over — making sure his audience understood that Newt was "getting a standing oh" each time.

Just as Newt did with the comely Kelly regarding judges and the Supreme Court, he turned Williams into a YouTube sensation over a failed attempt to play the race card. And by "sensation," I mean that both media personalities became famous victims of one of those classic on-the-spot — off-the-cuff — rapier-like Newt lectures. Schooled, taken to the woodshed, smacked down — take your pick of descriptions. All and more apply now to Williams. So good was the moment for Newt that Williams should put an "in kind" contribution to Gingrich for President on his tax returns.

The exchange is famous now. YouTube, Rush, and Sean Hannity made sure of that. If you missed it, it's worth the time it takes to find it on Google or any search engine.

But make no mistake: this is more than just a great debate moment. This should be a moment of instruction for the GOP primary voter and for Newt himself. This is how you win elections. This is how you win arguments, and this is how you handle the national conversation. You express the conservative vision for America without apology and with boldness, and you do not buy into a single liberal premise while doing so. You play offense, not defense, and you *don't slam capitalism!*

For the record, Gingrich also handled the foreign affairs section of the evening masterfully. Middle Eastern terror — the assumed instigating factor behind the dreaded 3 am phone call in the first place — is right in Newt's wheelhouse. Deftly mixing in a little parochial South Carolina history, the former Speaker showed total readiness for the 3 am phone call, as well as the 10 pm question.

You will not get the 3 am phone call, however, if you don't handle the 10 pm question. That's a fact. Newt showed Monday night — as he has in most of the 16 debates — that he is the king of the arena of ideas. It is that reality that slowly boosted Newt to the top of the polls in November and December.

Then he got sidetracked by the astounding array of negative ads aimed directly at him in Iowa. Yet responding directly to Mitt Romney was a huge mistake. Mitt was not Newt›s problem, and he should have spent his ad money and stump time doing just what he did Monday night in Myrtle Beach. He should have simply, directly, and succinctly put liberalism in its place in the manner that only Newt can do. All of the anti-Bain money should have been spent doing this, and not attacking capitalism. This is what I always thought, and the incredible response to him last night seals it for me. For what it's worth, Rush said the same thing yesterday on his show.

Whether or not it would have worked, we'll never know. But we do know this: Newt handles the 10 pm question better than anyone. He will definitely surge in the polls over the next couple of days. He has another debate on Thursday night. Whether it will be enough to win South Carolina is the question.

Now just imagine if Mitt had responded to the media regarding "47%" the way Newt did to "food stamp President." We would we have a different President today, plus an entirely different tenor of discussion regarding spending and the role of government in our lives. This is why the GOPe problem is not just an election problem; it's a reality problem.

As a result of the debate, Newt zoomed up the polls and drew an important media lesson. They had just seen one of their own taken apart, and they were frightened by the crowd response. They tried to ignore the issues Newt touched on by calling it an attack, but it was a really a reasoned demolition of several liberal templates in one short exchange. Newt's ability to do this shocked them. Any Republican who can do that he must be stopped, since this could embarrass the entire notion of "hope and change" on the big stage.

The Republican establishment quickly joined in this refrain. Their fear was palpable. Mitt has many talents, but he is not capable of doing what Newt can do in such a setting. Thus, the assault from Romney supporters like Jennifer Rubin and George Will was endless and shocking in tone. The unparalleled Mark Steyn joined in, too. I suppose such a target was irresistible for a man of his considerable abilities. I remember thinking, "Okay Mr. Steyn, your points are indeed valid, but *who* then? Reagan is gone, and you won't like Mitt or Rick any better." And he didn't, by the way. It was rare and unnerving to be in disagreement with Steyn.

In fact, many establishment commentators agreed with the insulting interpretation that Newt was only appealing to rednecks who like seeing reporters taken down a peg. Well yes, the media take down was part of it, but taking down the liberal media is, in and of itself, a valid issue and something the establishment is blind to. Newt's combination of a fearless style plus powerful substance was what encouraged me, and I figured eventually the consultants and other candidates would figure this out on the road to beating Obama.

Or not.

Quite the opposite. The subject of the awful Obama was not what the establishment wanted, because Mitt was not very good at talking about that. And besides, soccer moms wouldn't like it either, or so we're told. The arrogant and controlling establishment was telling us to shut up, sit down, and listen to our betters, then everything would work out just fine. In this way, the GOPe is similar to very thing we fight against in the federal government: the arrogant controlling assumption that the elites know what we really need. This problem is inherently limiting when your message is about decentralizing control. This is why Mitt's message was inherently limited.

Anyway, CNN ran the Thursday debate. They much preferred Republicans attacking each other, and had a plan to promote just that. They let it out that they were going to let the candidates go after each other with "no interruptions," baiting the trap for an intramural blood bath.

ARE THE GOP DEBATERS FOOLISH ENOUGH TO TAKE CNN'S BAIT?
American Thinker, January 19, 2012

So CNN's executives have let it slip (at least to Drudge*) that they are "going to let them just go at it" in what they are calling the "Republican Debate of the Year" tonight in South Carolina.

Let me translate:

'We are going to do our damnedest to get the candidates to go at each other and totally ignore Barack Obama. We're going to ask those cute little questions like 'Governor Romney, with Speaker Gingrich standing right here, will you say to his face that he's the biggest son of a blah blah blah...'

So please tell me, Republican candidates, that you are not foolish enough to fall for this. Please? No one has gained anything in this cycle in the debates by trashing other Republicans. Quite the opposite. Consider the travails of Newt:

Gingrich had an unprecedented standing ovation from most of the crowd Monday night in a now famous exchange with Juan Williams. To gain that kind of amazing response, Newt uttered not a single syllable about any GOP opponents. Instead, Newt overwhelmed the liberal Williams and his typical template with logic and history and power and passion and — get this — conservative principle!

The response was amazing. His standing ovation was so

loud and universal that it had to include many folks who entered the hall supporting others instead of Gingrich. This is not everyday stuff. Not only that, but it gained Newt millions of dollars worth of accolades on Rush and Hannity, and other talk shows the next day. All of this has given him huge bumps in both national and S.C. polls.

And it worked because this is what the Republican base voters are so obviously craving. That is why they responded so powerfully. And Newt's other great moments — on terror, local control of schools and unemployment compensation — were all in response to a logical Gingrich lecture of conservatism that over-powered failed liberal prescriptions for these problems.

Actually, if you go back through the 16 debates and track the big crowd moments, most of them result from Gingrich decimating some liberal premise, and usually a liberal questioner in the process. It's the primary reason Gingrich went from around 5% support to 35- 45% a few weeks ago. He didn't have any advertising to speak of. It was all the debates and that was all about attacking liberalism and doing it very effectively.

(Snip)

In other words, the problems we have in our country today are not the fault of Mitt Romney, Newt Gingrich, Rick Santorum, Rick Perry or Ron Paul. The problem is Barack Obama and the solution is removing him, and as many liked minded members of Congress as possible from office. Period. Why these candidates and their consultants and strategists can't understand this is agonizing and symptomatic of a Washington culture that does not understand the nation it tortures.

(Snip)

The attacks in the debates have backfired, and all of

that was started simply for the amusement of the media moderators in the first place. And it is driven by an inside the Beltway culture — blind as it is — that looks at all of this as a game, instead of understanding that this is about the future of our Republic and whether it survives or not.

The voters, however, largely understand the gravity of the situation — and once again are way ahead of most of the candidates and their consultants as well as the pundit class. Thus, they respond on those occasions when the candidates figure it out as well. On Monday night, Newt figured it out. He put the Bain disaster behind him and re-focused on the problem: Barack Obama and liberalism. He aimed, fired and scored several direct hits and might have saved his campaign in the process.

Tonight he and all of the candidates have another opportunity to do the same. There is the Keystone Pipeline issue just lying there for the taking, not to mention the recess appointments made by Obama, and the NLRB assault on Boeing's North Charleston plant. The debate is in Charleston after all!

The candidate who ignores the CNN bait and his GOP opponents and focuses on the real problems will win this debate. If nobody figures this out, we all lose, and it's a win for CNN and Barack Obama. You know that, and I know that instinctively. Why is this so hard?

This was the debate that started off on the subject of the Nightline interview with Newt's very bitter ex-wife Marianne, which no one knew about until hours before the debate. Should anyone doubt the dread liberals had at what Gingrich would do to their entire worldview on the stage of a Presidential campaign, this attempted ambush should put it to rest. The media knew what they should fear, while the GOP establishment had no idea what they should promote.

Another continuing theme was the churlish side of

Santorum, who for some reason continued to get a pass on it, including on talk radio. It must have been due to the doggoned sweater vest, because his demeanor was observably petulant and he spent more time attacking Republicans than Obama. Video evidence will confirm this. Yet, after the final S.C. debate, some pundits reached the absurd conclusion that Santorum had gained ground, would pass Newt, and finish second behind Romney. I'm not sure what planet they were watching from, as this debate cemented the obvious to me. South Carolina voters disagreed with the pundits, too, and Newt steamrolled to a massive 13 point win over Romney, more than doubling Santorum. With record turnout, Newt piled up a total that dwarfed all candidates in Iowa and New Hampshire combined.

Psst: Hear the Roar and Pay Attention
American Thinker, January 22, 2012

After Thursday's debate in Charleston, I assumed that Newt had not only survived the Marianne episode, but had benefitted from it. I also figured he would win S.C., and that Santorum would fade as a challenger to him. Santorum fade? Yes. All he got were polite 'golf claps' you hear when someone out of contention taps in for bogey. Pay attention. This means the attacks Rick was selling were not being bought.

So where did the crowd roar? They roared when some premise of liberalism or some particular liberal was taken apart, and no Republican on Republican attack was rewarded. Even Mitt, no favorite of the red meat crowd, got his loudest moments when he finally decided to support capitalism with some fervor. Newt got the big reaction of the week by attacking liberal members of the media who were either assaulting conservative beliefs on the whole (Juan Williams and the race card) or protecting Obama by focusing on personal lives (John King).

The math is clear. While negative ads can be effective if run in huge numbers — as in Iowa — what the voters want from the debates and on the stump is someone who can look liberals squarely in the eye and tell them why we are right and they are wrong. The American conservative base has had to put up with being called stupid, racist, greedy and unfair for decades by not only the Democrats but also the vast majority of the media. The pent up frustration of these decades is magnified by the fact that George H. W. Bush, Bob Dole, George W. Bush and John McCain would not, or perhaps could not, confront this.

In fact, rare is the Republican candidate at any level who refuses to put up with this and fights back. When they do, they become sensations. Even Chris Christie and Donald Trump — neither one a true conservative — earned the love of the Republican base by simply deigning to fight back. Marco Rubio and Allen West are far more popular and well known than they have any right to be, simply because they refuse to accept the argument on liberals' terms. They fight. They elicit the roar.

(snip)

It wasn't merely the few thousand in attendance who rose to give Newt his standing ovations per se, it's that there were hundreds of thousands cheering at their television sets across the state, and the nation, as well. Something like 60% of all likely voters in South Carolina did watch these two debates, merely confirming just how important the crowd reaction should be taken.

Yet the elites ignored the roar. After all, the roar came from the unwashed, from the fans of cockfights, from Tea Party folks and other such rabble. Inside the sterile cable studios and on their laptops, the pundits scored their debate and their election prospects without the roar. They have their little formulas about who has to raise doubts here, and who has to score points there. What they don't understand is what the roar means.

Memo to the pundits: listen and learn.

The roar is passion. The roar is intensity. The roar is pent up frustration. The roar, put another way, is the national mood of conservatives. It is a roar that will demand a fighter, and it will demand that those who want our votes must not cower in the face of the liberal template. If fact, it is a roar that demands that we do not accept any liberal templates. That's why Newt has gotten most of the roars, and why he has vaulted into serious contention only days after being written off. Anyone else who wants the roar should heed the lesson. It's available to every candidate running, and yet the roar comes only at the expense of liberals and liberalism. You won't get the roar attacking others on the stage. Tell your consultants to take a hike if they tell you otherwise.

The roar was an easy predictor of what would happen Saturday night in South Carolina. I and many others knew late Thursday night what would happen on Saturday. Seems like few inside the Beltway understood...until Saturday evening.

Newt had discovered the key to charge up the base, turn voters out, and beat Obama, which was to defend conservatives against the forty years of charges about being racist, sexist, greedy, stupid and unfair. This is powerful because we have lived through two Bushes, two Doles, one Kemp and a McCain damn near confirming that we are those things. Newt was awesome in combating those narratives. Call it the opposite of the 'new tone.'

Now, before defenders of conventional wisdom throw a hissy, let me say definitively that a passionate defense of beliefs is not merely a pander to your base. Conviction, well articulated, is the key to changing some percentage of the hearts and minds you need to win a national election. Newt was making a compelling case for what the base believes, and why those beliefs were right. It was also an effective assault on the inherent flaws of liberalism, two concepts that continue to evade the GOPe consultant.

Pundits may drone on about moderates and independents and low information voters, but nothing turns moderates, independents and low information voters into higher information voters like a campaign that draws sharp and clear distinctions, and one that generates enthusiasm. I remain convinced that such a message, even delivered by Romney and his PACs, could have convinced about 2% or so to flip sides. That is all it would have taken.

Unfortunately, even as Newt headed to Florida with a clear message that was drawing massive crowds, all momentum was about to evaporate.

Just prior to Florida, Santorum was finally declared the "winner" in Iowa, by thirty-four votes over Romney. Paradoxically, this ended up helping Mitt in the long run. For weeks, Romney had been the presumptive winner by eight votes, yet this late, final recount showed Santorum plus thirty-four. Artfully, Santorum claimed that he had "won a state just as Newt and Mitt had" done, and declared a mantle of equality with Newt for the non-Mitt semi-final.

Technically this was true, but there was no real equality in terms of voter mobilization. Santorum spent a year in Iowa, polled less than thirty thousand votes, and would have never won Iowa without all six candidates running specifically against Newt. By comparison, Newt spent a week in South Carolina, got nearly two hundred and fifty thousand votes, and routed the field based on his ability to attack Obama. Newt was running against Obama for President, while Santorum had run for Congress from Iowa. Those are just not comparable, yet as they went to Florida, there was still widespread perception that the non-Romney semi-final was tied 1-1.

This suited the GOPe and Team Romney fine, since they never feared Santorum. There were even rumors that establishment sources were financing Santorum to divide the non-Romney vote. With Perry effectively out, Santorum was the only foil to Gingrich. This was only feasible due to Santorum's Iowa "win."

The other development in Florida was round two of the breathtaking anti-Newt advertising. The freaked-out Romney campaign, the Super PACs supporting him, and the establishment media types were more obsessed with Newt than they ever were with Obama. Again, setting the particular candidates aside, when our establishment attacks our guys harder than they attack Obama, we have a big problem. And as we know now, we damned sure have a big problem as of November 6.

In the first Florida debate, Newt played right along. It's as if he and his campaign were simultaneously standing on both sides of the divide in the Republican Party. The good Newt, the one focused on Obama, became the bad Newt on a dime. All Newt had accomplished in South Carolina, for himself and the combined effort to defeat Obama, evaporated fifteen minutes into the debate. He took Mitt's bait and was off on all kinds of negative intramural tangents. It was an awful display that served neither. Gingrich seemed unhinged by the negative ads. Quietly, Santorum benefitted from the simple fact that Newt and Mitt ignored him.

Since New Hampshire, I had warned WOF that Santorum was not to be taken lightly and that his support was firming, but that Newt could still get some of it if he played it right. But like Newt and his official staff, the consultants inside WOF were so obsessed with Mitt's campaign that they forgot about Obama, whoever the hell he is, and refused to acknowledge that Santorum even existed. Those were two awful mistakes.

At any rate, Mitt did get his victory in Florida, by 15% over Newt. Santorum got less than half of Newt's vote in Florida but still clung to the mantle of equality in the non-Mitt semi-final. In an odd twist of voter sentiment, Santorum "won" by finishing way down, but Newt "lost" by finishing second.

(Could it be that damned vest?) Florida, like Iowa, was ugly, and the stench of both primaries was still in the air all the way through the general election where Obama won both states. So predictable.

MITT'S SCORCHED EARTH WIN

American Thinker, February 1, 2012

While Mitt Romney may have taken a step closer to the nomination Tuesday in Florida – the scorched earth he leaves behind tells me he took a few steps further away from the White House – and what's more, he knows it.

No man who really thinks he has a chance at occupying the Oval Office would ever find it necessary to use 99 per cent – yes, that's right, 99 per cent – of his own massive advertising budget to tear down his chief opponent. I'm not talking about Super PAC ads, and I'm not even factoring in the mega bucks worth of anti Gingrich publicity provided by the establishment media. No, I am talking only about the rich Romney Campaign advertising budget for Florida. You know, the "I'm Mitt Romney and I approved this message" budget.

And you read the figures right. Ninety-nine pennies out of every ad dollar these folks spent were invested in the destruction of Newt Gingrich. With so little to brag about apparently, one penny per buck was used in a positive way. And to add insult to injury, Romney and his campaign operatives found it necessary to go around claiming that they were merely responding to Gingrich's efforts. Puh-leeze. Mark Levin called them out on that fantasy Tuesday evening on his show.

Congratulations Governor. You have just won the shallowest and most negative and destructive victory in modern American politics according to a study quoted widely on Tuesday nights' Levin Show. And as for those who insist that this is just a normal ordinary political campaign – with due respect folks, history says otherwise.

There was something that stunk to high heaven about the Iowa campaign, and the same thing is true of Florida. Thanks to the Campaign Media Analysis Group for putting numbers and hard facts to what we already instinctively knew. This has indeed been an awful campaign for the past 5 or 6 weeks, and in no way is it normal.

And what the Romney Campaign put the poor folks of Florida through was shameful. And do not buy any assessment that this was a two way street or that both sides were equally guilty. The numbers make liars of anyone who tries to float that point of view. In addition to the stunning figure of 99% quoted above, nearly half (47%) of Newt's supporting groups' advertising was positive. Over all, some 68 per cent of all advertising by all candidates and PACs in Florida was aimed directly at Newt. In total, Mitt and his PACs outspend Newt and his PAC's 6 to 1. Yes, six to one.

All of which led to a dark fantasy kind of a win for Mitt Romney. He had no reason to ask people to vote for him, and thus he didn't invest much to do so. The scorched earth of Florida will in no way, shape or form resemble any other state, let alone the General election. The carpet-bombing of Iowa and Florida simply cost too much money to duplicate nationally. Further, the media support will not be there against Obama either.

In other words, Mitt won Florida and New Hampshire, but he showed in both states that he is totally unprepared to take on Obama. And he knows it. He's given no one a compelling reason to vote for him, and he knows he's in trouble if he has to go off script. There's no other way to explain the salt the fields tactics he felt pressured to resort to.

Any legitimate study of 2012 will take note that the entire Republican nomination campaign season changed during that week, and not for the better. The torpor over the entire process after Florida was so obvious that I figured, for the first time, that Obama would win re-election. It's as if the negativity in Florida wiped away four years of the building anti-Obama wave. Newt and his consultants were to blame, as well as Team Romney and his Super PACs.

NEWT STRUCK GOLD, PROMPTLY ABANDONED MINE
American Thinker, February 2, 2012

In South Carolina, Newt Gingrich correctly attributed his success to the fact that he had simply "articulated the deepest felt values of the American people." Then the former speaker promptly went to Florida and abandoned that in favor of the most deeply felt values of Beltway consultants — a childish food fight with Mitt Romney.

Bad idea.

Thus, with gravy stains on his tie and mashed potatoes in his hair, Newt Gingrich will limp away from Florida with less chance of becoming the nominee, let alone president. This is a stunning turn of event for a man who had spent months explaining why any of the Republican candidates would be far better for America than Barack Obama.

That very notion actually is one of our "most deeply felt values." Voters are interesting in but two things this cycle: a vision for defeating Barack Obama, and a vision for rolling back the red tide after this is done. Anything and everything else is theatre of the absurd. What Newt was tapping into with his "any of the eight would be better" proclamations were the deeply felt values that priority one is defeating Obama — because Obama's deeply felt values scare the hell out of us.

Also scary are the deeply felt values of San Francisco radicals and Marxists, and while we're at it, the values of the mainstream media. This is generally what the Tea Party and the midterms were all about. America as founded is being ripped out from under us in broad daylight, and this rip-off is being propelled and celebrated by our education, entertainment, and media elites. Far deeper than the "economic versus social" meme debated by facile and isolated strategists and pundits, something much more foundational is going wrong, and so few are willing to confront this fact. (Snip)

In what are still largely misunderstood moments, Newt again tapped into the most deeply felt values and righteous anger of the Republican base. Yes, it felt good to see Juan Williams and John King put in their place, but that was not the main point. No, the main points were the real issues of race and unions and schools and Iran and bureaucrats and so on — and, moreover that someone was *finally* willing and able to look liberals squarely in the eye and tell them you are so damned wrong on all of those issues. That by itself is also an important issue!

But then, for some inexplicable reason, he wiped that campaign gold off his hands and abandoned the gold mine. He quickly returned to the tar pit of the food fight with Mitt. And it has been all down hill from there. Frankly, it was stunning to observe.

The entire process was now a shameful food fight, and the winner was all but determined. Voter turnouts started to tank in all the subsequent primaries, and this proved to be a horrifying forerunner to the reality of the general election in November. A couple of dead horses are whipped again in this article, but appropriately so, since the establishment still doesn't understand what killed them. Their primary campaign in Florida predestined -- nine months in advance -- that Romney would suffer from low turnout in the general election. The primaries one week later were another indication of the same.

TURN OUT PROVES MITT *REALLY* *DID* SCORCH THE EARTH
American Thinker Feb 9, 2012

The real story of the three results from Tuesday night is not that Rick Santorum picked up some wins – thought that is big. No, the real story is that three states held votes, and nobody came. Almost nobody that is. Consider that the total turn out for Missouri, Colorado and Minnesota combined was *barely over half of the turn out of South Carolina alone,* and worse yet –barely over half the turn out for the same three states in 2008.

Thus after South Carolina's record setting primary turn out, the Republican Party has now seen a total of five events in a row where turn out was down compared to 2008. This includes the three events from this week, along with Nevada and Florida. Yes, something has made Republicans less excited about beating Barack Obama than they were about John McCain maybe replacing George W. Bush. *Who knew that was even possible?*

So what gives?

The answer is fairly clear. The candidates have forgotten about Obama. What has turned folks off is Mitt Romney's scorched earth campaign, which has sucked all the rest of the candidates into a circular firing squad of a childish food fight that is of zero interest to the Republican base voter. Given that all have entered the negative arena, you might ask why blame Mitt?

Good question, but there is an easy answer. The Romney campaign and their PACS have the lion's share of the ad money and thus can dictate the ground rules. Also, for the record, they started all of this, along with Ron Paul in Iowa, in a panicked response to Newt's double-digit lead in the polls. In Florida, it got so bad that 99% of Mitt's ads were negative towards Newt Gingrich and only 1% positive about Mitt. I guess the Romney Campaign forgot a person named Barack Obama. They damned near forgot about a person named Romney. At the very least, they thought he was irrelevant.

And yes Gingrich jettisoned his winning strategy of focusing on liberals and also joined the ugliness. Predictably, he has started losing again. More importantly, the voters stopped turning out. They were turned off. In South Carolina, the proper focus excited voters, and the Palmetto State had a 35% jump in participation over 2008. They were jazzed.

Which begs the question. If this is what everybody wants, why is it so doggoned hard for candidates and consultants to figure it out? There is a case to be made that negative ads "work," but you have to define "working." The way they work is that voters stop caring and don't vote, and to achieve this result you have to run a ton of them. So, if you're willing and able to run a scorched earth campaign, and just mercilessly hammer an opponent with a big budget, you can keep his or her numbers down and win a contest. Consultants love it!

There is one teeny tiny little problem. Once you scorch the earth, the earth is, well, scorched. The fields are salted so to speak, so they quit bearing fruit. What Mitt Romney in particular, and the entire party in general should understand from the past five contests is that this is an absolutely losing strategy in the long run. Obama will be easily beaten if the GOP has an excited base that donates and talks up the candidates and turns out and is aggressive about yard signs and bumper stickers and other iterations of intensity – because it is positive intensity that attracts new voters.

Conversely, a depressed or even disgusted conservative base means another McCain or Dole or Bush 41 campaign – in other words – four more years of Obama. Put another way, the choice is a raucous enthusiastic election a la South Carolina – or the low turn out models seen in the past five states. The only way to regain what the party (not necessarily just Newt) had in South Carolina is to refocus on Obama and liberals.

When I wrote on the day of the Florida primary that Mitt had earned only a flimsy and costly victory, I was accused of merely having sour grapes and of not having a case. Perhaps my grapes were a bit sour, but that doesn't change the fact that the analysis and prediction were right on the money. Mitt's scorched earth has indeed come back to haunt not only him, but also the entire party. Even Santorum can only claim wins with tiny voter populations that have been carpet bombed with negativity. He has shown zero ability to promote enthusiasm or turn out either.

In a cycle when primary turn out should be at an all time high, the hatred the candidates have for each other is trumping their love for the country and turning voters away in droves. There is no way this is a winning strategy in 2012. In one of them does not re-apprehend what the voters are demanding, we will all be losers.

Well, that nailed it. Mitt and the establishment had their clinching victory, pyrrhic as it turned out to be, and turnouts were a disaster in the general election, as predicted.

Santorum and Gingrich kept their campaigns active into April, but this was academic. What had started out as a terrific contest in mid 2011, riding the wave of electoral defeats suffered by Obama for years, limped home as a tired romper room episode of survival at any cost. As in ALL costs.

Mitt had survived, but not as the anti-Obama champion. He had survived because he had the money and the media influence to savage Newt Gingrich twice, and then used Santorum and Newt against each other down the stretch. Rick Perry's inspiring firebrand defense of states' rights, Bachmann's audacious stands in Congress, Ron Paul's love of the Constitution and hatred of debt, Cain's refreshing attacks on stupid people, Newt's sharp indictments of liberalism in general, and even Rick's vest were all just faded memories.

Instead of serious discussions about taxes and the economy; the liberals who caused the mortgage mess; and the liberals who want full-speed, total amnesty for illegals, our candidates were awash in the muck about Bain Capital vultures, Fannie Mae irrelevancies, and the green card status of who mowed whose yard. The GOPe did not get their smooth coronation, nor was the base allowed to have a dynamic anti-Obama contest. It was a shabby lead-in to what would be a failed Romney Campaign in the fall.

10

DID ROMNEY'S CAMPAIGN ENDORSE OBAMA?

Before the mess of Mitt's campaign could start in earnest, the rest of the first half of 2012 was slammed full of fabricated campaign narratives as well as real stories, some of which overlapped the final weeks of the Republican primary season. Many of these offered obvious openings for Mitt and his Super PACs to turn at least a few low and mis-information voters into slightly 'mo information' voters by connecting a few low hanging dots. Naturally, they missed them all.

In late February, the real story behind the bizarre contraception question from Stephanopoulos in New Hampshire was revealed as the start of the "Republican War on Women." The hostilities ramped up when a well off thirty-year-old law student was called to testify before Congress about how Republicans wanted contraception to be rare and unattainable. To hear Sandra Fluke (rhymes with yuk), one would think that women could only have birth control pills, sponges, diaphragms or condoms while Democrats were in the White House. Fluke attends Georgetown Law School, allegedly dates a wealthy heir, and we're not sure why she was chosen to speak for all careless and promiscuous women other than she is past President of something called the Georgetown Law Students for Reproductive Justice (GLSRJ). (I did not make that name up.)

This "civil rights" group, a description they use with a straight face, was formed because put-upon students were forced to "attend a Jesuit law school that does not provide contraceptive coverage in its student health plan." Silly me, I thought "coverage" could be purchased for seventy-five cents a throw in any convenience store or truck stop. I never really contemplated that it was the responsibility of a Jesuit law school to provide it. Besides, I must have missed the memo that Georgetown Law School had become an arm of the Republican Party.

Moreover, I'm not aware of any real world impact of the so-called "barriers erected by Georgetown's policies," a phrase Fluke used in her testimony. She further added that this was cruel because "students have faced financial, emotional, and medical burdens as a result."

Fluke's point was that Georgetown should pay her and others to sleep around, for which I think there is a descriptive word. In late February, Rush Limbaugh merely spoke that word after saying correctly that Fluke "wants you and me, and the tax payers, to pay her to have sex." Rush did the math and used the words "slut" and "prostitute." While I'm not sure what the problem is with such an assumption — Fluke more or less said the same thing in front of Congress — Rush faced an immediate firestorm of typical liberal outrage.

At any rate, the next thing we know, there was a raging "war on women." President Obama even found it necessary to call and check on Fluke's emotional state related to her publicity from the Limbaugh Show, which was clearly a coordinated campaign stunt. If only Obama were this concerned about things like daily security briefings and dying Ambassadors...

Although no one bothered to read it, the actual testimony that Fluke had given was imbecilic, irrational, and non-sequential, and was born of an astonishing sense of entitlement. It was a huge opportunity for the Romney campaign and the GOP, had they simply focused on her moronic words instead of buying into the liberal misdirection ploy.

At this point, it was obvious that both the Stephanopoulos question and the elevation of Fluke to chief uterine spokesperson were part of a calculated AstroTurf media campaign. Apparently, in the mind of Democrat consultants, women should vote the concerns between their legs over the concerns between their ears.

For a while, the harder the Democrats pushed this issue, the smaller Obama's advantage with women voters became. The entire charade should have insulted women of intelligence everywhere, and it appeared to be doing just that. Romney was surging in all the polls and was fast erasing the "gender gap." The momentum and the message were there for the Republicans to turn the tables on this theme, but instead they stayed away from it.

"I'll just say this, which is, it's not the language I would have used," said Romney of Rush's comments specifically, no doubt reading talking points drawn up by some unnerved consultant. "I'm focusing on the issues I think are significant in the country today, and that's why I'm here talking about jobs and Ohio."

This is typical establishment consultant 101 speak, and there's a lot of mind-numbed establishment thinking going on in just that one sound byte. First, Romney was allowing the issue to be couched in terms of whether or not what Rush said was properly polite or not, instead of the real crux, which was Fluke's nonsensical Congressional testimony. Second, there was an obvious blind spot to the biggest issue, which was not "who" or "what" Fluke was doing, but who was going to pay for it. With due respect, Mr. Romney; those *are* significant issues in the country today. You know, freedom and government spending? Third, this exemplifies the formulaic return to a "jobs and Ohio" sound byte, which could have been "jobs and Pennsylvania" or "jobs and Florida" or even just "jobs jobs jobs." This entire non-response was obviously driven by fear and not intellect.

Truth be told, almost every issue fumbled away during

2012 could be deconstructed this way, and it was all the result of the multiple-decade drift away from hard truths and towards the meaningless pabulum of formulaic talking points. Rest assured there was focus group research behind every jot and tittle of the quote above.

This was an opportunity for the social wing, the fiscal wing, and the Libertine wing of conservative voter nation to find common ground, as the only relevant issue was who was going to have to pay Sandra to do the dirty. On that, most people, even Ohio soccer moms agreed, and Fluke's own words should have been used against Obama. And the liberals had handed it to us!

* * *

In the meantime, the Democrat campaign continued to hammer the notion that Romney was a cold, heartless, capitalist bastard. While the war on women and the cold-hearted messages were going unopposed, the GOPe consultants were approving huge consulting fees for each other with the donors' money, assuring themselves that the wise thing to do was to sit on the PR money until later in the campaign. This was a disastrous decision, since, the war on women aside, voters came to believe that one of the most astonishingly generous candidates ever to run for office was instead a cold, heartless SOB. I'm not particularly enamored of Mitt, but facts are facts on his lifetime generosity.

This aspect of Mitt should have been a vital fragment of the campaign's message. When you ask for a party's nomination, you owe it to your party to fight like the dickens for the Presidency, and that means bragging when necessary. Romney might have thought he was being magnanimous, but all he was doing was ensuring that you and I would live under the regime of a *true* cold-hearted bastard for four more years. Nice has nothing to do with it. Similar to Bush and Rove's refusal to fight back for eight years, Romney was falling on swords that were not his to fall on. I include the consultants to both men as party to these poor decisions.

Obviously, it's no surprise that both the war on women and the heartless bastard themes were taking root in the minds of the voters, and exit polls later confirmed the significance of both.

In an early May development somewhat related to the war on women, the Obama Campaign released the "Julia" cartoon. This was a total dud, featuring Julia as a cradle-to-grave entitlement child. Never needing a man, or any other relationship for that matter, Julia weaved her way through life by bouncing from one government program to another. This creation was so bad that you would have thought it was satire from our side, until you remembered that the GOPe consultant class doesn't have the creativity or the cojones to pull off such a strategy.

This embarrassing and typical caricature of our opponents was handed to us on a silver platter, and any decent Republican campaign would have kept it alive and well to the very end. To have the confidence to do this, however, one has to recognize Julia in the context of the government siege and be able to explain how Julia is part of the cabal that is stealing the country. You have to understand that making fun of Julia will not offend soccer moms in southern Ohio, and realize that the real Julias already hate Republicans, anyway. This kind of big-picture understanding is intellectually out of reach for our consultant class.

The calculus in the Romney campaign was to ignore both Fluke and Julia, so eventually both narratives turned back in favor of the Democrats, showing the impact on an argument when only one side is participating.

On the subject of not participating in an argument....

Obama's Bureau of Labor Statistics (BLS) continued a pattern of dubious calculations regarding the unemployment rate into the summer. It wasn't that hard to figure out how they were monkeying with the figures (is that racist?), yet for a campaign supposedly obsessed with "jobs and Ohio," Team

Romney was inexcusably ineffective, even uncurious, about it.

The jobs fabrication was another example of letting assumptions marinate in the early stages, making it much harder to reverse down the road. Predictably, the BLS jobless rate started to tick down leading up to the election, even as the reality around the country was getting worse and people were giving up. The Romney camp was still stubbornly sticking to their "over 8%" strategy, flawed for many reasons, not the least of which was the callow faith that the official statistics would remain an honest measurement. It also set up the obvious, that the BLS would figure out a way to get it below 8% before the election. I mean really, who could have seen *that* coming?

Romney and his team were like a bunch of Charlie Browns, thinking that this one time Lucy would leave the football in place. The childish naiveté was almost other-planetary. How could they not see what was going on? Many talkers and bloggers certainly noticed!

In an article published June 4, I predicted that Obama would statistically break even on jobs. There were two key pieces to Obama's tomfoolery: the change in the scoring metrics is one, and the aforementioned and lesser known issue of jobs lost right after Obama's election was the other. As established in the chapter about the aftermath of Obama's 2008 win, business owners jettisoned some two million jobs between Election Day 2008 and the Inauguration. Those losses are officially attributed to Bush, but anyone with any business sense understands why those are Obama job losses. This realization apparently did not include anyone in Romney's campaign, an astonishing situation considering Mitt's business background.

It's not like any of this was hard to understand, and many normal, average people understood it four years ago. Now, by saying this, am I indicating that normal, average, main street business owners are that much smarter than Republican consultants? Uh, yeah, I am. And while we're on the subject, perhaps the business community and not the Congressional staffer community is where our consultants should come from.

Compelling data indicates that the decision to go along with the 8% sham would be the single most devastating decision made by Team Romney. When you loop in Bush's eight years of capitulation, McCain's inability to speak coherently on the economy, plus Romney's mistakes, you see a pattern of losses all resulting from unchallenged economic narratives. We have truth on our side, and yet our establishment wizards have ignored it for many years.

Talk show hosts and columnists often do a good job of articulating the truth, but it's imperative that campaigns and the party do so, as well. They did not, and this issue came back to hammer them later on.

There was, however, some great news on June 5th from Wisconsin. After eighteen months of the persecution of Scott Walker and two recall bites at the apple, Wisconsin held their *super-official, final, sure to work this time* re-call election. This was only nineteen months after Walker took office, and only twenty-one months after he won the election in the first place, proving the point that liberals never admit to losing and are perpetually campaigning. This whole exercise was a colossal waste of time and money, but it ended with a terrific result nonetheless. As an added bonus, it was a purely ideological fight. Wisconsin was a ground zero of sorts in the government siege against those of us who pay public sector unions, and on this night, without any input from the GOPe, the good guys won.

BIG LABOR'S BIG BOO-BOO
American Thinker, June 6, 2012

Wow. Where to start?

The media assured us it was "gonna be a late night in Madison," and yet it was over by the end of Happy Hour — which no doubt did cause some very late nights in places like Washington and Chicago.

(snip)

The real story is this: what happened this spring in Wisconsin was not a recall election at all. Pure and simple, it was a mulligan, or a childish do-over. Moreover, it was a fight by government union members and their families against pretty much everyone else. And when this reality crystallized in the minds of the voters, the unions' cause was doomed. The name Tom Barrett (Walker's opponent) is irrelevant here. The biggest losers last night — and there were many — were big labor generally, and public service unions specifically.

Succinctly, the petty, protected, pampered lefty government unions — still indignant over Scott Walker's 2010 win — simply threw a 75 million dollar tantrum as a third do over on that same election. And the unions' reward from the citizens of Wisconsin for a year and a half of hell was a resounding "go to hell" of epic proportions. And if anyone doubts that there is a God — and that He has a sense of humor — the Wisconsin State Motto is, yep, "Forward."

You can't make this stuff up.

Making stuff up, however, is what the entire leftist media-Democratic Party complex is doing today, blaming everything and everyone from the Citizens United decision, voter fraud, a bogus robo-call, George Bush — and probably even Brett Favre. MSNBC's Lawrence O'Donnell went one better - as his show pretended the election didn't even take place, focusing on Mitt Romney's job creation record in Massachusetts instead. It's all very funny and satisfying.

Now to the losers:

Big Labor: Virginia Governor Bob McDonnell didn't want to admit it on Fox, but big labor was absolutely the huge loser last night and in fact, they have been losing ever since Walker took office. It was the behavior of the unions in the Madison riots that really started the general public's focusing in on just how much these "public servants" are now making in salaries, pensions and health care, and how doggoned entitled they feel to all of this. That is what started all of this mess. The public was also tuned into the unseemly nature of public sector unions per se and their relationship with politicians they get elected. And perhaps most devastating of all is the fact that some government unions in Wisconsin have lost over half of their own membership during this protracted campaign. And oh by the way, public sector unions *started* in Wisconsin. In 1959.

Democrat Party: it goes without saying that if big labor loses, the Democratic Party loses. Actually, we have Wisconsin to thank that this now goes without saying. The past 21 months have been a highly visible object lesson for all to see. Moreover, the Democrats have lost much of their built in fund raising via the union mechanism thanks to some of Walker's reforms.

MSM and their Exit Polling: As 9pm EDT rolled around last night, all media outlets were buzzing with the word that the exit polls were 50-50, and Ed Schultz was settling in "for a long night." He had no idea at the time. These exit polls excited the media fantasy that "the race was tightening" in the final week, when actually, it was not tightening at all. One thing the exit polls showed was that almost everybody had long ago made up their minds. And why not? You›re either on the government gravy train or you're not, so what's to decide? How this escaped the shamans in the media is another story. But they lost last night in a big way.

Obama: This one is a no brainer, and was pretty much obvious when he decided to avoid Wisconsin this week like yellow in the game Twister. But it goes deeper than that. His failure to do more than send a last minute Twitter message in support of Barrett has to rankle the unions, who have in the past done so much to get Obama and other Democrats elected. Looking ahead to November, their coffers are depleted, and their enthusiasm for giving money to Obama and manning phone banks is diminished.

GOP Establishment: Setting Reince Preibus aside for a second, the GOP Establishment took a bit of a whipping last night — because Walker is exactly the kind of Republican the establishment constantly warns us is poison for the party. Preibus gets a lot of grief because he is RNC Chair and they normally deserve it. But Preibus was important to Walker's first win as well as Ron Johnson's defeat of Russ Feingold in 2010.

GOP Consultants / Conventional Wisdom: See above, but the consultant class deserves their own space in the biggest loser category. They have cost us many elections over the decades, and last night was a huge blow to their entire foundational template. This may be Walker's biggest gift of all to conservatives.

Bi-partisanship / No Labels Crowd: The stunning vitriol and passion in this election, along with the results of the recent Pew Research findings, have dealt the notion of "getting along" and bipartisanship a huge blow. Actually, reality is the problem with bipartisanship. This is a nation divided on the role of government and government unions and all of the attendant spending and control in our lives. Many of us knew that already. Those that didn't surely should now, after seeing the last 21 months unfold in Madison and after perusing the Pew results as well.

Julia: The entire nanny state government dependency mindset — as demonstrated by the Obama 2012 cartoon character Julia — took a big whipping last night. The folks who pay for all of the government union members and for all of the Julias have had a collective awakening and said enough is enough. If there's another installment of Julia, and I suspect there will not be, she would be very unhappy watching MSNBC in last night's episode.

Now, as pleasing as this result is, this is not an indication that Mitt Romney can necessarily come rolling into Wisconsin and win. While Walker, his Lt. Governor Rebecca Kleefisch and several State Senators won last night, surveys indicate that even in this environment Romney would have lost. Rarely has Romney shown the cojones on any issue that Walker has shown consistently, which is the problem.

Compared to Brown in 2009, the Walker win is even sweeter and more significant. Scott Brown campaigned on tea party principles, and while avoiding the term celebrated those principles in his victory speech. But he has not always voted that way — and will run against Princess Warren as a moderate and likely lose. Scott Walker campaigned outwardly as pro Tea Party in 2010, governed that way — campaigned that way again this year — and won an even more substantial victory. Last night Walker said, "he's committed to working together" and determined to "put this election behind us." He was just projecting the obligatory good winner attitude, but we all know better. The liberals, their unions, their President, their media — all have to be defeated because there is no working with them.

And last night, we did. Soundly.

That night in Wisconsin should have been a harbinger of disaster for Obama and the Democrats in 2012, as almost every single election of consequence since December 2008 had been. The Democrats had every advantage against Walker, and yet they got crushed. Being the good liberals they are, they refused to look upon the result as "the election is over," much less that Walker's reforms were "the law of the land." They are still trying to reverse Walker's reforms in the courts, and in January 2013 they lost another round in the Seventh Circuit. They' won't give up, though.

Even though Obama ultimately won re-election, I still say the Wisconsin result caught his team off guard. He seemed rattled on the trail afterwards. Moreover, the viewers nationwide got to witness countless images of government union employees screaming incoherently into video cameras. Negative images about their unsavory relationship with the Democrat Party were seared into voters' memories by way of viral videos and news reports. Whenever Richard Trumka, Andy Stern, or union hoards are seen on camera, it's a good day for conservatives. Team Obama knows this, which is why union goons were rarely seen in the final months of the campaign. You can trace this directly to the disaster of Madison.

How did the Romney-Ryan Campaign capitalize on this anti-union fervor? They didn't, because they fear angering union members. In fact, the word "government union" was hardly uttered by either side during the final weeks of the campaign. Romney's statements were restricted to the peripheral issue of dues. He never delved into the deeper philosophical points about how unions are bankrupting the public and private sectors. The only people talking about Romney and unions were the union goons, using their typical scare out the vote tactics late in the campaign.

And it turned out that the ever helpful Ryan, perhaps reading from an AFL-CIO campaign brochure, had said in 2009 that unions are "people who are just trying to make their lives better, people trying to collectively negotiate a better standard of living for themselves. What is wrong with that?" There is a lot wrong with that fatuous statement, and Ryan knows it, but he vacated his intellect in favor of his inner Wisconsin liberal. With no appetite from the GOP to mention the issue, government unions remained the 800-pound gorilla in the room. Speaking of 800-pound gorillas, now that the election is over, you can't sling a dead Twinkie without seeing Trumka everywhere, especially in or near the White House. Unions, with their actions against the Hostess Corporation and ports in California, are proving to be very sore winners. In Detroit, after the state legislature passed Right to Work legislation, they are proving to be sore losers, too.

Walker didn't really help Romney either, saying a week after his win that "police, firefighters and teachers are not big government." This is almost verbatim the leftist talking point of "hiring more teachers, firefighters and cops," which, as we know, is the Democrat answer to every single economic question. This is why I insist Walker is not the answer for conservatives on the national stage; his Wisconsin inner liberal sneaks out at the darndest times.

At any rate, Walker's re-call was very good news, even if Romney could never capitalize on it. However, after the good night in Wisconsin, unexpected bad news was just around the corner.

* * *

In mid June, The Supreme Court was about to rule on ObamaCare, and since Romney had signed "RomneyCare" into law in Massachusetts, this had not been the clear winner for the GOP it should have been. In fact, RomneyCare was the basis for much of the anti-Mitt sentiment from conservatives in the first place.

In fairness, Mitt promised to repeal ObamaCare on day one, but he never handled the philosophical disconnect between that promise and concocting RomneyCare during the primaries. Let's just say Mitt is no Ben Carson, and he ignored the issue completely for the general election. The issue was further complicated by Romney mouthpiece Andrea Saul's astonishingly tone deaf response to the abominable Democrat Super PAC "cancer ad.". With the Democrats pushing the dark fairy tale that Romney killed a woman who had never worked for him, Saul retaliated with the unforgivable response that "if

[they] had been in Massachusetts under Governor Romney's health care plan, they would have had health care."

Face palm!

This typical "we can be good liberals, too" response reinforced the unhelpful notion that Romney was the godfather of ObamaCare. It was inexcusably vapid on Saul's part and indefensible that Romney didn't fire her immediately. What happened to Mr. Bain's propensity to downsize? Saul was clearly over her head, so naturally she was Press Secretary for the Campaign.

The Saul example is noteworthy because she has just the kind of resume the GOPe likes. She has worked for John McCain twice, Orrin Hatch, and Charlie Crist. Crist? Really? Well of course she has, bless her little establishment heart. I doubt she can explain today why conservatives don't trust Crist, and she probably thinks it's a bad thing he is out of the party.

She went from liberal Vanderbilt University straight into political communications, and on a routine basis proves she doesn't understand a damned thing about the real world. This is preordained, since she's never been in it. But she'll be employed in the next cycle, and will continue to make indefensible statements. She is another great example of how the consultant class fails each other up. One thing the GOP *must* do is clean house of all the little naive "Daddy got me a job" consultants and hire some folks who have actually been in the real world for a while.

At any rate, as the Court's ruling approached, many conservatives figured the Justices would do for us what Mitt could not. This ended up being a false hope. For months, I had been writing about the risk of making the individual mandate our main argument against ObamaCare. Certainly, the mandate was an intellectually sound and morally correct way to oppose this monstrosity, yet it was only one of many ways to do so. What concerned me was that we were putting too many eggs in the mandate basket.

Whenever conservatives do this, that single basket always turns over and everyone forgets we have more baskets. We experienced this with the WMDs. There were many reasons to remove Saddam Hussein besides WMDs, yet when the report came out, suddenly all the other reasons were forgotten and we were stuck with "Bush lied people died." We are still dealing with fall-out from that invention today, and I feared a similar single-basket problem with ObamaCare and the mandate from the start.

FEAR THE 'MANDATE ONLY' RULING
American Thinker, June 21, 2012

While a lot of reasonable musing has been done as to whether or not any particular Supreme Court ruling on ObamaCare advantages Barack Obama politically – it is plausible that the ultimate liberal goals are advanced the furthest by a split decision, as opposed to any other outcome.

By ultimate liberal goals, I mean goals way beyond how ObamaCare will play as 'an issue' in the election cycle of 2012. I refer to the grander goals related to "fundamentally transforming" America by way of damaging the private sector – which we all know is still doing fine. And by split decision, I mean the much discussed scenario where the Court strikes down only the individual mandate - while leaving the rest of the law in place. With such a focus placed on the mandate by Ken Cuccinelli and Rick Santorum and others, I fear that conservatives have perhaps put too much emphasis on the mandate - and too little emphasis on the rest of the awful 2700 page bill.

Certainly the mandate - as drawn up in ObamaCare - is the most blatantly unconstitutional part of the bill and therefore considered the low hanging fruit of legal opposition. But it is far from the most malignant part of the bill.

Separate from the mandate, the rest of the bill is awful. It is unworkable, and it hands over our collective futures with respects to life and death to an army of bureaucrats whom we did not elect, cannot defeat, and whom we will never see. In fact, it is the rest of the bill – not the mandate – where the Sarah Palin 'death panels' reside. When you think it through to its unavoidable conclusion, the entire bill is signing us all up for a ride on the death panel train eventually. It is simply a matter of time. It can play out in no other way, and this has nothing to do with the mandate per se.

Consider the NIH in England – one of the models for ObamaCare. As reported by the Daily Mail, they have a particular "care pathway" impacting over 130 thousand patients a year. And this is a one-way pathway that does not require the dropping of breadcrumbs, because there is no return trip involved. It is one way, and all of the decisions are made in bureaucratic cubicles.

You think that's an over statement? Consider this: ObamaCare – even with 2700 pages – is amazingly vague. It bestows incredible authority to Kathleen Sebelius to determine when, what and how this monstrosity will be put into place. She will have hundreds of thousands of DMV type functionaries carrying out her orders and tens of thousands of IRS agents backing them up. You don't think those folks will have data base access to your voter registration info – or perhaps even your internet search history?

Let's see, Mr. Smith is registered Republican. He searched a bunch of articles ridiculing Bloomberg's soda and salt bans, while Mr. Jones is registered Democrat and signed up for a lot of LGBT groups online. Hmm. I wonder whose by-pass we should approve – we only have the money for one...

Far from being an over statement, the term death panel is almost overly benign when you consider the nature of how

ObamaCare turns our entire lives over to the government bureaucrats. This is horrifying and will mean nothing less than the end of our nation as we have come to know it.

But back to the Court and a potential mandate only strike down. Let's work through this scenario:

Off the bat, some in the pundit class would consider such a ruling a win for conservatives opposing ObamaCare - while others would argue that it gives Obama and the Dems a powerful populace issue to run on. Those are both defendable assessments in a purely political sense and both are probably true to some extent. However, this misses the main calculus I think is going on in The White House now.

According to the AP, "the Obama administration plans to move ahead with major parts of the president's health care law if its most controversial provision (the mandate) does not survive." Their sources were "a leading Democrat familiar with the administration's thinking (and) a high-level Capitol Hill staffer. The two Democrats spoke on condition of anonymity to avoid appearing to be out of step with the administration's public stance." Note the wording "out of step with the administration's public stance."

For the record, the official public stance came from David Plouffe on ABC, saying "we do believe (the mandate) is constitutional, and we hope and expect that's the decision the court will render." Since it is untenable for Plouffe to admit anything else, his comments were predictable. He did not stop there, adding "we obviously will be prepared for whatever decision the court renders."

Prepared indeed, and perhaps even rubbing his hands together in anticipation. As the AP story says, "the remaining parts of the law would have far-reaching impact, putting coverage within reach of millions of uninsured people, laying new obligations on insurers and employers, and improving Medicare benefits even as payments to many service providers get scaled back."

Now think about this for a second. New obligations on insurers? Great, and with no mandate, there are no new customers for them either. New obligations on employers? No problem. They are the 1% anyway. Reduced payments to service providers – meaning doctors, nurses, hospitals, clinics, etc? Fine, that serves them right for all those unnecessary tonsillectomies and amputations.

All of this is exactly what Obama and other statist liberals want to accomplish with ObamaCare. It's why they pushed it in the first place! The 'mandate only' ruling from SCOTUS is Obama's fantasy.

Let me channel my inner Obama: *these darned private sector folks are doing fine, and we just can't have that. Don't you know this is all about destroying the private sector in healthcare totally? I told you before I was elected that this single payer thing would take a while. Well heck, I finally figured it out. We can get there sooner without the mandate. Let 'em strike it down. Go ahead Court. Make my day.*

Or, as the AP puts it "overturning the mandate would have harmful consequences for the private insurance market. Under the law, insurers would still have to accept all applicants regardless of health problems, and they would be limited in what they can charge older, sicker customers." In other words, for an industry operating now on 2 and 3% margins, it would be bye-bye. And that's the point. Then we have socialist healthcare by definition. Totally.

Now anyone using any modicum of business and economic sense understands that ObamaCare really cannot function without the mandate. After all, the revenue from the mandate was theoretically going to fund all of this expansion of coverage. (This is voodoo economics, but it is the theory at least.) Thus, from a logical and business standpoint the law cannot stand without the mandate. But this is not logic. This is not business. This is the Court. And this is politics. Court makes rulings all the time that defy business logic. Even the highest courts in the land do so.

While not predicting a split decision necessarily, I think we'd be remiss not to consider it a possibility. And if such a possibility comes about, the liberals will be cheering. They will get to act put upon in public, and run sanctimonious political ads – all the while knowing their ultimate goals just got closer.

Be afraid of a split decision. Be very afraid.

We did, as conservatives, put way too much emphasis on the mandate and, as it turns out, the Court's ruling was even worse than the feared split decision. I didn't see this coming and neither did Antonin Scalia or Clarence Thomas. Nonetheless, some of our intellectual superiors in the establishment insisted that we were missing the hidden genius in the Roberts' ruling. Our own pseudo-intellectuals insisted that we sit down, shut up, and like the ruling.

JUSTICE ROBERTS PLEADS: 'LIE TO ME'
June 29, 2012

When the shocking ObamaCare ruling came from the Supreme Court Thursday morning, the reaction from the conservative pundit class started with befuddlement – then worked through confusion, shock and then anger. Later in the day, however, the pundit elites started to furrow their brows and dust off their elbow patches - and proceeded to try and convince us rubes that we had over reacted. They treated us to all kinds of contorted rationalizations and justifications full of pseudo-intellectual gobbledy goop.

We got this from Charles Krauthammer, George Will, Erick Erickson – among others.

And while I really tried to like it – and really tried to find solace or a silver lining – there are just some basic fundamental things I could not ignore. The bottom line is that John Roberts just told Barack Obama and Nancy Pelosi figuratively to "lie to me....lie to me, and I'll like it!" One can only wonder if he liked it as much as Chris Matthews liked the leg tingle or as much as David Brooks liked the sharp crease.

Apparently he did.

Whatever the case, our Harvard educated Chief Justice– undergrad and law school – just made it the law of the land that as long as a President and House Speaker and Senate Leader lie long enough, and bald faced enough, to the entire nation about a societal changing piece of legislation– what they pass is just fine and dandy - as long as we can eventually admit it's a tax.

Actually, it's more of a stretch than that. Technically, neither Obama nor Reid nor Pelosi have yet admitted it's a tax. Roberts even did that for them – and thus he found a perverted way to call it Constitutional. He did it to himself, so I guess you could say he committed judicial masturbation. Don't Ivy League folks say and do the cutest things sometimes? Next thing you know we'll have an Ivy League Treasury Secretary who can't figure out Turbo Tax – or perhaps an Ivy League Fed Chairman unfamiliar with the Weimar Republic.

Oh, wait....

But the Chief Justice's crimes against the Constitution did not stop with memorializing and rewarding dishonesty.

He gave rationality and reality a good whipping too.

"Under (my) theory, the mandate is not a legal command to buy insurance," Roberts wrote. "Rather, it makes going without insurance just another thing the Government taxes, like buying gasoline or earning income."

Huh?

Yes, Roberts actually wrote those words – in what will certainly go down as his most famous and studied work ever. Our Ivy League credentialed Chief Justice just wrote that going without insurance can be taxed just like income and buying gas - without realizing that many people do not make income or buy gas. It must have escaped Roberts that you can avoid making income – which is ironic since many of the folks celebrating his ruling do avoid making income. And he missed that you can also avoid buying gas. Hell, Obama's Energy Secretary, Steven Chu, avoids buying gas. But now, under Robert's own theory and using Robert's own words, you and I cannot avoid buying insurance without being taxed as a result. And as we mentioned, our Treasury Secretary – not to mention the former Ways and Means Committee Chair, manage to avoid being taxed.

Beam me up Scotty!

This ruling is just beyond foolish. This is from a parallel universe. Antonin Scalia said in his dissent "the Court today decides to save a statute Congress did not write... and regards its strained statutory interpretation as judicial modesty, it is not."

Let me translate: you just wrote a bill that did not really exist so that you could uphold it on arguments that were not made– and you are not half as smart as you think you are in doing so. Yes, Scalia pretty much said just that.

And he continued: "It amounts instead to a vast judicial overreaching. It creates a debilitated, inoperable version of health care regulation that Congress did not enact and the public does not expect."

Which reveals what is so shockingly naïve about the Roberts ruling. He thinks he showed restraint by virtue of what he ruled on the Commerce Clause – all the while performing a larger contortion under the guise of taxation – to create something that cannot work, and is not wanted, and has not been passed.

What Scalia says, and I reiterate, is that ObamaCare was not enacted as a tax program, and as such, Roberts was writing a new bill so as to call it a tax program. Scalia's words are obviously directed only at Roberts since he is the only one who ruled on the basis of taxation. It is shameful and scary – and there is no way that any of our Founders would approve.

Ah, but our Founders were not privy to the wisdom of our current day so-called conservative elite pundit class. I speak of masters like George Will, who called it "a substantial victory" for conservatives by improving "our civic health by rekindling interest in what this expansion threatens — the Framers' design for limited government."

So let me get this straight Mr. Will: We had to lose to win? We had to snatch defeat from the jaws of victory so that, theoretically we can one day perhaps maybe win again on this very issue? Maybe perhaps? Huh? Well.

And oh, no one had been rekindled until Robert's ruling? Earth to Mr. Will: have you heard of the ObamaCare town halls? Have you heard of the Tea Party? Did you hear about Scott Brown, Chris Christie, Bob McDonnell – and oh, the 2010 mid terms? Things have been rekindled for a while here.

Yet this is elite conservative wisdom. Frankly I think Mr. Will needs to get out more. Out of DC that is.

And then there's Charles Krauthammer, whose tortured justification includes the notion that Roberts pulled off "one of the great constitutional finesses of all time.

"He managed to uphold the central conservative argument against ObamaCare while at the same time finding a narrow definitional dodge to uphold the law — and thus prevented the court from being seen as having overturned, presumably on political grounds, the signature legislation of this administration."

Again, we have to lose to win because, um, why exactly? And to clarify, Roberts upholds the law by finding "a narrow definitional dodge"- and this is finesse? I think Sherman Potter called such reasoning "chinchilla chips."

To be fair, perhaps we just don't appreciate the munificence of Roberts the way Krauthammer does: "Why did he do it?" writes Krauthammer, "because he carries two identities. Jurisprudentially, he is a constitutional conservative. Institutionally, he is chief justice and sees himself as uniquely entrusted with the custodianship of the court's legitimacy, reputation and stature."

Translating Krauthammer - we must be willing to sacrifice the Constitution today - so that the body singularly charged with being the final gatekeeper of that document can maintain its moral imperative to maybe save the Constitution at some point in the future....maybe...perhaps someday.

Sorry folks. As we say in fly over country, 'that dog won't hunt.' We just saw The Court sanction unlimited taxation on behavior and given permission to lie about it at the same time. And no amount of tortured ruminations from elites can put lipstick on that particular pig. Please. Don't lie to me.

The Roberts' ruling and the defense of it from luminaries like Will and Krauthammer illustrates the tension within the GOP. ObamaCare is the main weapon in the liberal arsenal to steal the nation through government fiat, and yet to the elites and others in the GOPe it is merely another issue to be finessed and discussed in esoteric terms that mere mortals cannot understand. They have no idea, isolated in their little cloister, what is really at stake with ObamaCare, Obama's re-election, or anything else, for that matter.

Naturally, ObamaCare will not be stopped unless the Republicans can do it. Unfortunately, Republicans will not do it unless conservatives and the base retake command of the party, because evidently only the conservatives understand what is really at stake. As shown by Wisconsin and Robert's ruling, the elites in our party are wrong when we win, and wrong when we lose. They are just wrong, period.

As late June turned to mid July, Obama himself changed the subject in our favor. In an off-teleprompter speech in Roanoke, he gave the Romney campaign a nuclear bomb. Romney managed to turn that nuke into a mere grenade, but no one will soon forget this speech. The following breakdown includes some ideas that have been covered before, further demonstrating that our elections are points on a continuum of ideas and reality and not isolated events involving just people.

OBAMA OF ROANOKE: WE SAW YOU COMING
American Thinker, July 21, 2012

Now that Brit Hume, perhaps the best network anchor of our time is on record that it's "fair to say that we know more (after the Roanoke speech) than we ever have about the President's view of business and the economy," the real Obama is finally starting to be recognized in the truly mass media. While Mr. Hume and many others have been reticent, Obama of Roanoke has been out there for all to see for years quite frankly.

What might be "fair to say" is that Obama let slip in a momentous way what many of us knew all along about him.

Ayn Rand saw Obama of Roanoke coming way back in the 1950's before Barry Sotero was even born. Ronald Reagan saw him coming in the 60s and 70s — and was especially prescient on how he would use the medical industry to advance his goals — even though our current President was but a choom boy "doing some blow" back in the day.

Obama of Roanoke is not merely a specific person named Barack Hussein Obama. He is Van Jones. He is Elizabeth Warren. He is Valerie Jarrett. He is Steven Chu and Cass Sunstein. He is Jeremiah Wright and Frank Marshall Davis and Karl Marx and many others. Obama of Roanoke is not some benign elegant speaker. Obama of Roanoke is a malignant mindset, and his fingerprints are all over some of the biggest disasters in world history. For this reason, Obama of Roanoke was utterly predictable long before Friday last.

And many utterly predicted him, though for some reason, the elite pundits and elected Republicans are not among them.

All through the campaign of 2008 Rush Limbaugh, Mark Levin, Sean Hannity and Joe the Plumber saw him coming. Why do you think Rush said "I hope he fails." The millions who flocked to see "Atlas Shrugged" also saw him. Way back in early 2009, I outlined why we were systematically dismembering my business of twenty years — that I actually did build — and why I knew instinctively that millions of others would do some iteration of the same thing we were doing.

Why did we do this and how did we know it was the thing

to do? Obama of Roanoke, that's why. It mattered not at all that he waited until July of 2012 to give the Roanoke speech. Obama of Roanoke is exactly who he has always been and has done exactly as many of us expected him to do. The Roanoke speech was not a contextual problem nor was it an aberration or a teleprompter misprint.

Roanoke was Obama, and Obama is Roanoke. As I paraphrased before his 2009 inauguration, we already had in place plans to avoid those who naively think "we didn't do that" in our business:

Atlas has shrugged all over the country. Like many business owners, we are no longer willing to take all of the financial and legal risks and put up with all of the aggravation of owning and running a business. Not with the prospects of even higher taxes, more regulation, more litigation and more emboldened bureaucrats on the horizon.

It is no secret that owners circulated endless emails leading up to election day discussing lay off plans were Obama to win. Entrepreneurs instinctively understand the danger posed by larger liberal majorities...the risk-reward equation and fierce independence spirit of start up businesses are anathema to the class warfare, equality of outcome and spread the wealth mentality of the left. [...] We got into business to be independent. We will get out for the same reason.

Now at the time, we had not met folks like Jones and Chu and Sunstein. It didn't matter. We knew Obama of Roanoke, and we knew exactly what kinds of people would be put in charge of our lives without having to know the specific names. And Roanoke may now become synonymous with the moment that others figured this out too.

Yes, history has a way of soft morphing big truths into events or even speeches, and I suspect that the term

'Roanoke' will cease to connote a small town in Virginia populated by Hokie football fans, and will instead live throughout this entire campaign, and perhaps even have a long life in the annals of Presidential politics as a seminal moment. It may well be the moment that Mitt Romney and his advisors and the so-called conservative pundit class finally had to admit that this particular emperor has not a stitch of proper economic or even pro American clothing. It may be the moment where on some level, the elites in Washington and Manhattan had to come out of the closet of doctrinal denial and join the enlightenment that so many so-called normal average folks had from the get go.

It may well be the moment when the budding momentum by Democrats to shun the Charlotte Convention and to leave Obama there all by himself reached critical mass. As we saw in 2008, when all Republicans ran against George W. Bush, a party that runs against its own President is a party in deep trouble. The same was true in 1976 with Carter V. Ford (Nixon).

It may also be the moment that the independents and the moderates finally 'got it.' It may be a point of realization that the problem is not what Mitt Romney was doing with his money, but what Obama of Roanoke is doing to their dreams and their money. It could be the time where they say "actually, I hope I can one day send my money to the Caymans too."

And because of Roanoke, I am more confident than I was a few months ago. Maybe Roanoke will be the term that defines when that "over 50%" tide started to turn. Maybe it will be the day the Beltway Republicans realized that while Obama of Roanoke is many people, but he is not the same old Democrat Party of Tip O'Neil. It may be the day that Obama's electoral coffin - and the coffins of many other statist liberals, were nailed shut by a rare act of candor.

Okay, so I got that one wrong; the door was not slammed on Obama. I still insist the opportunity was there to do so. Wisconsin and Roanoke had returned my confidence in an Obama defeat, which had evaporated during the Florida primary.

Roanoke should have been the point where a critical mass of evidence was reached, causing light bulbs to go off in even in the minds of some who do not necessarily possess the brightest of bulbs. To be fair, Romney and Ryan did make use of the "didn't build that" theme for a short while, and it helped. The fact that Team Obama insisted on clarifying and re-clarifying, and insisted that he didn't say what he said, was just icing on the cake. Every repeat of those words was good news for those who wanted Obama to be evicted from 1600 Pennsylvania Avenue.

This situation, however, demonstrates what Caddell meant when he said that the GOPe thinks they can "beat narratives that build over time with just a single message." Romney had this nice single message about "didn't build that" handed to him. The problem is, our establishment has run like scared cats from every other similar statement Obama has made over a period of years. Roanoke should have linked Obama to a four year Republican message about him being a "spread the wealth around" socialist. Instead, the GOPe has been too busy criticizing Tea Party members and talk show hosts who have made these linkages.

Repetition of the truth is how events build over a period of years. It's how the public comes to believe certain narratives. Our opponents will repeat lies time and time again but our establishment is too timid to repeat truths. In their 24/7 cable internet universe, the official pundit class remains consumed with the optics of the moment, as if issues happen in a vacuum and are merely topics that come and go. This is why they tend towards a series of single messages instead of long-standing truths.

They clearly do not understand that, for real business owners, real managers, real parents, and so on, these issues do not come and go. These issues are not confined to a vacuum of momentary optics. These issues come, they stay, and they screw up our lives every day. That's why we don't worry about the optics of the moment, because optics don't change reality.

As an aside, Roanoke also added more fuel to the "off-prompter" meme that Obama doesn't sound smart or smooth when the teleprompter is missing. The GOPe is scared to mention that as well, opting instead for self-congratulations on how open-minded they are by insisting that the black guy is the most intelligent being to ever grace the planet. In truth, Obama the statist/Marxist/socialist is destined to slip up when the prompter is gone, because he's not really that smart — the Ivy degrees and the David Brooks pant crease notwithstanding. Thus Roanoke, with the twin memes of socialism and off-prompter stupidity, should have been a wide open fairway for Romney and Ryan, but they were unable to tee up the ball because the prissy establishment had run from these two notions for four years.

* * *

In mid July, Chick Fil-A CEO Dan Cathy was given an "ambush" question in an economic interview about his personal views on marriage. To the shock of no one, the CEO of a restaurant chain that has never been open for even one minute on a Sunday said he supported traditional marriage. Now who could have possibly seen that coming?

This entire episode is a fabulous object lesson in the differences between the establishment consultants of the two parties. Liberals are always looking for an excuse to be offended and run with one of their pat deceptions, so they took advantage of this situation immediately. Never mind that Mr. Cathy does not impose his beliefs in any way, shape or form on employees or customers of Chick Fil-A, because facts are not relevant in the AstroTurf world of Axelrod and Company. They live for the chance to pretend that they have been offended or had their rights violated.

Of course, faux offense was never the crux of the issue to begin with. Mayors of Boston and Chicago came out and self-righteously threatened Chick fil-A not to even think about building stores in their cities, and it was this raw use of power to constrain trade and to punish assumed political enemies for words and not deeds which was the real issue. As with the conversation about paying Sandra Fluke to sleep around, the Chick Fil-A situation was a tailor made opportunity to unite social and libertine leaning conservatives, because both groups certainly agree on the abuse of government power, whether or not they agree with Mr. Cathy on marriage. This angle was there for the taking, and is what messaging should be about: connecting the dots for voters from time to time. When Paul Ryan was picked eleven days later, with his understanding of Ayn Rand's work, one would think he might connect some of these dots. He didn't, only mentioning the issue with short answers to a couple of questions, while Romney was sprinting to the microphones to make sure people knew that this was "not part of my campaign."

No Mitt, we wouldn't want the unchecked audacity of thuggish government to be "part of your campaign," by God. Who cares about that?

In the world of Republican campaigns, strategists are obsessed with what voters already think and with attempting to position the campaign in front of that belief, whether it is right or not. Many voters thought this was about gay marriage, and that Chick fil-A hates gays, so Team Romney let them think that and just got the heck away from the issue. This is a self-perpetuating problem, letting one phony narrative stand and spending the rest of the time avoiding that particular narrative by letting even more phony narratives stand. We literally get cornered as a result of the GOPe's fear of almost everything.

Millions of Americans did not stay cornered. On August

1, a massive, unofficial national straw poll took place. Chick Fil A "Appreciation Day" saw vast throngs of good natured, happy and supportive customers jam the restaurants and drive thru lanes. The response was staggering, and it was not just a gathering of social conservatives. This amazing show of support demonstrated that the situation was indeed a blue print for uniting the social conservative wing of the voter base with the libertarian-leaning wing. But remember, it was "not part of (Romney's) campaign" and it was just a one-off in a campaign full of them.

Mistakes like this one are fear based and symptomatic of the Republican consultant. Because he lives in a vacuum of venial and un-related single issues, he assumes voters live there, too. The idea of melding a socially conservative principal with libertarian disdain of unlimited government power is a bridge too far for the Lilliputian consultant mind, especially one frozen by the irrational fear of being called homophobic.

11

TEAM ROMNEY TIP TOES
TO THE FINISH LINE

Later in July, the conventions started to become the focus of attention. That might have contributed to the Romney Campaign missing yet another fabulous opportunity, one handed them by a Congressman from Michigan named Mike Kelly. On July 28th, on the floor of the House, Kelly told an astonishing story about bureaucratic meddling which should have been a galvanizing event for the Romney Campaign and all Republican candidates nationwide. This moment should have been the next installment of the Roanoke story line, and it was a great way to keep that theme going. Instead, after a day or two of viral fame, Kelly's speech chronicling how bureaucrats were destroying our nation was lost in the shuffle.

What is ironic is that Kelly's story put real life credence to the words spoken in 2008 by Romney himself, when he warned us of the problems our country would face when "bureaucrats have more opportunities than entrepreneurs." I wonder what happened to *that* Romney. Consultants probably shut him down. Bureaucrats are also shutting down Kelly's life, and the country.

IT'S THE BUREAUCRATS, STUPID

American Thinker, July 28, 2012

It is hard to know whether Congressman Mike Kelly knew that his fabulous diatribe on the House floor would be the perfect follow up to Obama of Roanoke or not. But it was.

Thus, all you really need to know about the two general visions for America being debated in this election cycle can be summed up by contrasting the Pennsylvania Congressman's now famous rant and Roanoke. It perfectly illustrates the liberal "you didn't build that" government centered mindset in action on main street - as it plays out every hour of every business day destroying businesses, hopes, dreams and lives.

Once the very foundational nature of this insidiousness is understood, everything else falls into place. Perhaps even in the minds of the precious moderates and independents. It's the bureaucrats, stupid!

Vote Obama in 2012, and you have cast your ballot for more rules and more paperwork and more bureaucrats to answer to should you dare to try and carve out your little piece of the pie without government help. Vote against Obama, and you are at least saying "no" to the Roanoke vision - and whether or not the other side is worthy of your vote is another question altogether.

Yes, bureaucrats and their bureaucracies and their red tape of endless and mindless regulations are the real cancer that is sapping the freedom from not only our economy but from our very lives. As many are beginning to find out and as Mr. Kelly so passionately described, red tape and bureaucrats cripple or destroy potential business deals on the surface every minute. But the ominous impact is that below the surface, this dynamic depresses and numbs the human spirit of the would-be self-starting entrepreneur.

And do not think for a minute that this is by accident.

True entrepreneurs naturally embrace the challenges of competition and marketing and of building a team, because those are but inherent hurdles in a great game where the winners — and there are many winners — can achieve freedom and independence and self-actualization. And in this game, you win by having a good idea and by working hard and working smart and by innovation pursued with courage. You win when your customers and your employees win too. Win win win.

There is nothing in *this* great game that will ultimately defeat the entrepreneur. It is simple human nature. There is, however, one way to defeat the entrepreneur and thereby ruin an entrepreneurial economy.

Change the very nature of the game.

Yes, rig the game so that honesty and hard work and innovation are merely coins of a foolish realm. Rig the game so that the little microbial rules become more important than the game itself - thereby elevating the little human microbes who sit in government cubicles 40 hours a week with no risk above the dreamers who work 100 hour weeks and who are willing to risk everything.

Moreover, continue to confiscate more and more of the fruits of entrepreneurial success in order to can give more salary and other benefits to those destructive bureaucrats who are paid to destroy those same entrepreneurs. And then to top it off, have a President who gives a speech letting everyone know that not only does he approve of this and want more of it, he enjoys insulting folks who deigned to have an American dream in the first place by giving credit for their success to the very folks who are making it damned near impossible to succeed.

This takes irony and chutzpa to new levels.

And don't think for a minute that these bureaucratic Barney Fifes don't know inside that they don't have the stones to risk a start up business - and don't think for a minute that they don't enjoy the power they are given over those that do. That's why the crowd in Roanoke was high-fiving and giving Amens to brother Barack as he was taking the movers and shakers down a peg or two. The resentment was palpable.

Yes, this is how you kill the entrepreneurial spirit. Kill the entrepreneurial spirit, and you kill America. I think the appropriate euphemisms are "hope and change" and "fundamental transformation." Do those ring a bell with you?

In Kelly's particular case, he was describing how government red tape is suffocating his business by coming between him and his banker. Kelly is in the auto business, and has a banking relationship with a man he grew up with and who has an office near Kelly's establishment. Everything that a banker would need to know about the credit worthiness of Kelly's business is readily available through the very nature of their relationship and their proximity.

Now one might think that what government should want is for bankers to have a good idea of the credit worthiness of their clients so that we have a viable business environment. You might remember that little sub prime mortgage meltdown and all of that, right? This was the result of government mandated NON-assessment of credit worthiness.

What Obama of Roanoke government really wants is raw power. One real good way to have it is to take a common sense and mutually beneficial business relationship away from Kelly and his neighboring banker in Pennsylvania - and give it to nameless, faceless bureaucrats in Washington who now have the power of Dodd Frank and

1100 pages of forms to wield over Kelly and his banker.

And to folks who believe "you didn't build that," this is music to their ears. They either believe it in ignorance or cheer it with their resentment. Or both. And it's not just Dodd Frank. This is what will make everything about ObamaCare like pulling teeth, including pulling teeth. This is the EPA and the INS and the IRS and the TSA and all the other alphabet agencies becoming the focus of our lives.

And as Kelly said, this is the government agent who refused to allow a ballpark to open after 2 million dollars of improvements were completed because the "mirrors in the men's room were a quarter inch too low." Let me reiterate that in case you glossed over it. A newly renovated ballpark, with 1500 paying customers waiting outside and the teams ready to go, were told "no" by some smarmy paper pushing government inspector who is supposed to be working for them. And the reason had nothing to do with the mirrors. It was for the same reason male dogs do what male dogs do. They can.

This bureaucrat dominated his little corner of the real world because he could. Period. This IS Roanoke America. When government agencies choose to do business with us, we do not have the freedom to take our business elsewhere. We just have to take it. I hope the liberals among the 1500 disappointed folks at the ballpark realize they are responsible for this madness.

The result of this madness is we can't get anything accomplished – because we have to get approval on this and triplicate on that and on and on it goes. Forget the new seats and the new paint and a new scoreboard and the fresh sod. Forget the folks who paid for a ticket and are waiting outside. The paper says the damned mirrors are a quarter inch too low!! Shut her down!

This is the same mindset that informs a banker and a customer who have known each other for 40 years that they must get their business relationship put on 1100 pages of paper and then blessed by someone in Washington who has never met either of them before they can proceed. This mindset is foreign to the entrepreneur's very fiber. This kind of thing is what keeps the movers and shakers from moving and shaking. This is what motivates Atlas to shrug. This is what liberal elites know. This is what they want.

Remember, it was Dodd and Frank – and all the others who joined their vision of home ownership and mortgage underwriting - who killed the economy by telling bankers what loans they must make. So naturally, the Roanoke answer is to have more Dodd and Frank. Since bureaucrats killed the economy, we must give more power to bureaucrats to revive it.

Yes, it's the bureaucrats stupid. And the stupid bureaucrats too. Congressman Kelly tapped into that sentiment. This is why his speech has gone viral, and why the lessons he gave are central to this campaign.

Well, I guess I should amend that now, to why the lessons Kelly illustrated *should* have been central to the campaign. What Kelly's story demonstrated was the very essence of America being "fundamentally changed" in front of our eyes. It speaks to what I called the perfect crime and the grandest of larcenies -- the stealing of America in broad daylight. Mystifyingly, this message didn't fit the pre-approved Rove-Romney campaign template.

This is a shame, because when Obama is in office, this should be the theme of every opposition campaign against him. Clearly, however, this is a topic that the GOPe and their consultants are not even familiar with. Instead, they continued to focus on making it clear that Obama was a "nice guy," who was simply "over his head."

With due respect, Mr. Romney, Obama is *not* a nice guy. And while he is over his head in some ways, in other ways he is perfectly suited for what he's doing. Marxists are not nice guys. Presidents who divide American on purpose are not nice guys. Government bureaucrats who use their undeserved power to lord it over us are not nice guys, either. That's the point! People who want to destroy our businesses, our country, and us are not nice under any definition with which I am familiar.

This distinct lack of niceness is not particularly difficult to grasp, and yet we had a candidate and campaign determined to run a phlegmatic, shallow, timid campaign. Many knew that, if the Beltway establishment was the only voice in the campaign, it wouldn't be effective, and this proved to be the case.

Pundits and consultants like to dodge blame by pointing to events like the "47%" comment, or Christie's shenanigans, or even Todd Akin's disastrous candidacy as the main problems. In fact, a story from Rasmussen came out recently showing that many in the Republican establishment are basically blaming the entire Romney loss on Akin's lone comment.

That idea is vapid and even nutty, and supports my thesis that our consultants are, among other things, not very intelligent. One clear sign of intelligence is being able to take a set of facts and events and reach correct decisions and conclusions. You know, much like that hick ex-governor from Alaska always seems to be able to do. Our establishment gurus, meanwhile, have failed that test at almost every turn for decades, and they continue to do so daily.

Besides, no single comment by Akin, or even Romney himself, would have mattered with a strong coherent message. It's precisely because our establishment ran a campaign of isolated single messages that allowed a single moment to stand out in the first place! A confident and cogent conservative campaign wouldn't be vulnerable to such a moment, and such a message isn't hard to construct since conservatism has truth on its side. In fact, the "47%" comment would have been part of that message in proper context, instead of an embarrassing sound byte out of context.

As we mentioned earlier, we know now that people routinely use the electronic version of food stamps — the EBT card — to obtain cash from strip clubs, bars, and X-rated video stores. You cannot tell me that the 47% comment was wrong, or that it was a losing issue. Allow me to whip the dead horse again and remind the consultants that sometimes the truth requires a bit of repetition to sink in, but it is still the truth nonetheless. Instead, Romney, Ryan and the GOPe ran away from 47% remark because they feared losing a narrative. They never stopped to think that perhaps the reason they would lose it was because they never bothered to counter it in the first place!

Another installment of this pattern -- refusing to contest narratives — repeated itself related to the August jobs report, which is widely considered the most critical jobs report leading up to a November election. Inexplicably, the Campaign, and both candidates in the debates, managed to lose this issue.

SHOULD MITT HIRE JAY LENO AND PAT CADDELL?
September 27, 2012

There's an old saying that if you torture the data long enough, it will confess to anything. Proving the point, the Obama administration has put national employment statistics on the Procrustean table, and the poor numbers remarkably now "confess" to an *improving jobs situation* with an 8.1% unemployment rate — even as fewer and fewer Americans are actually working each day. Obviously, if fewer folks are working, the jobs stats can improve only if the calculus is severely flawed. And it is. (More on this later.)

This data corruption renders the employment metric

useless for its stated purpose, which is to provide a realistic snapshot of the health of the economy. It is now merely a tool of political expedience. If Americans even had a rough understanding of the true employment situation, Obama and liberal economics would be guaranteed a generational defeat this November. This is Team Romney's opportunity, and our future depends on them taking advantage.

Tragically, however, Mitt and his campaign are actually collaborators in this peculiar fiction, repeating the line in their ads and campaign speeches that headline unemployment (U3) "remains over 8 per cent." And technically, U3 *is* over 8 per cent. In fact, U3 is a shocking 11 %-plus according to numerous serious students of the history of unemployment. And the concept that explains why it is really 11 and not 8 is relatively simple to understand — so simple that even a liberal comedian and his audience can do it.

In fact, last week on Leno, they did.

And yet, Team Romney is still loath to mention the real U3 rate. I suppose it's an interesting commentary on the insulated nature of political consultants that Jay Leno thinks more highly of his liberal audiences' ability to see through the preposterous 8.1 figure - than Romney's media sorcerers think of everyone else's ability to do the same. Getting two enlightened responses from his audience last week, Leno said the following during his opening monologue:

"Well, according to the Labor Department, unemployment fell from 8.3 to 8.1 % last month. But that was because only, that's because, rather, 368 thousand Americans gave up looking for work." (NERVOUS AUDIENCE LAUGHTER) "And today, President Obama said that's a step in the right direction, and he is encouraging more Americans to give up looking for work so the numbers will come down a little bit more!" (ROBUST AUDIENCE LAUGHTER).

Let me translate: Leno and his audience get it. Leno was accurately mocking our boy president and the bizarre machinations used by the Bureau of Labor Statistics (BLS) to push our official unemployment rate down to 8.1%. And his audience was tracking. They understand not only who put the BS in the BLS, but also how they did it.

And why shouldn't they? The explanatory concept is almost Occupy Wall Street easy. This is not really a matter of the confusing seasonal adjustment ruses — nor is it even related to the somewhat confusing "UN and UNDER employment" rate, known as U6. No, this is simply a matter of "shrinkage in workforce participation." So how technical is "workforce participation"? Not very. What Leno used as his first punch line — "because, rather, 368 thousand Americans gave up looking for work" — more or less defines the concept. I think the more technical term is that more Americans are "sitting on their butts."

Yet Romney's wizards now deem this notion too risky. They must figure this is too confusing of a concept for the campaign to mention.

So how ill-advised is this strategy? Extraordinarily so. Pat Caddell, who as a Jimmy Carter adviser in 1980 knows a thing or two about trying to re-elect a failed president, put this particular aspect in perspective last week. «This is, I've said all along, Romney's election to lose and by God he's losing," said Caddell. "I swear to God…this is the worst campaign in my lifetime. Hundreds of millions of dollars - they're still not on the air explaining to people that with the labor participation rate - if it was the same as he came into office the unemployment would be 11.2%."

What Caddell is saying is that if we kept score for Obama the way we kept it for Bush, the rate would be 11.2%. Under Bush, the participation rate of adults was 67.5%.

Now it's only 63.5%. That's a four-percent grading curve for Obama in effect. Without getting too deep into the weeds here, what it means is that a full 4% of the would-be work force is simply vaporized out of the math equation for all intents and purposes — and for Obama's benefit.

But that 4% reduction is not good news for those who care about reality. That 4% is still here, and its members are still eating and still living somewhere and still talking on cell phones. We are paying for most of that. And with due respect to Romney and his advisers, I maintain that it is not too technical to explain. Remember, the explanation is a Leno punch line, for crying out loud! James Pethokoukis of The American Enterprise Institute has real U3 at about the same rate as Caddell, and the website Zero Hedge has it at 11.7%. The point is this: Obama cannot possibly be re-elected if Team Romney will but tell the simple 11% story. And yet, they won't tell it.

One can only guess that in the groupthink world of the consultant bubble, they have opted for the path of least resistance. Conventional wisdom says no one gets re-elected at over 8 %, so let's just leave it at that. Easy, flaccid, infantile calculus like that is what passes for political genius these days in the strategist class. That›s their story, and they are sticking to it.

But betting the farm on these crazy eights — as in the 8% figure — will backfire though, I guarantee it!

Obama and his BLS will manage to get the official U3 rate down below 8 %. You know they will. If they can lose a quarter-million jobs and still drop 0.2 in a month, getting below 8 before the election will be a piece of cake. Rush Limbaugh has been predicting this for many months. As have I. Why is this so hard for the consultant class?

Moreover, why is this so hard for the man who would be CEO of the United States? Why won't Mitt lead on this issue? He showed a great anti-groupthink daring streak with the pick of Paul Ryan. An effective leader must set the tone for his team. Perhaps Mitt should fire some of his Boston wunderkinds. They are not up to the job. Hell, hire Jay Leno and Pat Caddell. At least they understand basic unemployment math.

Well, Mitt did not fire any of his Boston wunderkinds, nor did he hire Leno or Caddell either, and we all know the exit polls concluded that the main reason he lost is due to voter interpretation of blame for the sour economy. Part of that losing effort was allowing the fallacious jobs reports to go uncontested.

Blame, in fact, is a great concept that gets a bad rap. In our culture, and to our consultants, blame is always personal. This is nonsense, as who we blame is necessarily connected to *what* we blame, and properly assigning blame is the only way to learn from past mistakes. If we must name a "who" to define the proper "what," so be it. And yet, GOP handlers would rather play into the notion that blame is personal, and thus shy away from ever properly assigning it. On that score, they succeeded brilliantly. Blame has not been properly assigned to this day for the economy, dooming us to more of the same misinformation.

In fairness, starting with a Virginia speech on October 5, Mitt did change his talking points a tiny bit when he said that Obama was "nine million jobs short of his promised recovery." This only partially addressed the phony "8%" issue, though it was the closest he ever got to the truth. The take-away is that this tepid response only reinforced the pathetic focus group narrative that Obama is a nice guy who broke some promises, and was simply not very fast at over turning Bush' failed economy. Romney and Ryan droned on about a promise to keep an Ohio plant open, mentioned that Obama "broke his pledge" on taxes related to ObamaCare, and ran ads about "broken promises" related to the economy and the national debt.

Broken promises were never the point. If broken promises were an effective message, Bill Clinton would have never been President and there would be no Democrats in Congress. Besides, our problems have nothing to do with Obama's broken promises and everything to do with the one promise of fundamental transformation that he is keeping. It doesn't matter that Obama promised this or that and didn't deliver. What matters is that Obama favors big government policies that have never worked in world history, and a state run existence that saps the freedom and liberties away from all of us. Obama was not trying to over turn a failed Bush economy he inherited, because he and others with similar beliefs are the ones who drove it into the ditch in the first place.

The biggest lie of this campaign, and of the campaign in 2008, and one that will probably still be the biggest lie of the 2014 and 2016 campaigns, is the foolishness about what Obama "inherited." This is also known as "what got us into this mess in the first place." Heck, it was the biggest lie in the ongoing Fiscal Cliff debates, and naturally John Boehner played right along with it. We'll never win elections or have good policy until we straighten this one out.

OBAMA 'INHERITED' ONLY OBAMA
American Thinker, October 16, 2012

"Did they come in and inherit a tough situation? Absolutely." —

Paul Ryan spoke those words, in the worst moment of the VP debate. Damn Paul. What were you thinking? (Snip)

Mitt Romney and Paul Ryan both left some easy low hanging fruit untouched through the first two debates, and now they need to collect. The Romney/Ryan team can win, and their mandate will be even bigger, and effective governing afterwards will be more viable, if they but correct the media narrative of what Obama "inherited." The notion that our fearless young president *innocently* inherited a mess of biblical proportions is just not correct. Neither is the idea that we are in a recovery that is merely too weak to justify re-election.

The total of those arguments is that Obama should maybe be fired - because although he's a nice guy gosh darn it - he simply has not lived up to his promised timetables for fixing this mess. You know the mess — the one caused by a 40-year reign of John Galt, where government disappeared, regulations were rolled back, and we had too much American energy while businesses were writing their own rules.

If only we really *were* in such a mess.

That entire notion is preposterous, yet widely accepted. What Obama inherited in January 2009 was *Obama*. Maybe not personally Obama, but he inherited economic problems resulting from implementation of too many Obama pipe dream policies.

Consider some history: the economy Obama inherited had been dominated for two years by radicals named Reid and Pelosi — with a certain Senator from Illinois voting with them every step of the way as it turns out. This inheritance included energy prices that had been skyrocketing off and on for years thanks to forty years of policies written, implemented, interpreted, and enforced by leftists at every level of government. These policies prevented this country from accessing our own incredible energy resources to the extent our economy required.

Obama and Biden firmly support all such policies.

Obama also inherited a housing disaster caused by radical lending policies also written, implemented, interpreted, and enforced by liberal apparatchiks at various levels of government. Meanwhile, people at the center of all of this voodoo were giving each other sweetheart mortgages, promotions, and seven-figure bonuses inside Fannie Mae and Freddie Mac — while the rest of the population was suffering for their very decisions.

Obama and Biden support all of this too.

In fact, when you examine the "many decades" Obama refers to as the precursor to his inheritance, you will find that liberals have been in the White House almost half the time, and have controlled Congress the vast majority of the time. Moreover, they naturally control the bureaucracy all of the time — since the bureaucracies they put in place never go away. And they are liberal by definition.

Setting party labels aside for a second, the key point is that our economic successes have resulted from conservatism being enacted while our failures result from liberalism run amok. You can observe this in many of our cities and states today, as liberal utopias gone wild are bankrupt, failing and losing their citizens by the millions. Everywhere liberalism is put into practice, be it California or Cuba or Illinois or Detroit — it fails.

Think about how intellectually destitute you have to be to bankrupt territories as teeming with beauty and resources like California and Cuba. I wager Mitt could turn a profit in a single quarter managing Cuba. I think I could!

And yet Mitt's campaign continues to go along with some iteration of Axelrodian history as spouted by Obama, Biden, or their many surrogates in the Jurassic media. "Let's take a look at the facts. Let's look at where we were when we came to office," blustered Biden in the debate, temporarily unaware that he has been in office since mules pulled Amtrak. "The economy was in free fall. We had the great recession hit; 9 million people lost their jobs...$1.6 trillion in wealth lost in equity in your homes, in retirement accounts for the middle class."

You see, Obama and Biden were innocently attacked by "the great recession" that just "hit." Ever intrepid, they soldiered on for us. As Biden put it, "we knew we had to act for the middle class. We immediately went out and rescued General Motors." Biden didn't mention that GM is technically insolvent today, or that the "rescue" involved pilfering the company from the bondholders and giving it to the unions. His summary failed to acknowledge that GM needed rescuing in the first place only because unions had too much power and because radical energy policies had decimated sales of SUVs. This is the same Biden who just days ago told us the middle class has been "buried these last four years." Who does "just Joe" think has been in power those four years?

Of course, it's not Joe's place to point out the hypocrisy of his own arguments. But it most certainly is Paul Ryan's place to do so. Yet Ryan demurred, simply stating "we're going in the wrong direction...the economy is barely limping along. It's growing at 1.3 %. That's slower than it grew last year, and last year was slower than the year before."

With due respect to Mr. Ryan, our problem is not that our GDP is limping along or that the recovery is too slow. Nope. Our problem is that the statist policies of Obama and Biden have not worked because they cannot work. The problem Obama and Biden inherited was an economy under attack from policies favored for by Obama and Biden for their entire careers. It's not that they haven't effectively reversed their inherited course. It's that they have effectively doubled down on the *same* course.

Now I know what some are saying. Romney is surging, so don't complain — or Obama and Biden are imploding, so don't confuse voters with the facts. I suppose there may be some merit to those thoughts — in a poltroon inside-the-Beltway RNC strategist sort of way. I just so happen to think America is as Ryan has said, an idea. And that idea is a Republic of limited government, and it is worth fighting for.

Moreover, the 2014 midterms start the day after the 2012 election is over. If the notion that Obama inherited problems caused by limited government is allowed to stand, then any potential Romney-Ryan victory won›t be as big as it should be, nor will the Congressional elections turn out quite as they should. Any mandate interpretation will be weakened.

And more to the point, governing properly after the election will be impossible if the public still believes that Obama inherited a mess resulting from conservatism. Obama did not inherit anything but Obama. And he tried to solve it with more Obama. This is critical truth. We will never get out our republic on the right course until more of us understand that, given that one election runs right into the next.

We all need a lot less of Obama. That idea is easy money. It›s still on the table. Any talk of Bain Capital or the 47% will tee this up for Romney. I hope he grabs it.

As we know now, Romney did not grab anything, which guaranteed that Bush would still get the blame and that Obama would win the election. He left the truth about the workforce participation rate and the real jobless rate on the table also. That meant that Obama falsely got credit for breaking about even on jobs, which didn't sound too bad considering "the mess he inherited." (See how these phony absurdities multiply each other?)

Mitt also left Benghazi on the table. In fact, for the final three weeks of the campaign, including the final two debates, he went into a prevent-defense and left everything on the table. There was not a peep about anything philosophical or directional, and while the second debate was confrontational, Romney was not ideological. As these debates unfolded, there was a sense of helplessness among many that our team simply refused to defend the truth on so many important issues. Romney and Ryan were both sanitized. As a result, we have Obama still in office, unchecked by any need to win re-election, and we still have Bush and Republicans to blame for the economy. As Glenn Beck would say sarcastically, "that's fan-TAAA-stick!"

* * *

To get some insight into the foolish and superficial thinking of the GOPe consultant class and the Romney campaign, one only needs to examine what Rove and Haley Barbour told big money donors at a special fundraiser in Tampa during the National Convention. "The people we've got to win [over] in this election, by and large, voted for Barack Obama in '08," Rove said, defending the namby-pamby campaign message. From focus groups, he learned that "if you say he's a socialist, they'll go to defend him. If you call him a far out left winger, they'll say no, no, he's not."

Now that may be correct, as far as it goes, but did Rove ever stop to think that perhaps people believe this nonsense because the GOPe never bothered to say otherwise? So what if an Obama voter from 2008 defends him in a single focus group setting? What else would you expect after five years of our side reinforcing these cockamamie ideas?

Even though the very notion is nonsense, Rove insisted he had uncovered "an acute understanding of the nature of the voters" as a result of focus groups. Think about the sheer insanity of that statement. What about stepping outside your laboratory and getting an acute understanding of day-to-day life, Karl? What Rove was admitting to was an acute *misunderstanding* of human nature, not to mention reality. Rove was confirming my accusation: that his preferred tactic is to conduct a focus group to find out what misinformation the voters believe, and then positioning his candidate to agree with that level of misinformation. According to Mr. Acute Understanding, if a voter thinks Bush is to blame for the economy, we must *agree* with him. If the voter thinks Obama personally took out bin Laden, *agree* with her. If the voter thinks Republicans want to stop all sexual activities, run away from the issue. If the voter thinks Palin is a dolt, reinforce that idea. Mr. Acute Understanding thinks we can actually win this way. Who is the dolt again?

Rove and like-minded consultants never consider the crazy idea of trying to change a few minds, and they remain blind to their own culpability in this massive voter ignorance in the first place. The proper thing to do is to look at focus group or poll results as starting points for voter education. Conversely, the Rovian mind considers it an end point that results in candidate capitulation. Thus, with these people in charge, our candidates get painted into corners, and that leads to super safe responses that paint us into even smaller corners. We will never break this cycle until we take the establishment's brush away.

For the record, Reagan never campaigned this way, and neither did Newt, when he was the "good Newt" in the 1994 campaign and during part of 2011-2012. The 2010 campaign was not like this either, as the message to the independents and disaffected Democrats was pronounced, conservative and distinctly anti-Obama. The same is true of every campaign after Obama's 2008 win. Even Scott Brown and Chris Christie, who have disappointed recently, ran confident, even audacious campaigns, far to the right of Martha Coakley and Jon Corzine. There is a thirty-year pattern confirming this, and it was recounted right after the 2010 primary season.

Which brings up the inherent flaw with conservatives depending on focus groups in the first place. Frank Luntz and others who place so much emphasis on focus groups are destroying the Republican Party. Conservatism is an intellectual pursuit, and often takes longer to resonate with voters than the emotional pursuit of liberalism. A focus group, by definition, is a single point in time, and not reflective of how people form their foundational opinions. A single moment may determine whether we choose honey barbecue over sour cream and onion, because we can always switch next week.

The beliefs that Obama is brilliant, that Bush and free enterprise ruined our economy, that Dick Cheney is the devil, and that Democrats had nothing to do with screwing up the Katrina response were formed over much longer periods of time. Reversing those delusions will take some time, effort, and courage, and the girly men establishment lacks the latter. They demonstrate time and again a refusal to do for the truth what the other side routinely does for the lie, which is to repeat it and repeat it and repeat it — even in the face of initial push back. Focus groups, by their very nature, cannot account for repetition, and will always indicate a preference for an emotional appeal over an intellectual one.

There is a reason Rush says it takes six weeks to understand his show, and a reason young liberals often become conservatives when they grow up. Conservatism takes longer than the confines of a single focus group to understand, and yet Rove insists that he can gain "an acute understanding" on the basis of focus group data. That's ridiculous.

Moreover, focus group inspired thinking also misapprehends the dangerous nature of what we face. The 2012 election was one thing, and the war for the heart and soul of the Republican Party is another. Yet the real issue at stake is the preservation or destruction of America as founded. A campaign will never succeed if it's built on the premise that offending soccer moms in southern Ohio is a fate worse than losing the entire American experiment. Such campaigns are inspired by focus groups and isolated from reality.

Yet armed with all of this focus group claptrap and isolated from reality, Rove and Barbour insisted on the need for "a respectful tone." Then they turned right around in the same meeting and admitted that Democrats were scoring points with extremely non-respectful tones, unaware of the obvious contradiction they had just stepped in.

"Romney is a vulture capitalist who doesn't care about the likes of you," Barbour said, mocking the Democrat campaign. "He doesn't even know people like you — he'll lay you off, cancel your insurance."

Those absurdities are exactly what the Democrats said, and repeated and repeated and repeated, and damned if a lot of folks didn't end up buying them. This no doubt includes some of those Ohio soccer moms our establishment lives in fear of insulting. For some reason, only confident conservative truth offends soccer moms, while hateful liberal lies never do. Must be something in the Ohio River.

None of the above is true or even makes any logical sense as an effective lie. And yet it worked, because Romney's Campaign never countered the nasty folly about who Romney really is, nor ever tried to define Obama as the cold, calculating statist he is, a man who does not believe in America as founded. As long as we run low information campaigns, we will suffer at the hands of low information voters. This rationale never entered the picture in Tampa. Thus, the big money threw in with Rove and his groups, and they, along with the official Romney Campaign controlled the entire message. This messaging strategy included all advertising, stump speeches, and surrogate appearances, as well as the debate strategy. It was all non-confrontational, non-philosophical, and ineffective. In a word, it was, "Obama's a nice guy, but he hasn't quite solved Bush's mistakes as fast as he should. And yes, he did get bin Laden, which Bush couldn't do, so we congratulate him on that. Vote for our vulture capitalist and his granny killing veep anyway."

This obviously was not the way to win. Why Rove, Barbour, or the billionaires who donated to them ever thought it would work is beyond me. I do not know if the good guys, with truth on our side, will win the battle for the heart and soul of the Republican Party or not. And even if we win that battle, I'm not convinced we will do so in time to stop the destruction and save the country. But I know this for sure: both are pursuits we must join, regardless of the odds we face. All is not lost, but it is certainly misplaced at the moment.

12

OKAY, WHAT NOW? ARE WE TOAST?

Bill Whittle is a gifted communicator whose reputation is rightfully growing. Shortly after Romney's loss, he said in an astonishing presentation that victories for the good guys should always be "a foregone conclusion for months in advance." He's right. The paradox is that we'll never have those easy victories if the focus is on elections for election's sake. The real emphasis must be stopping the grandest of all larcenies and the most perfect of crimes -- the theft of our nation in broad daylight.

To boil it down even further, we need to stop obsessing about what and focus on why. We'll never win the Presidency again until we focus on *why* we must do so. Any focus on "what" leads to temporary, government-centered solutions, whereas a focus on "why" inclines towards permanent liberty.   Liberals will usually win "what" elections, and yet the typical GOP consultant strategy is to run on certain whats in Ohio and talk about some other whats in Virginia in order to niche our way to two hundred and seventy electoral votes. This is a foolish attempt to run up a down escalator, and fails to contemplate the emptiness of any such victories we might win. Bush family what victories led to Bill Clinton and Barack Obama. More damaging still, they led to absurd national assumptions that free markets are a failed economic system and that liberals will keep us safe from terrorists.

The what focus in 2012 had people in a dither about a failed economy and celebrating a dead bin Laden without ever asking why the economy failed and why Seal Team Six was able to kill bin Laden. A focus on what suggests auto bailouts as the way to temporary "jobs in Ohio," whereas a why focus informs that a strong auto demand from forty-nine other states, and more American energy is the way to achieve "jobs in Ohio" permanently. An emphasis on what always favors the shallow appeals of liberalism.

Conversely, Reagan's "why" victories led to the end of The Cold War and the greatest economic opportunities the world has ever seen. There was a national understanding of why the Soviet Union was evil and why free markets work and are moral. Reagan is gone, but the truth of why is not. The free market is still moral and superior to any other economic system, and there is still evil in the world. And yes, the why takes a little longer to teach and invites more scorn initially, but once the sale is made, it is a done deal. Besides, history is clear: when we forget why, we usually lose, and even when we win, we lose.

Mr. Whittle's idea of huge victory is far from fanciful, and his reason is impeccable. We happen to have truth on our side. Moreover, even as misguided as Romney's campaign was, a flip of merely 2% of the voters would have changed the outcome. We only need to turn a few of the low and mis-information voters into higher information voters, and we have the weapons to do so.

While the truth is our ultimate weapon, it is the first thing GOP consultants jettison when the going gets tough in the focus group. Whittle was quoted because he is one of many brilliant and talented people from that strange dimension known as the real world outside Washington whose message is ignored by our inbred and obtuse establishment class. Dr. Ben Carson is another, although after his latest speech at the National Prayer Breakfast, he will be impossible to ignore.

Carson did more damage to Obama Care in forty-three

seconds than Karl Rove has done in forty-three months. The country is full of talented yet unknown conservatives, and they've posted messages that could decimate Obama (and every other liberal for that matter) all over YouTube and other places for years. The establishment, isolated and only interested in protecting their over-paid gigs, avoids this universe of extraordinary citizens, which, in and of itself, is un-American and anti-conservative. We will never reach the low information voters until the wisdom of people like Whittle and Carson replaces the stale formulas of the Beltway masterminds. Conservatism appeals to the doers while liberalism comes naturally for the serial commenters. We need to start recruiting pundits and consultants from the world of the doers, not from the professional commentariat.

We must also dismantle the groupthink suppositions about voters and elections. If we continue to look at elections as isolated events as consultants do, we will fail. If we continue to look at people as "education voters" or "social conservatives" or "jobs voters," to be pandered to on pet issues, we will fail. If we continue to allow the liberal narratives to soften the battlefield in their favor heading into every election cycle, we will fail. If we continue to accept voter turnouts exceeding 150% in select minority precincts, we will fail. If we continue to pretend our candidates agree with whatever lies the low and mis-information voters happen to believe, we will fail. Put another way, we must abandon the mistakes of the past twenty years as outlined in the previous hundred thousand words or we will allow the theft of America to be complete.

Below are a few specifics places to start, with an emphasis on the big picture. We are right, and our message is superior. All of human history validates this, as does by every fiber of human nature. If you are a consultant and don't believe it, then get the hell out of the way and make room for those who do.

FRAUD:

I've only mentioned voter fraud briefly, simply because I'm not qualified to write on the subject. I hope someone who is, will. It is beneath contempt that the establishment remains remarkably uncurious about mysteriously high turnouts for Obama and mysteriously low turnouts for Romney. Succinctly, if the Party refuses to lead on this issue, then they are dead to us. This is a battle they must fight and one properly under their purview. A good place to start would be to reign in early voting, since this invites fraud.

FOCUS GROUP AND POLLS:

We must throw out our entire playbook regarding focus groups and start over. Currently, the strategists rely incessantly on these devices, with no regard for how flawed they are. As stated earlier, a focus-group-driven campaign will be one built upon the premise that offending a soccer mom in Ohio is a fate worse than the death of America. We will never win campaigns, much less save the country, if we continue down this path. A focus group should be the starting point of voter education, not the end point of candidate capitulation.

GET OUTTA DA BUSHES:

(First time I've ever quoted Jesse Jackson in agreement.) Any consideration of Jeb Bush for 2016 is beyond ridiculous. Even if he were doctrinally solid -- and he's not -- and even if he were fearless -- and he's not — nominating him would be a disaster. It would be to admit that we are merely subjects, not capable of being free citizens, and that we are in need enlightened royal families to guide us. Read my lips, NO NEW BUSHES.

QUIT OBSESSING OVER PRESIDENTIAL ELECTIONS:

The people already talking about Jeb are the ones who obsess over the Presidential elections and nothing else. Ideas are more important, more timeless, and less fallible than people, and as conservatives we should understand this. Great people will always let us down at some point, but great ideas never will.

NIP IT IN THE BUD:

Gore really won Florida in 2000, Sarah Palin is dumb, Clinton was impeached over sex, Obama is brilliant, conservatives are racists, Romney is greedy, Chris Matthews is heterosexual, the Tea Party is racist, Halliburton created Katrina, oil is bad, Bush lied people died, Wall Street favors Republicans, guns kill people, capitalism destroyed America, all Republicans are racist, SUVs are destroying the planet, Obama saved GM, whites are racist, etc. Did I mention racism? All these memes are false, yet they are believed by a lot of Americans. The GOP is too scared to fight back on any of them. Which, come to think of it, is why they are all believed in the first place. We must directly contest liberal narratives, or they will destroy us.

Priority one right now is to beat back the narrative that Bush, conservatives, all Republicans and free enterprise destroyed the economy. This is a lot harder in 2013 than it would have been in 2008, but we'll never win another election or save the country if this fabrication is not turned around. John McCain and Mitt Romney conceded this point and got crushed, because blame on a Republican President automatically attaches to all conservatives and even free enterprise itself, even though all of the carnage stemmed from liberal policies making borrowing too easy and oil production too hard. Why is this so hard to figure out?

DON'T FALL FOR LIBERAL PSY-OPS

Liberals will publish purposefully constructed polls in venues like The Daily Kos to play on the fear of the Republican establishment, which they did with great success after Scott Brown's 2010 win and during the Ground Zero Mosque debate. They will also target unwitting Tea Party and conservative voters with misdirection ads, a ploy the McCaskill Campaign used by "accusing" Todd Akin of being "the most conservative" candidate during the Republican Primary for Senate. The left played establishment consultants, and non-establishment voters, for suckers in each of these situations. There is a war on, and all too often, only the left realizes it.

REBRANDING/TECHNOLOGY:

There has been a lot of talk about how the Republicans need to "rebrand" themselves, and how this should be done by marketing wizards. Let me think about that for a second... OH HELL NO! We have too many "marketing" wizards involved now, and that's the problem. Saving a Republic is not the same as selling potato chips or smart phones, because we're not necessarily trying to appeal to what people think they want. It would be easy if that were the case, but it's not, and we need to grow up and realize it.

We must turn low and mis-information voters into higher information voters, and only well articulated conservatism, repeated and repeated, will do this. It helps to have humor and to tailor the media mix to the modern consumer, and we must achieve tech equality by hiring the best and brightest technological and social media minds, but the message cannot be dependent on anything other than the truth. This is not rocket surgery, but technology will not replace the message, and we don't need shyster ad men to fool independents and moderates into the booth in hopes they'll vote the right way.

FIRE LOW INFORMATION CONSULTANTS:

Most consultants in both parties are political animals, trained in the art of politics and immersed in a government-centered life. This formula works well for the Democrats since their entire philosophy is government centered. This cannot possibly work for the Republican Party or any conservative candidate or cause, because people immersed in government have no understanding of why we believe what we believe. The only way to get our message out is to hire people who live it, and understand it, which discounts almost the entire current consultant class. The establishment consultants are not the victim of low information voters, they are the cause.

NOT ABOUT PARTY PER SE:

When he was on his high horse, the mastermind Rove assured us he had a strategy for securing a "permanent Republican majority." He actually said, with a straight face, that he could stitch this together by targeting single issues voters here and there for this permanent majority. It obviously did not work, and begs the bigger question: with no common philosophy, what would you accomplish by this anyway?

VOTERS AS AMERICAN INDIVIDUALS:

George W. Bush and Karl Rove were worried about "education voters" after doing poorly among those who rated education as their top priority in the 2000 election. Their solution was to let Ted Kennedy and John Boehner write the No Child Left Behind (NCLB) Act, which you and I are paying for today in so many ways. In the world of Rove, this is a smashing success since Bush scored much higher "among education voters" in 2004.

This is a fabulous object lesson about how the Rove mind malfunctions. Moreover, it shows how dividing voters into little affinity groups will lead to bigger government by definition. It cannot work out any other way. This kind of left brained, small picture, pandering must be done away with for a number of reasons.

Many of those "education voters" in 2004 became "hope and change voters" in 2008 and "GM voters" in 2012. In other words, "Obama voters." This temporal focus is the downside of running campaigns micro-targeted at voters as single-issue creatures. A big picture appeal to voters as individual Americans is far more effective and far more permanent. Once someone understands the role of government and their role as an individual, appeals to soccer moms or a Wal-Mart voters or energy voters or jobs voters will never be needed again. Besides, Republicans will never out-pander the Democrats.

DON'T BE ASHAMED TO BE RICH:

We cannot apologize for who we are, especially when we are

apologizing for successful people like Mitt Romney. Romney has a fabulous personal story of discipline, family, generosity and success -- stunningly so with regard to generosity. We need to trumpet this, not to brag but to show what is possible in a free society.

Conversely, we can't be scared to point out whom our opposition is especially when that opposition is wealthy due to crony schemes or from marrying into Republican fortunes. We should also celebrate that our political adversaries include the "Obama stash" woman from Detroit and the "Obama phone" woman from Cleveland. We should be proud to be opposed to those voters, and should at least pose the question of which country would be better, one full of Romneys or one full of Obama phones? It's an intriguing question.

FOOLISH TO JOIN ASSAULT AGAINST PALIN:

One of the favorite hobbies of GOPe figures is to prove that they hate Sarah Palin even more than the liberals do. This is beyond idiotic. She has been appointed -- like it or not -- as the top surrogate for everyone in the country who believes that life begins somewhere besides the Ivy League, Manhattan Island, or inside the Washington Beltway. If you are living a life that does not revolve around the universe mentioned above, then she is your champion, even if you're not aware of it.

Moreover, we will never win the argument about what America should be if we lose the Palin versus the Elite argument. If perpetual failures like Obama and Jamie Gorelick are automatically considered superior simply due to their pedigree, then we are guaranteed perpetual failure. There is no way around this for voters who believe in limited government and individual liberty. Besides, every decision and every controversial statement Palin has ever made has been validated by the passage of time, and, unlike Obama, she doesn't wear mom jeans.

OCCUPY THE HIGH GROUND:

We need to compare, in every way possible, Occupy Wall Street and the Tea Party. Compare the grounds after rallies are over, compare the sound bytes, compare the language on the signs, and anything else you can compare. One vision is of a third world banana republic and the other is a clean and polite society. Do not run away from this contrast, run with it. And while we're at it, Chicago and Detroit are good examples of Occupy societies to poke fun at too. We can't run scared of this message, because anyone who is offended by it is not a prospective conservative voter in the first place. Who cares if they're offended?

GIVE TRUTH A CHANCE:

The conservative message is an intellectual pursuit. As such, it will naturally elicit some emotion-driven push back when people first encounter it. So what? Liberty is hard. We must do for the truth what our opponents will do for the lie, which is to repeat it and repeat it and repeat it. Our successes in the past thirty years have always come as a result of just that. The Rove method is to try a message in a focus group, and, if that message gets the least little push back, discard it and try something else -- even when that message is the truth!

EMBRACE JULIA AND FLUKE:

The only thing that demonstrates the emptiness of the liberal mindset more than a middle class cartoon figure who depends on government for everything is a rich grad student who thinks her Jesuit law school should pay for her casual sex. We should embrace Julia and Sandra Fluke, not by agreeing with them, but by exposing them... often!

FISCAL V MORAL:

John Adams stated, "Our Constitution was made only for *a moral and religious people*. It is wholly inadequate to the government of any other." He also said, "The moment the idea is admitted into society that property is not as *sacred as the law of God*, and that there is not a force of law and public justice to protect it, anarchy and tyranny commence." What? Property is as sacred as anything else in the mind of a God-fearing Founder Father? That's what he said, and it's not a contradiction.

Translation: Property is what you receive in exchange for your God given time and talents, and therefore is the expression of the sanctity of life outside the womb, which, like life inside the womb, is indeed sacred. It is the issue we all share, whether we realize it or not, because a loss of property means we lose everything else to tyranny by definition. You can't save a single unborn child if a bureaucrat or the taxman owns the fruits of your labor, and therefore owns you and your time. This is powerful common ground.

Politically, the GOPe ignores the fact that Republicans win by running social conservatives. Social conservatives often ignore the fact that these candidates won by stressing other issues. Reagan's focus was on the greatness of the free market and the evils of the communism, though his intellectual consistency was morally based. The historic wins in 1994 and 2010 included mostly social conservative candidates, but neither election had an emphasis on social issues, other than the moral component of limited government.

In other words, what all of us have in common is an interest in property rights, regardless of what our individual hot button issues are. Social liberals are being naïve when they discount the fiscal cost of moral depravity, and social conservatives are naïve to ignore the moral cost of fiscal depravity. Pastors enjoying tax-exempt status are being hypocritical and intellectually bankrupt when they impugn "fiscal only conservatives" or sit out elections. The Bible talks a lot about the moral component of money, and even the atheist Ayn Rand recognized it. We must all recognize it, or we'll have a nation with no morals and no money. This divide threatens our ability to ever beat the liberals.

IMMIGRATION:

This is the new "third rail" issue, and it's threatening to destroy our ability to ever stop the liberal agenda again. It's a very complicated issue to be sure, but this self-immolation is not necessary since we all agree that we must secure the border first, and most of us agree that until that's done, nothing else matters anyway. Even so, in the last GOP Primary season, the Perry campaign was ended and others were damaged as a result of ridiculously hypothetical arguments over theoretical mass deportation fantasies that are not possible to execute.

Illegal immigration is a cancer that has metastasized for sixty years and been fed by the laws of supply and demand, plus a porous border, and there is simply no way to unravel this sixty-year problem quickly. Until the border bleeding is stopped, any argument over what we do next only tears us apart and strengthens the electoral prospects of the party that will never secure the border in the first place. We need to win a few elections first, secure that border, and then the debates about what happens next will be relevant. Until all of that happens, they aren't.

CONCLUSION:

Mitt Romney, with a conservative Congress, might have been a decent President -- or even better. Whether President Romney, or any President, can reverse the decline of our country is an open question. If you've visited a courtroom, an emergency room, a public school or a college campus lately, you might be inclined to answer in the negative. What many of us did know is that Mitt would be a phlegmatic and ineffective candidate, surrounded by predictable formulaic political pros with no tether to reality. We knew this would likely lead to the re-election of Barack Obama, a catastrophe that will exponentially decrease the chances that we'll ever pull this car out of the ditch. Winning elections in the future is not enough to save the country, but losing them will seal our doom.

And winning elections is hard, but it's not complicated. The lessons of history and human nature are very clear: the truth can only be sold with the truth, and the lie can only be sold with lies. Our cause is right and just, and like all such causes, can only be supported by a courageous defense of the larger truth. Trying to ignore the big ideas and appealing to voters on the basis of temporal single issues like "jobs and Ohio" is the coin of a fool's realm. Karl Rove and our establishment consultants are fools, and this is been their failed realm for a couple decades. Or maybe we're the fools. Perhaps Rove and his coterie are perfectly happy losing a few games, as long as they have our money to play the game with. Or maybe it's a little bit of both.

Ronald Reagan said the problem is not ignorance, it's that too many people "know so many things that aren't so." Rove and our establishment know so many things about how to win elections -- it's just that they aren't so. And this is why Rove and our establishment lost.... again.

AUTHOR'S BIO

C. Edmund Wright has been observing and commenting on the failures of the Republican Establishment since 1992, first dealing with them as part of the N.C. Bush Quayle Campaign. He has been warning about the most overrated political guru of all time, Karl Rove, since 2000. The disaster of the 2012 campaign, not to mention Rove's comments since, have suddenly validated Wright's long held contentions.

Ensconced firmly outside the Washington Beltway, Wright draws on his experience in reality as a businessman, husband and father, as well as his sublimely singular way of explaining cause and effect, to make his points. Telling stories that are punctuated by a sharp sardonic sense of humor and irony, Wright's specialty is weaving seemingly tangential issues into his main theme.

Living in North Carolina with his wife and youngest child, he contributes to the American Thinker, ghost writes for some well known political and media figures, and works for Marketel Media, among other business interests. His hope is that his books will inspire equal parts "finally someone said that" with "wow, never thought about it like that" responses.

CPSIA information can be obtained at www.ICGtesting.com
Printed in the USA
LVOW06s2157260114

371070LV00014B/218/P